GOLLY GEE
– IT'S ME!

The
Howie Meeker
Story

CHARLIE HODGE

Published in 1996 by
Stoddart Publishing Co. Limited

Distributed in Canada by
General Distribution Services Inc.
30 Lesmill Road
Toronto, Canada M3B 2T6
Tel. (416) 445-3333
Fax (416) 445-5967
e-mail Customer.Service@ccmailgw.genpub.com

Distributed in the United States by
General Distribution Services Inc.
85 River Rock Drive, Suite 202
Buffalo, New York 14207
Toll free 1-800-805-1083
Fax (416)445-5967
e-mail Customer.Service@ccmailgw.genpub.com

Cataloguing in Publication Data

Hodge, Charlie, 1955–
Golly gee — it's me! : the Howie Meeker story

ISBN 0-7737-2977-1

1. Meeker, Howie. 2. Hockey players – Canada – Biography.
3. Hockey – Canada – Biography. I. Title.

GV848.5.M44H6 1996   796.962'092   96-931242-3

Cover Design: Bill Douglas @ The Bang
Text Design: Tannice Goddard
Computer Layout: Mary Bowness

Printed and bound in Canada

To
Sharon, for sharing the dream
Mom, for fostering it
Eileen Cassidy, for encouraging it
Phyllis Kitson, for believing in it
and, Ron Elliott for financing it

Also to
Robert "Old Steve" Stevens, Harvey Stoltz, and Herb Sullivan
for
"just being there"

Contents

Foreword

Who is this "Golly Gee Whiz" character, Howie Meeker, whom Charlie Hodge — no, not the ancient goaler — is bringing back into such clear focus? Can it be the Howie Meeker who as a Maple Leaf popped five goals into the Chicago Blackhawks' net, on the night of January 8, 1947? It couldn't be. Meeker scored only 83 goals in his eight-year NHL career as a player. He was a winger who specialized in preventing the other guy from scoring. A careless media call them grinders today, but Meeker had a kinder name for members of his cult: "defensive specialist."

Is it the same Meeker who came out of New Hamburg, Ontario, back in the early forties to play for a kids' team which had been entered in the Stratford city league, much to the disgust of the lead-footed beer bellies who cluttered up the rosters?

These kids would only create an imbalance, they cried. It was a prediction that turned out to be valid. The New Hamburg kids skated away from the clods who had despised them.

One of the speediest burghers was this Meeker fellow. Dave Pinkney, a noted Ontario sportsman who operated junior hockey in Stratford at the time, took notice. He was overheard to remark: "The kid has big feet and a big heart. I like him."

The comment was to be recalled a couple of years later, when Pinkney was putting together a Junior B club that was destined to win the Ontario championship. Meeker was one of the first players he signed. But it turned out that Pinkney was not the only hockey person who had compiled a book on Meeker.

The Waterloo club claimed that Meeker's home in New Hamburg was closer to their arena than it was to Stratford's arena. Since New Hamburg didn't have a Junior team, Waterloo claimed him. The Ontario Hockey Association ordered a measurement taken, portal to portal, and to Stratford's disman, Waterloo was the winner.

But Meeker preferred to play for Stratford. So a young executive of the Waterloo club offered a compromise. Meeker would train for a couple of weeks with the Waterloo club. If he still wanted to play for Stratford, Waterloo would release him.

Such promises in hockey rarely were kept, but this one was. The young Waterloo executive gave Meeker his release and went on to other things. He became publisher of the Toronto Star. The name: Beland Honderich.

Is Hodge's Meeker the same player who won the Calder Trophy as rookie of the year in 1947 and played for three consecutive Stanley Cup winners, alongside Hall of Famers such as Turk Broda, Syl Apps, Max Bentley, Teeder Kennedy? The Meeker who went on to coaching, teaching, and broadcasting?

The answer, of course, as the pages you're about to read so ably attest, is that Hodge's Meeker is all these characters — and much more.

MILT DUNNELL
Toronto

Acknowledgements

Numerous people assisted in this project, only a few of whom are mentioned below. Thank you for your assistance, research, support, or simply inspiration:

Editors Don Bastian and Lloyd Davis, Sharon Hodge (editor, typesetter, idea bouncer); Joyce Elliott (in memory of); Rhonda and Tom Roy; Bob MacPherson (the wake-up call); Tom Dier; Paul Buckowski, Phil Rygg; Shauna and Chelsea Fagan; Vic Ingram; Suzanne Lubzinski; Barry Mathers and Curtis Tulman (The Cruzeros); Pete Quigley (Newfoundland interpreter); Kitty Stolar; Craig Hodge; Gerry Halpen; Milt Dunnell; the Toronto Maple Leafs; Dick Irvin; Jack Whyte; Cam Purdy; John Carter; NHL Statistician Dan Diamond; Stoddart Publishing; Jim LeGuilloux; Karen Wendelboe; John Van Herwaarden III; Maurie Jackson; Tom, Mike, Ken, and Andy Meeker, and of course, Howie and Grace Meeker.

Thanks also to Sanky, Oodie, Muggie, and Bear without whose help this book might have taken half as long.

One

The First Time

"There were many times in the following sixty years, a great many times actually, that I should have, or had very good reason to say, 'No, some other time,' to a request for an autograph. Whenever that happened, though, I remembered Busher Jackson and then would say smilingly, 'Sure boy, it's a pleasure.'"

The night sky had rumbled plenty already that evening, although this time the sounds had mercifully been provided by Mother Nature. A real storm, English style: torrential rain, wind, and then, of course, fog. For hours now the rain had pounded down. The rumbling sounds had been compliments of the ominous black thunderheads — and not the all-too-familiar drone and moan of German bombers, loaded with their cargo of carnage. When the storm finally passed, the old woman steadied herself for what she

1

knew would surely come next. Now that the skies were clearer, hell would be on its winged way.

She would not have to wait long.

When the first one hit that night it was bang on her block. The piercing, wailing air-raid sirens eliminated the drone of the German bombers. Radar — the modern warfare version of Paul Revere. She longed for a quieter warning. How she loathed those horrible sirens.

Then came the tumultuous scream of falling bombs bringing the latest salutations from the madman across the water. Their descent lasted only seconds but paralysed all who heard.

The first bomb to land in London that evening sent her sprawling across the room, dazed. Soon afterwards she shook her head and wavered to her knees, too stunned from the impact to know or really care how long she had been out. Her tiny living-room wall was cracked — and the roof as well; her skull had been more fortunate. She would have much to clean up, again, but it seemed that for now she was alive, and God could be thanked for that as well. The bomb had only blown off an outside corner of the flat; nothing that couldn't be repaired.

The next morning, the neighbourhood survivors on Threecolt Street resumed their lives within the smoking rubble. Much of the street was flattened now, and the few houses that remained were badly damaged, but Annie, her husband, Charles, and son George would remain. The area wardens visited again that day, imploring them to relocate for their own safety.

"Why don't you move out of here," the concerned worker asked the old lady, staring over his glasses at Annie. "The ministry will find you a place."

"Thank you very much, but I've already told you, I wouldn't give Old 'Itler the satisfaction of making me move. This is my home and I've too many memories to leave now," she said. And Annie never did leave.

Indeed the house on Threecolt Street did hold a lot of memories for Annie and her family. Her own children were born there and she had lived in the same house when her first grandson was born in Canada nearly 20 years earlier, to son Charlie Jr. and his wife, Kathleen. She'd written it down in her book: 'Nov. 4, 1923, eight pounds, eyes blue, baby boy — Howard William Meeker. Home — 29 E. Eby Street, Kitchener, Ontario.'

According to the doctor, the young lad arrived in the world strongly voicing his thoughts on the situation. Seventy-three years later not a lot has changed for Howie Meeker.

Charlie Meeker Jr. had joined the Royal Canadian Dragoons soon after moving to Canada in 1912 and wound up quickly returning overseas when the Great War broke out in Europe. The RCDs were a cavalry unit and the experience developed his love of horses. While in England during the war, Charlie met Kathleen "Kitty" Wharnsby, a charming woman who certainly charmed Charlie. When the war ended the two were married and returned to Canada.

Howard would prove to be the first of five boys for Charlie and Kitty; Dick, Ken, Chuck, and Tom would follow, and with them the long hard hours of work needed just to survive. For the most part Charlie Meeker provided well, even during the ugly Dirty Thirties which crippled much of the new nation. An army man much of his life, during peacetime Charlie did what it took to look after his growing family.

At one point he had a Coca-Cola franchise and then took a Kuntz's Brewery franchise out of Waterloo, Ontario. He had two big Geoffesson trucks. He operated one himself in winter, and had NHL players such as Ott Heller and Earl "Babe" Siebert, who lived in the area, service the other in the summers.

"I'd sometimes go with him on his out-of-town deliveries of pop," Howie recalls. "During those road trips we'd stop at Baden, New Hamburg, Petersburg, and other surrounding small towns. I'd go with him lots in the winter and we'd bundle up and head out into the chilling cold. I remember that he'd often stop in Baden and we'd buy some fresh bread. Oh, man, we'd put it by the heater, which was just a direct pipe out the motor into the cab area, and we would get home and have this warm bread. The bakery place is still there."

Howie's father built him a little stable in their backyard in Kitchener and bought him a pony. "We overfed him too much oats and, of course, spoiled him," Howie says. "One day the pony got out of the stable, as he often did, and onto the street — and as luck would have it the neighbour had just seeded his lawn. I tried to catch the pony, but do you think it would come off the neighbour's new lawn? He would run, and stomp, and slide, and then run, slide, and stomp some more. I can still see the look on my dad's face as he came walking up the street and saw the lawn — it looked like the Rocky Mountains. I remember the neighbour coming out shaking his head saying, 'Charlie Meeker, you asshole.'

"We repaired the lawn and had the pony moved up to the Seagram's barn in Waterloo. Seagram's was big into horses in those days. I'd go up there and ride him on weekends in a covered quarter-mile track."

Even before Howie had his own pony, though, he remembers his favourite mode of travel and very first love — skating.

"We had a rink in the backyard even then, and I can never remember a time in my life when I couldn't skate. Kitchener was a great place to grow up — lots of room to play. The marketplace behind the majestic city hall building had room for every kind of sport and we kids in the area always had a softball, baseball, soccer, or football game on the go. Suddaby School yard was just a short walk away. Dad was not big on sports but he never stopped me from taking part and often supported my desire. The Polish people who lived behind us on Eby Street had a huge backyard and Dad somehow got permission to build an ice rink on it every winter.

"I remember at age three or four pushing a chair for a short period of time. That same afternoon, Mom told me later, I grabbed a hockey stick and away I went. I also remember every Saturday and Sunday playing shinny from about 8 a.m. to 5 p.m. on the lake in Kitchener Park.

"It was a huge lake, cleaned, flooded, and lit by the park staff. There was an area in the middle with music for skating and the children skated in a huge circle. In the fringe areas there would be about ten to twenty hockey games going on."

Howie says the kids did something that the adults who run minor hockey in Canada haven't been able to do in the last fifty years of trying. "We sorted ourselves out by size, speed, and skill. On an average day there would be 300 to 400 kids on the ice with hockey sticks and thirty or forty games going on. All you did was pick an area, find someone with a puck, get a couple of frozen shoes or lunch buckets for goalposts — 'You five in black play the rest of us' — and away we'd go. It really didn't matter that players in some other game infringed on your ice. Depending on numbers, size, speed, and skill, your goals could be 50 feet apart or 150 feet apart and miles wide. Miss a pass and it took five minutes to go and get it. That's when the ice was good."

"In a group of twenty boys the same size there is good, bad, and indifferent talent. My buddy and I were pretty good. We'd get on a team and have the puck most of the time and after an hour, to even things up, it would be six of us against fourteen of them, really no fun for anybody. So some sensible kid would suggest we go play with the bigger kids. 'Get the hell out of here so we can touch the puck.' It made sense so we moved on."

After an hour or two of trying two or three different games on the lake and politely being told to "F . . . off," Howie would find his game, usually with the fellows a little bit older and a little bit bigger, some with as much talent as he had, some with more. "We eventually had twenty guys approximately the same age, size, and skills who came together through common sense. We often left home on Eby Street with eight kids, on the walk to the park pick up at least another four, and by the time we got into our skates, the dozen guys would go to six different games. No adults involved. The kids knew that if they were going to have fun, if they were going to handle the puck, carry the puck, shoot the puck, and score a goal, they'd better get on a team and play against opponents where they weren't physically and skillfully dominated.

"Years later, when I went back to Kitchener to play Junior B hockey at age fifteen, most of the guys on the team were fellows from our games on the lake in Kitchener Park. For the life of me I can't understand why modern minor hockey doesn't have the same philosophy.

"While we had a game going on of skilled eleven- twelve- and thirteen-year-olds and some small fourteen-year-olds, the skilled teenagers had one going of their own. When they were short a man it was a real honour to be asked to come and fill in until the others arrived. When some big, semi-skilled teenager bullied his way into our game, a quick skate to our older and bigger friends soon brought help. When that didn't work, my dad had a friend on the police force, 'Tiny' was his name. He was a big Scotsman, six foot six, 230 pounds — looked like a tiger, but I found out later in life that he had the heart of a lamb. Well, I'd go to the park's boathouse where we changed into our skates, get on the telephone and call Tiny. When word got around that if you disturbed the game with that 'snot-nosed kid' in it, Tiny would show up, we had less trouble than anyone else.

"It was just amazing that when left on our own to sort out our hockey problems we developed a natural system in which we all learned skills and enjoyed ourselves tremendously. It was only when the parents and bureaucrats got involved that the system deteriorated so rapidly."

Ɣ

Those early days of shinny provided the young freckle-faced Howie not only with social skills such as cooperation and teamwork but also with his first hockey lessons. He was the youngest and smallest at ten or eleven years of age, playing with and against kids twelve or thirteen, who were somewhat bigger and stronger. To that point, what had gotten Howie to the higher level of play was that he could grab the puck, stickhandle through and past everyone on the opposition team, and get a shot on goal. Against the bigger and more talented guys, he could beat one or two but never three or four. So when in trouble and surrounded by enemies, he would either shoot at the net (and risers weren't allowed so not too many shots went in) or throw a desperate hope pass towards centre ice (which more often than not landed on an opponent's stick).

"About an hour into the first game one day the leader of our team, Bobby Schnurr, called time. He came to me and said, 'Kid, what team are you on?' I said, 'Your team — we're mostly black.' 'Well,' Bobby said, 'how come every time you pass the puck you give it to those guys over there? You colour-blind or what? You keep giving the puck to them, boy, and you get your ass out of here.'

"Right then and there that was my first hockey lesson on how to play the game. I didn't realize the magnitude of the advice at the time. Here were twelve- or thirteen-year-old pond hockey players who had the game figured out. Adults and bureaucrats in fifty years still haven't figured it out. In minor hockey, coast to coast at every level, 65 percent of all passes land on the enemy's stick. What's worse, most coaches don't even know that it's happening and players accept it, coaches accept it, and parents accept it as part of the game."

Howie also remembers his first "organized" hockey game. Not surprisingly, the budding player — who never suffered from a lack of initiative — had a lot to do with inspiring the event.

"Suddaby School in Kitchener was ten minutes' walk from home and part of the yard there froze each winter. I encouraged the older guys to go to the principal of the school and ask him to build a rink in the schoolyard while I suggested to our teacher that maybe we should have a rink, form a hockey team, and play other schools.

"Miracle! In short order we had one. We had so many kids wanting to play that in our grade alone we had three teams. So we played a series at recess, noon, and 4 p.m. to see who would play against the other schools. There were no adults involved, no referees, no coach, no nothing."

After many games, Howie's team won the honour. "Somehow our teacher got sweaters for us and even persuaded another teacher to referee. It was a home-and-home series with King Edward School and the first game was in our own school's backyard, at our own rink. When we put on the jerseys with 'Suddaby School' across the front, man were we a proud bunch of kids. For all of us I think it was our first official hockey game. They were even going to keep score. I couldn't believe it.

"We had a ringer, Billy Hainsworth, son of the famous George Hainsworth of the Montreal Canadiens and Toronto Maple Leafs. He was our goaltender. Billy was the only kid in town who had all the goaltender equipment: snazzy goal pads, goalie skates, catching and stick gloves, shoulder and arm pads, special pants — he had it all, even a goal stick, which was unheard-of in those days. I played centre and when I looked back at our net before the face-off, there was so much of Billy I thought, 'Golly gee, the puck will never get by him into the goal.' Anyway, the King Edward guys were bigger and stronger and had considerable skill, and halfway through the game we were tied. I had the puck, made a sharp turn, and felt something give as I fell on my ass. I got up, skated, turned, and fell down again. When I looked at my skate, the heel of the tube skate had separated from the boot. The rivets had given way. The referee took a look and rang the bell — not a whistle, he had a school bell like all officials used in those days — called time, and took out some tape from his pocket to fasten the heel in place. It was better than nothing. We eventually lost the game, but we won the next one at King Edward's rink. Then came the spring thaw and no more hockey. It's funny, sixty years later I can still remember that game as if it were yesterday."

Like many Canadian boys during the past seventy-five years, Howie grew up idolizing hockey players. Magazine pictures of his hockey heroes and his Bee Hive Syrup hockey photo collection covered the bedroom wall. His favourites included goalie Roy Worters, Babe Siebert, and Sweeney Schriner of the New York Americans; goalies Andy Aitkenhead and Dave Kerr, the Colville brothers, and Ott Heller from the Rangers; Eddie Shore and Dit Clapper from Boston; and Toe Blake and Howie Morenz of the Canadiens. Best of all, though, was his prized collection of Toronto Maple Leafs, including the Kid Line of Busher Jackson, Joe Primeau, and Charlie Conacher; Red Horner; Bingo Kampman; Billy Taylor; Bob Davidson; Syl Apps; George Hainsworth; Alex Levinsky; and Hap Day. He had them all — all 105 in the set.

There comes a time in everyone's life when a dream comes true, and Howie Meeker's life has been blessed by a number of such fortunate experiences. Three of them involved hockey dressing rooms. The first was in Kitchener in 1936.

"My uncle, Harry Wharnsby, was the trainer for the Kitchener-Waterloo Senior hockey team. I wondered how he got the job and before long figured out it was probably due to the fact that he was the best rummy and poker player around. One day he asked me if I would like to be stick boy. Of course I would."

Harry told Howie's father that practice was Sunday at 8:30 a.m. at the Kitchener-Waterloo Auditorium. They picked Harry up, parked at the side, walked around the front, through a long, dark corridor into the arena area, through a door, up long, creaky stairs, through another door, and finally . . . a real live dressing room.

"There were men everywhere getting ready to practise; there were sticks all over the place, skates all over the place. I thought, 'Jeez, hey, this is really, really living.'"

Howie's eyes scanned the room and quickly focused on the far end of the long, narrow, liniment-permeated dressing room, where, stuffed behind a full-size poker table, sat a huge man smoking the biggest cigar he had ever seen. "Follow me," Uncle Harry ordered, and on the way to meet this huge person Howie did a little dance over the sticks, skates, shin pads, towels, pants, and pucks that he hoped would very soon become a part of his life.

"At first glance from afar, this guy sitting at the poker table scared me — looked angry, tough, maybe a little mean. Once I was standing in front of him, his bulldog face, kindly smile, and friendly eyes made me think, 'Hey, I'm going to like this guy.' Harry said to me, 'Howie, this is Heiney Wismer. He's the guy who pays all the bills so be good to him.' Heiney stuck out his huge hand, and as I slipped mine into his, he asked, 'You goin' to be a hockey player, kid?' 'Sure hope so, sir,' I replied. For the first time in my life I heard, 'Good luck' and 'have fun.'"

For Howie, being a stick boy was Christmas every Sunday morning. The seniors would practise from 9 a.m. to 11 a.m., after the very good junior team of the day which boasted future NHLers Bobby Bauer, Woody Dumart, and Milt Schmidt. He'd arrive at 8 a.m., walk through the corridor, say hi to the watchman there, and walk in. "Hah, I was a big shot! I'd watch the Juniors for half an hour, go upstairs with Uncle Harry, sort out and tape sticks, put the towels near the shower, put the skates that were sharpened and honed where they belonged, cut up the oranges into quarters, and help the guys get ready to go on the ice. The team had two hours of ice time and usually used just an hour and a half. Those who were recovering from injury, trying to make the team, the spares, and those who wanted to fool around stayed on the ice. One day the goaltender, Tommy Berner, said, 'Howie, next week bring your skates and come on the ice for the last half-hour.'"

Berner later became Uncle Tom when he married Howie's mother's sister Mae. Tom at the time was a very good goaltender and a young accountant at Kuntz's Brewery. He later had offers to turn pro with the Toronto Maple Leafs but finally said, "Thanks, but no thanks." Uncle Tom wound up running the E.P. Taylor soft drink and beer empire, earning maybe five times what the best-paid Leaf was getting at the time.

The next week Howie had his skates, shin pads, and gloves, and at 10:30 was ready to go. He wasn't on the ice five minutes when Heiney appeared with a hockey stick with a sawed-off blade. He took the adult stick Howie had repaired and said, "Here, kid, use this stick. You'll never learn to handle the puck with that stiff shaft and huge blade; it's got no feeling."

Howie didn't know what he meant at the time. Besides ice time, Howie got most of the broken and cracked sticks, free tape to repair the same, plus pucks, which made him the most popular guy on the pond. Pucks used to cost 15 cents then and they were hard to come by. Tommy Berner made sure he had goal sticks, and in the games Saturday and Sunday on the lake and all over the place, they were the only ones where the guys between the pipes, shoes, or rocks had goal sticks so they could raise the puck a little bit.

Soon after, Howie was to learn his main job. After practice, seven or eight players sat down at the poker table to play, at first gin rummy and then poker with a nickel-and-dime limit. Soon they were hungry and there was a delicatessen up the street open Sunday. Howie went back and forth a half-dozen times for sandwiches and Coke, each time getting a nickel or a dime tip — sometimes a whole quarter when the guy had just won a big pot. Sunday afternoons he'd head for home with a couple of broken sticks, tape, pucks, and a few bucks in his pocket. "What a country, Christmas every week," Howie says. "I kept the kids in the neighbourhood well supplied with sticks."

Along with hockey, the military played a significant role in Howie's younger life. Charlie Meeker had retained his connection, even though it was peacetime, with the RCDs, who were stationed at the Stanley Barracks in Toronto, and Howie often travelled there with his family.

"It was two and a half to three hours' drive from Kitchener in those days. It's forty-five minutes now. While there I spent many happy hours upon the gentlest horse in the stables. Every summer the battalion moved lock, stock, and barrel to their three-month summer camp at Niagara-on-the-Lake. Toronto to Niagara-on-the-Lake was close to 100 miles so the unit overnighted somewhere along the way. Dad would find out where they were, load the car up with chicken and chips and maybe six to eight thermoses of gin and tonic. No beer. Gin, tonic, and ice cubes in all of them. After the guys had been on their horses all day, Charlie and Kitty Meeker were very welcome sights to see."

The Meekers spent quite a few weekends with Charlie's wartime friends at Niagara-on-the-Lake. The battalion was the originator of the famed Musical Ride and toured at that time all over Canada. When the unit disbanded the Royal Canadian Mounted Police took over the creative cavalcade.

Howie got the hang of riding a horse and one day was asked by the regimental sergeant major if he'd like to ride the routine with the unit while they practised without the lance. "Talk about eyes as big as saucers. There comes a time and this was another one. At the time I thought I was in command, but heck, they put me on the oldest, best-trained horse in the barn who could go through the routine with her eyes closed and fast asleep. In essence I just sat there, posted in rhythm, and the horse did the rest. Over the years I must have gone through the ride a half-dozen times with the same mare, 'Sally.' What a ride, what fun. Talk about being king of the roost."

On one particular return trek from Toronto, Charlie and Howie noticed a disabled car by the side of the road. Charlie would stop and help anybody, but this time the troubled traveller turned out to be the best-known voice on Toronto radio, CFRB announcer Jim Hunter. "I had to listen to him mainly because he was followed by Wes McKnight, the only and best sports reporter in the business. Anyhow, Mr. Hunter was on his way to some big do in Kitchener as guest speaker, and time was short and he had to get there. So Dad packed him in his car, got him to the event, had a mechanic friend pick up and repair the car and deliver it to him, no charge. Jim Hunter and Dad became pretty good friends, and through him I met Wes McKnight.

"Here was the fellow who interviewed the famous Toronto Maple Leaf players and others, knew them by their first name. When he got me Charlie Conacher's autograph I was the most popular guy in Suddaby School."

Gaining access to hockey sticks seemed to be something Howie had a knack for, but so was getting himself in hot water. Sooner or later the two tendencies were bound to overlap.

During the mid-1930s, besides the normal soft drinks such as orange, lime, gingerale, and cola, Kuntz's Brewery had two specialties: root beer in a crock bottle, which looked and tasted great, and the other a tasty chocolate drink called Kayo. The brewery held a major promotion for their new product, offering a youth hockey stick in exchange for twelve Kayo bottle tops. The temptation was more than Howie could resist.

"My father's storage warehouse had a big sliding door which opened wide enough to let the trucks in to load and unload the cases of pop. Can you imagine the look on my face when the delivery truck from Kuntz's left two gross, 244, kids' hockey sticks? What a country!"

To supplement his income, Charlie Meeker — who was calling on every general store in the area — approached Silverwood's Dairy to see if he could wholesale their ice cream. Much to his surprise, they agreed. Approximately the same time as the hockey sticks arrived so did a huge walk-in deepfreeze in which to store the large supply of ice cream.

Howie couldn't believe his luck. Just two minutes' walk from his home was his dad's huge warehouse full of pop, ice cream, and hockey sticks. It hardly seemed fair to keep this good fortune to himself, so Howie decided to share it with some of his hockey chums.

"I knew that the hook at the far end of the sliding door opposite the locked end was loose and I could squeeze through; I'd done it before. So this day myself and three of my pals snuck up to the warehouse and three of us got in. 'Fatso,' our goalie, couldn't make it, so we told him to wait by the door and be our lookout.

"Everyone headed for the huge pile of hockey sticks and each picked out a couple. I headed for the ice cream cooler and opened a box of a dozen ice cream bars. We had one each and passed one through the door to Fatso. When the guys started talking about getting the hockey sticks out the door I said, 'No way, just mark the sticks and leave them here. Come on, I'll show you,' and I took them to a huge cardboard box filled with Kayo caps that dad had exchanged for hockey sticks. 'Take twenty-four each and twenty-four for Fatso, then later come and collect your sticks for caps. We'll have one more ice cream bar and get out of here.'"

While the boys were filling their pockets with caps, Howie took the opened box of ice cream bars, handed them one more each, went to the door, pushed it open a bit and said, "Here you go, Fatso, have another ice cream."

When no one reached for the bar Howie knew they were in trouble. As he headed over to put the box back in the freezer Howie said, "Boys, eat that ice cream as quick as possible." Just as he came back out of the freezer, the big warehouse door slid open and there stood Tiny and another police friend.

"What are you guys doing in here?"

"Nothing, sir, just . . ." Howie sputtered.

"Does your dad know you're here?"

Howie wagged his head no. "We're just picking out hockey sticks."

"No ice cream, no pop?"

"No, sir. Didn't touch a thing."

"Well, you've got to come down to the police station anyway — breaking and entering is the charge," Tiny replied as he waved the boys towards the looming doorway. One of the lads, before leaving the warehouse, started to take the Kayo caps out of his pocket and put them back in the bin. "Keep them in your pocket, kid, that's evidence," a gruff-sounding Tiny barked.

As they piled into the police car, Howie could just picture his old man kicking the shit out of him.

The Kitchener police department was on the basement floor of the huge city hall. When Tiny and his associate marched Howie and friends through the back door, the large sergeant leaned over his raised desk and asked, "What's the problem?" Tiny explained, and after taking the boys' names and insisting they give the name of the one who ran away when the police car came down the lane, the sergeant said, "Lock 'em up," dismissing them with a wave of disgust.

"We were terrified as Tiny opened the door that led to the four big, steel-barred cells. 'In you go, boys, while we call your parents,' he said as he locked the cell with this huge key. Nobody ever suffered more in silence than we three. Ten minutes later (it seemed like ten hours), the door opened. Tiny entered, and behind him was my dad. 'Charlie is not going to press charges, so you're free to go,' he said.

"After a very quick 'Thanks, Mr. Meeker' we were out the door sitting in Dad's Oldsmobile, ready to go home. Ten minutes later, Dad came out, got in the car, drove five minutes to home, stopped in the driveway, and as he got out of the car, said, 'If there is a next time — I won't bail you out.'

"The scenario had to be that people in the apartment saw us sneak into the warehouse, recognized me, and phoned Dad, who called Tiny and gave him and his friends the key to the lock on the door. After a healthy drink of gin and tonic, Tiny made the arrest while Pop watched from afar, then sat in the jailhouse office having a drink with the sergeant and friends while we shivered and shook in jail. Well it worked, that arrest. That car ride and interrogation, those fifteen minutes locked in the jail cell, left quite an impression. Only while overseas and in the name of war did I ever put myself even close to having to go through that very scary routine again."

Y

Charlie Meeker remained involved with the military reserve corps, which operated out of the top floor of the Dunker Building on King Street in Kitchener. Howie remembers spending hours playing badminton in the new building while waiting for his dad. Eventually Charlie took on the job of charity fund-raiser for a new legion building. In less than a year, he and the executive raised $250,000. Another year later they had the biggest and best RCL in the land. Charlie was the first president and remained so for as long as he wanted the job. "Years later, Mom indicated that Dad's business went in the tank because of time spent playing peacetime soldier, building the RCL, and drinking with friends. However, Pop did a helluva fine job and I am sure was rewarded when he was chosen to be part of the Canadian contingent that travelled to Britain for the coronation of King George VI."

At age ten, Howie watched his dad go broke. Kuntz's Brewery was bought out by E. P. Taylor of Toronto, and about six months later Taylor announced to all his franchise people and distributors that the retailer, or whoever bought the pop, now had to pay three cents for every bottle.

"All of a sudden my dad went to deliver pop and everyone said, 'You give us the three cents or else you won't get the bottles back (which they'd received for free) and we won't buy the pop.' So that broke my dad, and also a lot of other people. Mom and Dad sold the house in Kitchener in order to buy a hotel in New Hamburg. It was a small, rundown, three-story country hotel, the King Edward, for $10,000 from the Reinharts. With a big mortgage to meet there was no money to make the needed repairs. The hotel did not boast many rooms, or anything else, but the popular pub sold a lot of beer at 10 cents a glass and 15 cents a bottle.

For the Meeker clan it proved a wonderful step. They had ten acres, and the Nith River ran right through the middle of their property. New Hamburg-Kitchener-Stratford was a rich agricultural area and many people had 100-acre farms, mostly mixed farming, and everyone prospered. The majority of people spoke German. It often seemed to the Meekers that they were the only ones in the area who were of English descent.

"I realized later in life what a wonderful place it was to grow up. We had absolutely everything a family or a youngster could need: good schools, great teachers, room to roam as kids. We hunted regularly — groundhogs, squirrels, pheasants, cottontails, jackrabbit drives, and we trapped muskrats as well. I eventually got a ferret and we hunted cottontails with him."

Howie was no different than most lads of age thirteen, and when teamed up with his ferret, the combination was merely trouble waiting to happen. Add an elementary-school setting and a room full of young girls and pandemonium was inevitable. Howie regularly took his pet to school so he could hunt the banks of the Nith on the way home. He kept his furry accomplice in a canvas bag, which he hung on a nail outside the window next to his desk; the ferret slept happily throughout the school day. One afternoon while Howie was in the washroom, a classmate, Newt Thomas, took Howie's furry friend out of the sack and placed it inside the desk of a girl who'd also left the classroom. When both children returned, the ferret surfaced, much to the horror and surprise of the young lass. The shrieks and screams panicked the ferret, who scrambled about the room in fear, which only sent more young girls squealing and running in all directions. Howie finally caught his pet, and soon after also caught the discipline of a solid strapping from "War" Ruthig, the school principal.

"It was worth every smack," Howie giggles fondly. "Two skinned and cleaned cottontails, ready for the oven, got me back in Mr. Ruthig's good books."

Destiny also passed Howie's eyes for the first time at age thirteen, soon after the move from Kitchener. "We moved to New Hamburg in May, and in September that year Mom took Dick and me down to the New Hamburg Continuation School to register. We were standing around outside Mr. Ruthig's office in the hallway waiting to talk to him when this young girl came tearing up the stairs out of the basement, grabbed the doorknob, and flew by me into a classroom. Oh my God, what a girl. Her name was Grace Hammer and I knew right then she was the girl for me, but it took me a couple of years to finally get around to dating her. She was a very popular girl and had a steady boyfriend. I had to wait until that soured before I could nudge my way in. But I knew the first time I saw her."

Life in New Hamburg proved just as wonderful or better than in

17

Kitchener, and while money was not plentiful there was still plenty to do, compliments of Mother Nature. Howie, his friends, and his troop of younger brothers took advantage of all that was offered.

"We would go tobogganing, snowshoeing, cross-country skiing, and downhill skiing. I remember in those days I was the only one who had skis that had a harness on, but my feet came out of them. We used to hold our feet in position with rubber bands, get an old tube, cut it in half, tie them up. I tried barrel staves and they worked pretty good; the trick was keeping your feet in them. Between the five Arnold boys and the Meeker clan we didn't need any more kids to have fun.

"In the spring we'd trap muskrat and fish in the Nith River and the small lakes; we used to catch all kinds of two- and three-pound black bass, and suckers, big ten-pound carp, just for the fight, and boy, they were great fun to catch."

Sometimes the boys would amble up to a little lake in the Baden hills and catch three- to five-pound bass on a fly rod. "In those days I had the normal casting rod where if you didn't have the touch of a Las Vegas card shark the level wind would go out faster than the line would, so you'd have a bird's nest that would take all afternoon to untangle. To lessen this problem we would buy the longest ten- to fifteen-foot bamboo pole at either Lloyd Apple's or Becker's Hardware Store, add about the same length of strong line, use a cork and a Number Six hook and either a big dew worm or a wad of dough. Right across from the dam in the middle of New Hamburg was Luft's Bakery and we'd go see Herb and he'd give us a handful of newly mixed dough. It not only caught big carp but stayed on our hooks better than bread wetted down and squeezed into a ball. If you've never had an eight- to ten-pound carp on a fifteen-foot bamboo pole with fifteen feet of line — then you don't know what you're missing. It's like having a young heifer on the line. We caught zillions of carp of all sizes, although we hardly ever kept them except to dig in around the rose bushes, but they were fun to catch."

The Meeker boys also fished a string of rivers east of Tavistock for the only pike in the area. They would fish off the road bridges over the small creeks and catch at least one or two fish, three to six pounds each. "One day as we were travelling along from one bridge to another, we came upon a giant field, about five acres, flooded maybe six to twelve inches deep. Suddenly brother Ken hollered, 'Hey, there's fish in that water.' We stopped and sure enough there were dorsal fins moving about all over the place. So Ken, Chuck, Tom, myself, and our Newfoundland dog Pal bounced out of the car and headed for the fish-filled muddy pond, shoes, socks, clothes, and all. Soon Ken, with legs astride, walking along bent over, had his hands on the back of a huge fish. Sliding his hands up into the gills he lifted straight up and cripes, he had to be holding a ten-pound carp. For the next hour we caught fish after fish. Even Pal got into the act, tracking down and catching fish. You never saw a happier dog, tail just wagging like crazy when he'd lift his carp out of the water. He had more sense than we did, though, and took his fish and dropped it ashore. I don't know how Mother ever got our clothes clean."

Swimming was mostly conducted near the mud flats at Ritz's farm, at the Narrows, also known as the Willows, near the dam in the middle of town, or else at Holland Mills, about a mile and a half down the back road out of town.

The town boasted a community swimming pool, but the postage stamp–sized facility was often filled with cold, strong, sulphurous-smelling water. "It took at least three very hot days to warm the water even for the bravest person. The formula for a water change apparently was when someone stood at the shallow end and couldn't stop from sliding right in over their head to the deep end. Only then did they figure it was time to drain it, clean it, scrub it, and fill it up again. Before that the water got hot, dirty, and full of algae. It's a wonder we all didn't die, but actually, if the river didn't kill us — acids and dye from the felt boot factory and the Hahn Brass Works plus every sewer and septic-tank system in town flowed into the river — then the pool wasn't going to hurt us worse."

Ⅴ

Charlie Meeker's fixation with horses did not end with his son's lawn-stomping pony in Kitchener. The first thing he did when the family moved to New Hamburg was build himself a barn and buy a horse. He bought a mountain of a horse, which is what he called him — seventeen or eighteen hands high. "Dad wouldn't ride the thing. The horse was huge and it became my job to exercise him. I had a lot of fun with him and now, years later, I have kids who are crazy about horses and I blame it on him.

"Dad was quite the barterer, so it didn't take long before he got a few goats for a couple bottles of beer, then a few chickens, and then pigeons. He said, 'We'll raise pigeons and squabs and when they get big enough and fat enough we'll kill them and eat them.' Well, these were huge white King pigeons and there was no way in the world — I think my dad knew it — we would ever let him kill young pigeons. Eventually we got into pheasants and homing pigeons in a big way."

During the mid-1940s, Homer Pigeon Clubs were all the rage, with local clubs in Kitchener, Stratford, Guelph, and Toronto. Many of the clubs in the area sent their racing birds in wicker baskets by train to New Hamburg for regular runs. Stationmaster Clayton Engle would release the pigeons from New Hamburg at a set time and the owners timed their birds' journey home. Howie and brothers decided that a few of the hundreds of visiting pigeons would look nice added to their personal loft, so while Clayton was kept occupied a couple of birds found their way out of the wicker baskets into a gunnysack and home to Howie's. After a few such escapades the Meeker boys had about four or five pairs of pigeons. Then ingenuity kicked in and the boys realized that a lot of the birds at the railway release were flying for the first time and would follow veteran birds wherever they went. Howie and cohorts would wait until the railway birds were released, then would release their own veteran birds and King pigeons into the air.

Inevitably a few of the homers from the railway flock would tangle in with Howie's and wind up landing with the Meeker birds.

"It didn't take too long before we had at least twenty or thirty of them, most of them banded and really good birds."

Howie's love for birds and livestock led to a memorable moment in his young teenage life. Five or six of his friends went with him to the famous Royal Winter Fair in Toronto. They stayed to see the evening jumping competition and missed the last train home. Everybody there who showed horses fixed up one stall as a tack room and most of the owners or managers slept there to keep an eye on the horses.

"It was 11 p.m. and we wound up in this huge horse barn looking for an empty stall with hay in it in which to sleep. I found one, only there was a light and voices coming from the adjoining tack room. I knocked at the door and heard this 'Come in,' so I did and there sat the most beautiful girl this thirteen-year-old had ever seen. 'Yes?' she said, and I knew there was someone else sitting in the shadows but really didn't care. Cripes, I couldn't take my eyes off this lady. I finally explained our situation, six of us, no place to sleep, could we bed down in the stall next door? 'Sure, no problem, and here's some blankets to keep you warm,' she said. As I gathered them in my arms a man in the corner got up and said, 'Here kid, I'll give you a hand with them.' As his face hit the glow from the only light in the room my jaw fell open. 'Shit, that's Busher Jackson, the all-star left winger with the Toronto Maple Leafs,' I thought.

"Finally we got settled in the hay pile. Did you ever try to sleep in hay? If it isn't sticking in your ear or up your ass, then it's in your socks, even your underwear, try under your shirt — sharp as a pin. Anyway, before tossing and turning all night long with little or no sleep, I told the guys that Busher Jackson was the man in the next stall. No one believed me.

"I was awake most of the night and at 5 a.m., 6 a.m., 7 a.m., all is still silent next door, and then suddenly I hear someone talking.

By now we're all awake so I'm sitting on a bale of hay near the doorway waiting for Mr. Jackson. The door opens, he kisses this beautiful creature (even at 7:30 she looked super), and turns to leave. I said, 'Mr. Jackson, would you sign this program for me, please, and sign a page in it for the gang?' He could have said, 'Christ, kid, it's 7:30 in the morning and I am beat. I've just spent the last six or eight hours making love to a beautiful woman; I'm cold, and hungry, and really want a cup of coffee. I'll sign it another time.' He had every right to say that but instead it was, 'Sure kid, it's a pleasure.'

"Busher Jackson signed a card or piece of paper for all of us, answered questions for ten or fifteen minutes, then took us to the coffee shop in the building and paid for breakfast for all. Everything else that took place on that road trip to the Royal Winter Fair took second place to Busher Jackson. He made our day."

Howie recalls how Conn Smythe and others later kept the Busher, by far the best player on the Conacher-Primeau-Jackson line, out of the Hockey Hall of Fame because they said he lacked character. He may have liked a little wine and women, but he was big on character, Howie says.

"There were many times in the following sixty years, a great many times actually, that I should have, or had very good reason to say, 'No, some other time,' to a request for an autograph, interview, or event. Whenever that happened I remembered Busher Jackson and then would say smilingly, 'Sure boy, it's a pleasure.'"

That morning after breakfast with Harvey "Busher" Jackson, the boys visited the poultry bars and looked at the myriad of chickens and pigeons. "There was crate after crate after crate of pigeons. There were pigeons I had never seen: fantails, nuns, tipplers, tumblers, swallows, rollers, jaccomens, pouters . . . It wasn't long before we were copying names and addresses off the cages, saving money, and buying pigeons. In the next two years I must have ended up with twenty different kinds of pigeons. Our loft went from 20 pigeons to 150 pigeons and from one kind to eighteen or twenty different sorts. It's something that's stayed with me all my life, and my kids' as well.

"In the following years we acquired all kinds of pigeons, but in the process found out that highly bred birds don't necessarily mean they will be good parents or nesters. In fact most turned out to be very poor parents, either to nest and eggs or to the very young birds. We soon discovered that the best parents by far were the wild pigeons or barn pigeons, which we called 'scrubs.' We'd just swap the eggs — the swallows', pouters', jaccomens', and fantails' eggs — to the barn pigeon and hers to the others. It worked like a charm but some of the moms had puzzled looks when Junior's throat blew up, the swallow had leg-feathers six inches long while still in the nest, or the kid had a tail like a huge fan. Anyhow, the 'scrub' mothers did what we wanted very well and raised healthy and strong young birds. Soon we had more eggs than our four or five pair of scrubs could handle and we needed extra birds to look after the eggs. No problem.

"Ken, Chuck, Tom, and I, armed with flashlights, would steal into a farmer's barn each with a brin bag or potato sack cinched to our belt, climb up into the rafters, and scoff a few pigeons. Sounds simple, but have you ever noticed where the pigeons roost? Top shelf of the building — way up, no-oxygen height. From the top of the hay pile a third or halfway up you could spot the birds, but how to get there? It's dark as you climb up through cobwebs thick as a jungle, up a wobbly beam, across a creaking board, up and over and across more beams, and finally you arrive. You are fifty or sixty feet straight up and the bird is just three feet away. You've got to hold on, turn on the light, and catch the bird — but with only two hands, how do you do it? I remember holding on to the beam with one hand, sticking one end of the flashlight in my mouth, and then grabbing the damn bird with my free hand. There's the mate, now what? So you stick the first bird inside your jacket or shirt and as he's clawing you, trying to get out, you reach for number two, who has now moved. So you stretch a little further and luckily capture number two. Getting the brin bag open, both birds in it, and down safely back on the hay pile was another story."

The main reason the Meeker boys took youngest brother Tom on their pigeon-pilfering patrols was to distract dogs. "Tom had a way with dogs, always did. He knew every farm dog in the county, and they knew him, so when we picked a barn we sent Tom in ahead to make peace with the dogs. Then we could enter the barn unannounced to the owners.

"Sometimes we'd go to two or three barns a night; it's a wonder that we all weren't killed. One evening Tom was almost trampled to death by a big sow who thought he was trying to get her young ones. After the initial scare I never saw anything so funny in all my life. That night we were in Elmer Ruthig's barn and Elmer and I were buddies. We bought a six-battery flashlight to spot the birds and the route to them from the top of the hay pile while one of us climbed up and captured the bird.

"This day Tom is up about forty to fifty feet, has one bird that he put in the armpit of the hand he's holding on with, and is reaching to get bird number two when the captured bird claws him, escapes, and takes off. Tom loses his hold, slips, and falls. Elmer had a two-tiered hayloft, one about twenty feet above the other. Tom lands almost at my feet, bounces off, falls another twenty feet onto a haystack loader backed into the barn still loaded with hay, bounces off it to the floor, rolls over, and falls another eight to ten feet through a hole in the main floor where they threw the hay down to the animals, right onto the back of a big sow with fifteen to twenty piglets in the pen.

"You never heard such a fuss in all your life. The pig was screaming, but I knew Tom was alive because he was hollering louder than the pig. The dogs at the house were barking, the cows mooing, the horses neighing and jumping up and down; the chickens and ducks were squawking and hollering and flying all over the place. When the three of us finally arrived at the ground floor it didn't take long to get out of there because in my mind I could see the lights going on in Elmer's house and his wife (who hated me) grabbing the shotgun and heading for the barn — so I wanted out of there as quick as possible. I'll never forget Tom astride the sow's back hanging on for dear life as she ran all around the pen. We all died laughing."

One day the municipal people in Kitchener decided to sell their streetcars and bring in buses, so Charlie Meeker bought a streetcar and had it transferred the twelve miles from Kitchener to New Hamburg. It was a big job and just about everybody in town turned out when the trolley was brought in.

"We had a huge backyard including the big barn. Dad put the streetcar in one corner of the backyard and we used it as a dressing room. That left us a playing area in the yard of fifty to sixty yards long, forty yards wide. I was thirteen or fourteen years old.

"We played every sport, but nothing was organized in those days. Wilbur Reinhart, son of the people we bought the hotel from, stayed on to work there and took me golfing a few times. I continued to play every sport going: soccer, fastball, softball; then I finally caught on that tennis wasn't such a bad game because that was where all the good-looking girls were and they were all wearing shorts, even back in those days. I even went lawn bowling, got pretty good at it actually, but I was really there because of the girls."

γ

But the thing Howie and his friends did more than anything else was play hockey — morning, noon, and night. They would stick-handle a tin can or frozen horse bun to and from school. They played shinny on the grass, slush, or the school rink. After school they headed for one of the three rinks they had constantly on the go. There was the huge rink in the backyard next to the streetcar, a pond just behind their place, and then fifty yards down the bank a rink on the Nith River. Eventually lights were put on the backyard rink and they spent hours and hours skating and keeping it in top shape.

There was still no such thing as organized minor hockey, but

Howie's mom got him connected with a minister who had a Sunday school class in Shakespeare, just up the road. "One day one of us said we should have a hockey team. There were about fourteen or fifteen boys in the Sunday school, and the same number of girls, which was probably one of the reasons I was going there. He said, 'Fine — you get the team organized, I'll get you kids some games.' So that night the minister got on the phone and called up a number of other ministers in the area, and it wasn't long before we had a four- or five-team league. We were playing hockey all over the place, including a men's league where Dave Pinkney first spied Howie. Then I went to the school principal and said, 'Sir, we have a rink outside on the basketball court and I could get a hockey team together if you could get some other schools involved.' So we ended up playing quite a bit of hockey through the Sunday school as well as the school."

When it came to hockey nothing matched the National Hockey League, but in 1937 in New Hamburg, the Intermediate league with teams from towns such as Elmira, Milverton, Tavistock, Clinton, Seaforth, and Goderich was a close second.

"I think the local team was in the middle of the pack in the standings. Walter Geiger, a local grocer, and friends owned the small natural ice rink and was just delighted when 500 or 600 fans would show up for every game, paying 15 cents or a quarter. We used to scrounge up enough money for one of our gang to purchase a ticket and get in the arena and then ten minutes before the game he would open a pre-arranged shutter that would allow fifteen or twenty of us free entry to the game."

When watching the games, Howie often used to stand on a balcony behind the visitors' net and in those days the centre men faced off standing with their backs to the side boards, not the end boards as they do today. The balcony was built because the end boards of the rink were also the ends of the building. To clean the ice, workers simply opened the gates on the boards and the building doors and threw the snow from the scrapers directly outside. The setup caused a minor problem, though: where do you put the goal judge? The answer was to have the brave soul stand on the ice behind the net, and New Hamburg had a great (brave) goal judge.

"There was none better than Shorty Eichler, who unofficially led the league in assists and had the quickest feet in the league. He made more good foot passes from behind the net, right onto the tape of New Hamburg forwards, than Wayne Gretzky ever has. In fact Gretzky could have learned a few things from Shorty about playing behind the net."

Shorty's rule for opposition teams was that the puck crossing the goal line wasn't good enough — it had to hit the back of the net before he would reluctantly wave the white hanky, declaring a goal. "I remember the time Shorty wore new rubber galoshes with rounded toes and his passes were way off line in the first period, so they sent someone home to get his old reliable square-toed rubber boots."

Howie says they had great goaltending in Claire Pfaff, and great offence from Roter and Bumpty Roth, local farmers. Roter at one time led Buffalo in scoring in the American Hockey League. If he had had skating legs he'd have been a superstar in the NHL. "We never missed a game and I learned a lot about offensive skilled hockey by watching Roter Roth. Boy, was he smart. The only problem was that no one on the team had any idea of what he was trying to do; his mental game was on a completely different level."

Howie was the best of the fourteen-year-old players in the village, and one day he received an invitation from Irish Culbert to practise with the Intermediate club. "I'm a kid and get an invitation to practise with the men. I didn't tell Dad, he could care less, but I told Mother and she was delighted.

"For 6:30 p.m. practice I walked to the rink. I was there at 5:30; stood there and froze until someone showed up and opened the dressing room at 6 p.m. I followed three or four others into the room with my kit bag and stick and got cool looks from most of the men. I knew them all because I had been watching them for three or four years but they didn't know me and most were thinking, 'What the hell is this kid doing here?' I picked a corner, sat down, and began to look around. First thing that caught my eye was a big pot-bellied stove in the centre of the room which the trainer was trying to get a fire started in. Around the entire belly of the stove was a tin water jacket and I wondered why. Then I saw about fifteen suits of dirty, rotten, smelly underwear with numbers written on the back hanging from the ceiling. There were nails pounded into the walls all over the place, and a bench wall-to-wall in this twenty-by-twenty-foot room with skates, gloves, shin pads, elbow pads, jocks, in a pile on the floor.

"Players were arriving in ones and twos and so I got up and stood in the corner while everyone got dressed. But hey man, this was the big league, a warm room, with benches to sit on and finally a sheet of ice with boards around it. No more skating a quarter-mile after an errant pass or wasting five minutes trying to find the puck in a six-foot snow bank, or lying on your belly on the ice, gingerly trying to fish the puck out of eighteen inches of water with your stick."

It didn't cross Howie's mind that his 130 pounds on a five-foot six-inch frame might not stand up when pitted against men. Somehow he felt he belonged there. Finally Irish Culbert showed up, told everyone why Howie was there, and said, "Get dressed in a hurry, kid." Five minutes later, Howie was ready to go.

"I'll never forget the first time I visited that dressing room; it was every bit what this great game was all about and I am sure I made up my mind right then and there to make it part of my life as long as possible. Oh, the water jacket was for shower water, compliments of a teammate standing on a chair with a watering can held over you. Yes, it worked and I'll never forget my first shower with the guys in their dirty, smelly, stinky, lovable hockey room. It didn't take me long to figure out that if you wanted a warm shower you'd better get undressed quick after the game, and to add cold water to that which came directly out of the jacket, or get burned. There were only five pails of water in that shower and if you weren't one of the first ten, it was cold water only."

Howie didn't play any games that year with the Intermediate team but practised with them on a regular basis. The few times they put him on the wing with Roter Roth they filled the net. Howie was by far the quickest skater in the group and Roter would put him home free time after time. Howie says he's played with some great centre men but no one had more pure skill than the talented farmer.

"No kid in the world could have grown up in a better environment than I did in Kitchener and New Hamburg," Howie says. "Later on in life when I got married and started to have kids, I looked back with great pleasure and thanks to my father and mother for allowing me to grow up in that kind of environment. Whenever possible, I have done the same thing for my own kids — given them an environment in which to have a good time and live in the country. When we eventually moved to St. John's, Newfoundland, we lived there for two years and then moved out to a place with fifteen acres on the sea.

"When we transferred out of there we ended up again on the sea, at a great fishing and boating area next to a marina, with all the best things that Parksville, on Vancouver Island, B.C., could offer the kids: skiing, hunting, fishing, swimming. I don't apologize for that. I think Grace and I were very, very fortunate to be able to put our kids into an environment where they could take advantage of the outdoors."

Two

Big Fish — Little Pond

"We could have built the ark. There had to be a half-dozen homes in the area missing lumber and tools."

One Saturday morning, just after the thaw in late February 1938, a circle of boys clustered inside the streetcar in Howie's backyard. Between the Arnold, Klassen, and Meeker clans, they numbered at least eight or nine. Naturally, with spring's influence in the air, talk soon turned to trapping skunks, hunting groundhogs, and eventually fishing. After lamenting at length that none of them owned a fishing boat, one of the Arnold kids suggested they make one.

"My big brother and his buddy built one, and if they can do it so can we. My dad has some tongue-and-groove cedar stored away.

I can beg, borrow, or steal some," Fauts Arnold told his cohorts. They called him "Fauts" because he had the impressive ability of being able to fart upon command. With the boat-building seed firmly planted, a number of questions arose: how do you build a boat, how long will it be, how wide, what about the depth of the sides, how do you make it float, how do you waterproof it?

It soon became apparent a little adult advice might be needed on the project, but who should the boys go to? Llama Hunstein was the unanimous answer.

Llama had become a steady customer at the hotel pub and often helped Charlie or Kitty Meeker with small jobs. He was a huge man with various skills, but he didn't like constant work. "A circus came to town one year and held a big parade," Howie recalls. "Hunstein helped out and led a llama down the street. He was always called 'Llama' after that; we never did know his real name. He had a lot of patience with kids and was always happy to help people out."

However, neither Llama, Wilbur Reinhart, nor any other adult consulted seemed to have a clue about building boats. Undaunted, the boys proceeded and within two days the area between the street-car and barn looked like a lumberyard. Tongue-and-groove cedar, six inches wide and fifteen feet long, two-by-fours and two-by-twos by the dozens, planks, hammers, saws, chisels, screwdrivers, clamps, glue, planers, sawhorses, were strewn about the Meeker yard. "We could have built the ark. There had to be a half-dozen homes in the area missing lumber and tools."

It was time for serious planning and the boys methodically solved their concerns. "It's got to hold at least five of us — two in the back seat, two in the rowing seat, one in the bow. How wide?" Two boys sat on the board and measured — three feet — too narrow. "Let's make it four feet wide at the back. How long do we make it? Where's the middle seat going to be?" Someone said, "Two of us sit on this plank. Cut another one the same size, four feet wide. You guys sit on it facing us. Sit normal. Now stretch out your feet. Now, move that middle seat back a bit so our feet don't touch when we stretch out. Ah, that looks like about five or six feet."

"The bow seat. How do we do that?"

"Well, if the back half of the boat is seven feet, let's add another seven feet and make her fourteen feet long."

Someone asked, "What about the dog? Can't leave him ashore. Let's add two more feet for Pal. The boat will have to be sixteen feet long and four feet wide."

The project dragged on a few weeks and it looked as if the frame would never be completed. One day it rained, then it snowed, then it got cold. Ontario was no warmer in February and early March in the 1930s than it is today, and with only an hour or two of daylight after school to work on the boat it wasn't long before one boy suggested a change of building sites. "Why don't we build the boat in the streetcar? It's going to be warm and dry because we've got a stove, and we've even got lights so we can work at night."

By mid-April a proud gathering of boys stood around their completed vessel. The questions began again: what to name it, where to launch it, what colour to paint it?

Then, as they all sat there in the streetcar, Fauts said, "How are we going to get the boat out of here?"

"Jeez, boys, we never thought of that. Llama — help!"

Llama seemed confident the problem was easily resolved. "No problem, boys — just take off the end of the streetcar. The three windows that have to be removed will just drop down into the sides."

"But Llama, that means sawing off two supports. How are we going to get them back without Dad knowing it?" Howie worried.

"I'll bring four U-bolts, we'll screw them in, put the window frames back in, and your Dad will never know the difference."

That Friday afternoon, the crew dropped the windows into the back of the streetcar frame and Llama sawed the two supports, top and bottom, leaving a gaping hole five feet high and nine feet wide. With the aid of many bodies the heavy ship was extracted.

The final question — what colour to paint the boat? At least six partially filled, different-coloured cans of paint were discovered in

Charlie Meeker's shed. There wasn't enough in any one can to paint the boat so they decided to mix the red, blue, green, and white paint together.

"I'll never forget Fauts, sitting on the streetcar step, stirring a can of green paint with about two inches in it on his lap, working damn hard to try and mix the runny stuff with the junk stuck on the bottom. As he's grinding away the can slips — jeez, green paint everywhere. He looked like the Green Hornet. After a great laugh, Fauts began to cry. 'These are new pants — look at them. My old man will kill me,' and he would have, too. Mom saved the day. She gave him a pair of mine for the night and the next day sent him down with $3.49 to get a new pair at Becker's store."

At 7 a.m. Saturday, the boys were gathered to paint their boat and fix the streetcar, but there was no Llama. By 8 a.m., Howie led the crew off to Llama's place. He lived alone, so the parade of boys walked in. As usual, Llama was nursing a hangover. He gave the boys turpentine and three brushes and said he would be over later.

"With almost a full can of mixed white, red, green, and blue paint, we decided that three of us would paint the outside and three inside. We'd take turns. Well, with three brushes in the gallon can at the same time we damned near spilled the thing taking them out. Thirty seconds later we had a stream of spilled paint from the can to the boat, some of it on the ground, some over our shoes and pants, hands, and face; our parents were going to kill us when we got home. So, back to Llama's — he's still in bed. We dug out his oldest, dirtiest, working clothes, his painting stuff, rolled up the sleeves and arms and went back to work. What a funny-looking sight because Llama was about six feet tall. We had one half-full can of bright blue paint and painted the bow and the cover over the bow blue, so we called it the *Bluenose*."

Sunday was launch day in the Nith, about 100 yards away from the streetcar, but down a sloping, sometimes very steep, hill. "We got pretty smart and found six round fence poles, put the boat on them, three guys pulled the bowline, and two guys replaced the used poles, stern to bow. When we started down the path behind the barn, we had a hell of a problem; the boat rolled over the logs without our help and, had the guys not hung on, it would have ended up against a tree or in the river all on her own. We ended up with four guys hanging on to the stern letting her slide down by herself.

"So we made the shore and as much as we wanted to launch her right away, we had promised Mom, Dad, Llama, and Wilbur Reinhart, who all had considerable investment in this venture, that we'd invite them to the launch party. We had Cokes, I remember they were five cents a piece — five Cokes from the Imperial service station for 25 cents. The kids brought sandwiches and doughnuts from home and Mom had baked a graham wafer pie and also a chocolate cake for us. Dad had bought a cheap bottle of wine to christen the *Bluenose*."

Empty tummies and one look at the food dictated that perhaps the party should be held first and the launch after. It was a wise decision. When it came time to christen the boat, Charlie Meeker, half snockered by then, volunteered. He took first crack at the bow and hit it a pretty good shot, but the bottle didn't break. The next time he hit it harder — with the same result. The kids started to look at each other thinking, "If he hits it any harder he'll destroy the bow of the boat." As he drew back to break the bow or the bottle, Howie's mother wisely said, "Why don't we uncork the bottle and just pour the wine over it?" Everyone chirped quickly, "Good idea."

With the ceremony complete the marvellous *Bluenose* was shoved off shore into the four-foot-deep water to a rousing hail of cheers and whistles. The glory was short-lived — within thirty seconds it filled with water and sank to the shallow bottom, water up to and over the gunwales.

They didn't know whether to laugh or cry, but Llama said, "No problem boys, bring her out of the water and let her dry. Then we'll get some tar and seal every joint. She'll float fine." For once Llama was correct and with some tar on the joints the *Bluenose* was soon waterproofed and floating.

As Charlie Meeker headed back to the hotel, he could hardly miss noticing that the end of the streetcar was gone. "Howwwarddd!" he screamed. Howie, still down at the river, some 250 yards away, immediately started widening the gap. Llama and the boys had forgotten to replace the windows. "I knew I was dead but by the time we crossed paths again the next morning, Mom, Llama, and Wilbur had assured Dad that they would put the windows back in, which they did and I never did get a licking.

"We briefly lost the *Bluenose* in a flood that first year but found it unharmed in a farmer's field six miles down the road and had it trucked back. We often put it in the dam in the centre of town, where there was always water. Everybody used it; we swam and fished from it and spent many a moonlit night courting young ladies in it, making little waves. Eventually we lost the *Bluenose*. We had a launch site where we tied her up and one time someone didn't tie the boat after using it, we had a rain storm, then a flash flood, and the boat disappeared. We walked the river four to five miles, right to Haysville, trying to find her."

Ɣ

As for many people, the year 1939 held a lot of significant changes for Howie Meeker. Less than twenty years after the Great War had ended in Europe, a second and perhaps larger conflict had broken out. Two months before Howie's sixteenth birthday, England and Germany declared war.

Charlie Meeker, a veteran of the Great War, had been in the reserve army for years in the Kitchener area and when the second conflict began he quickly joined the Veterans Corps. He was a regimental sergeant major and wound up guarding various prisoner of war camps throughout Ontario.

The start of the war parallelled the opening of another school year — another change for Howie, who suddenly had to bus to Kitchener to attend high school.

"That was great, in my mind, because Grace was one grade

ahead of me and we'd be on the same bus. I'd never forgotten her from that first day at school a few years before, when I saw her run through the classroom door ahead of me.

"A number of us kids went down on the bus that first day to Kitchener and got lost, homesick, and lonely. We were from a school with about 100 kids and suddenly we're at a high school of 3,000. Man, were we out of our depth as a bunch of farmers' kids. One day during that first week I couldn't find one of my classes, and didn't really care to find it. I finally went downstairs and out the front door, and there was Grace sitting on the steps. I said, 'What are you doing here?' and she said, 'I don't know, I don't like this, I don't like what's going on.' "

Howie replied he felt the same way. "I've had enough of this, too. School in New Hamburg was fine but school here in Kitchener is for the birds." The two country bumpkins wound up quitting school that day. While signalling an end to their education, the rebellious step also started a friendship and eventual partnership.

"It took me maybe a year to finally break the ice with her. She disliked me for the longest time after our first meeting in junior high school, but eventually found I wasn't a total jerk and dated me. We hit it off pretty good after we came back home on the bus together; that was the real beginning. We went skating together — she was a great skater — and we went skiing, hunting, everything. We took the kids, my three youngest brothers Ken, Chuck, and Tom, swimming, and to all kinds of things. Grace and I did everything together, often with the kids in tow, and she was part of the Meeker family very early."

Leaving school may not have been as easy for Grace or Howie had their rebellion come in a different era. The war created quite a shortage of labourers and Grace immediately went to work at her father's Ford agency. Howie tried to fill part of the gap created by his father's sudden absence.

With Charlie in the army, Kitty needed help at the hotel. Howie, now almost sixteen, convinced his mom to let him leave school and help out. He worked at the hotel from 9 a.m. until midnight and enjoyed it.

"For a time we had the nickel and dime slot machines; boy, were we ever busy. That's where I got my love for playing the slots. We bootlegged Gooderham and Worts whiskey. I remember it was 25 cents for an ounce and a half of drink. A good friend in the law enforcement agency always made sure we were alerted well before any raids took place, and the liquor inspector looked the other way over the fact that I was only sixteen. I guess he figured with Dad in the army, Mom could use any help she could get running the hotel and bar."

When the liquor board finally decreed there were to be no more slots in the building, Howie and Wilbur moved them down to the barn. Regulars would order a beer or two in the pub, take them to the barn, and play there for hours. "Whiskey sales went way up then because it was a lot easier to take a bottle of whiskey down to the barn than a case of beer."

The hotel often held banquets for as many as 100 people, which meant horrendous work on Kitty's part, but she slugged it out. Saturday was always the big day and night for business: $125 at the till and $50 whiskey money was a great day.

Ɣ

Regulations in those years dictated that one had to play hockey for the closest team to home. The town of New Hamburg, however, sat nestled almost equally between Kitchener and Stratford, so Howie usually had his choice. In early September the *Kitchener-Waterloo Record* reported that the local Greenshirts Junior B hockey team was having an open tryout. Howie packed his bag, grabbed his stick, and hitchhiked the twelve miles to Kitchener.

"When I went to the Greenshirts tryout it was like returning home — same arena, same people. I walked into the huge foyer and got directions to the Junior B dressing room. I was halfway up the stairs, kit bag, stick, and all, before I realized, 'Jeez, this is dressing room number one, the same dressing room we used when I was the stick boy for the Kitchener Seniors — I've made it.' At the top of the stairs I stopped, and in my mind's eye I could see Uncle Harry Wharnsby, Heiney Wismer, Uncle Tommy Berner, and all the other wonderful men who made my life a dream world for three long winters. When I made the team, I insisted on using Karlo Kuntz's former stall. Karlo was the guy who'd spent time with me on the ice and was a very good hockey player, and also a generous tipper. All that winter, every time I dressed in that room, it brought back very pleasant memories."

Beland Honderich and Ernie Goman were partners in the Junior B club with Goman the organizer and general manager. Honderich later became publisher of the *Toronto Star*.

"It didn't take long to figure out I was the second-best skater on the ice. The best was Joe Iarnelli from Sudbury. I could almost skate with Joe but had no idea what the hell the game of hockey was about, why you would do this or that, nothing about playing the game. He became my centre man and I played with Joe all year.

"Joe later played minor professional hockey and years later moved to Victoria, B.C. He still lives in Victoria and now plays old-timers' hockey. We occasionally play together at seventy-plus years of age, only *now* I can outskate Joe."

The club had some imports, but mainly the players were from the Kitchener area and were the same fellows Howie had played with and against years before on the lake in the park. As a team they were so-so, winning as many as they lost, but no match for the stronger teams. They made the playoffs but lost in the first round. The coaching was iffy but Howie had a good year. He played one year of Junior B in Kitchener.

Hockey was not the only sport in which young Meeker excelled. Both he and brothers Ken and Tom showed strong softball skills as well. In the summer of 1940, New Hamburg had a competitive Intermediate softball team with most of the players in their mid-twenties and very adept at the game. One day the club invited him to a practice. Howie normally played infield — second and third base, or shortstop — but those spots were filled by "adults" and no one moved over, so Howie gravitated to the outfield.

In those years softball players didn't use gloves, and the ball was hard. The sixteen-year-old kid wasn't going to move any man out of a spot, but in the outfield Howie managed to catch most balls hit his way and when it was his turn at batting practice he sprayed balls all over the field. Howie made the team and helped them win the Oxford-Waterloo League championship. On the way to that championship they eliminated the Stratford softball team, which helped land him a tryout the next summer with the Stratford Senior baseball team.

Howie's success with the Junior B Greenshirts caught the eye of more than one hockey coach or general manager. The next year a chap by the name of Dave Pinkney from Stratford came to New Hamburg to talk to Howie. Dave had been in hockey all of his life, spending many years in the old Michigan-Ontario Hockey League and coaching or managing top-rated Junior teams in the 1930s. He organized and sponsored numerous teams over the years and eventually owned the Queens Hotel in Stratford. Howie says "Dave was a prince of a fellow and should be in the Hockey Hall of Fame as a builder. Of all the people I ever met in hockey, Dave was probably the finest gentleman."

Pinkney told Howie he was organizing a Junior B team in Stratford. "It's going to be a great club and we'd like you to play as one of our imported players. Another big reason to consider us is we can get you a job in the Canadian National Railway shops in Stratford as a machinist's apprentice. You get a job in there and you have it made for life."

Soon after that meeting a fight developed between Kitchener and Stratford as to where Howie should play hockey, and the clubs even got down to measuring the distance between Howie's home and the two towns. However, Howie had already started working at the CNR shops in Stratford, so the Ontario Hockey Association ruled to let him play there.

The night Kitchener-Waterloo reluctantly gave Howie his release, Stratford displayed no sense of gratitude and clobbered them 14–0. Howie scored three goals and added two assists. New teammate and slick centre Billy Cupolo had six points. Billy not only proved to be a great teammate but also a fine friend for Howie.

The five-year apprenticeship program paid 12 cents an hour to start, with a 3-cent raise every six months for two years. In the third year a lad stood to make at least 35 cents an hour. After five years, successful graduates would collect top pay as a machinist of around $2.50 per hour.

"I was not cut out to be a machinist, that I knew. It was the only job in my life I didn't enjoy. We worked 7 a.m. to 4 p.m. Monday to Friday, and 8 a.m. to noon every Saturday, and I didn't enjoy a minute of it."

Howie had two good years with Dave Pinkney in Stratford, one year of Junior B and the next in Junior A. Carl White was the coach and his assistant was Bill Gerby, an old hockey man from years back and wonderful person.

The 1941–42 Stratford Kist Canadians were a skilled hockey team with Billy Cupolo head and shoulders above the rest of the guys. "I'd be going down the ice full out and Cupolo would put the puck on my stick giving me shot after shot," Howie recalls. "I could skate and he could handle the puck, pass, shoot . . . he was always a threat. We had great goaltending in Dolly Dolson Jr., all five-foot-eight and 170 pounds of him. His father was an all-star goalie in the American and Michigan-Ontario leagues for years and like father, like son; Dolly was a winner."

On defence the club was big, strong, and mobile with Lou Ayres, Bear Huras, Larry Gatschene, and Bob Marshall. Up front the club had speed, skill, and finesse led by their two great centres Cupolo and Bruce Burdett. Both later played pro hockey. Herby Morrison from the Maritimes played with Bill and Howie, and on a wing with Burdett was Ken Ducharme — a stop-and-go, goal-scoring winger in the same mould as Cal Gardner, who later played with Howie in Toronto. He scored goals by the dozen, especially big ones, while Erle Burdett and Jack Mavity filled in wherever.

The Kist Canadians lost just one or two games during the regular season but got a few good scares in the playoffs. In the best-of-five final playoff series, Stratford was hard pressed but finally succeeded three games to one against Hamilton. "We won the final game 6–5 at home in Stratford with a packed rink," Howie says. "It was early April of 1942 and that night they had a huge parade with fire trucks, bands, and everything else. It was the first Ontario Hockey Association championship in Stratford in nineteen years, so they were due for a celebration."

Less than a week later the club headed for Copper Cliff, in northern Ontario, to meet the Sault Ste. Marie Rapids team starring a hotshot kid named Joe Klukay. Coach Carl White couldn't go with the team to Copper Cliff so Gerby, dubbed Father Bill, filled in as coach. "He was the last guy in the world you'd want as coach. I'm not sure what he knew about hockey, if anything. During the whole year Father Bill didn't say two words, but we all loved him dearly; he was at all the games and practices. We wanted to win for him and Dave more than for ourselves. The first game we go up 2–0 early; Sault Ste. Marie ties it 2–2 in the third and we are being outplayed. Billy and I are coming off the ice at the end of a shift and Dolly is keeping us in the game, and there's Gerby at the end of the bench, head on the rail, with the most forlorn look on his face I'd ever seen. I can close my eyes and still see it; like he'd just lost his best friend. Billy and I both burst out laughing, and soon the whole bench was laughing, and on the next shift Bruce Burdett scored two quickies, game over, a happy Father Bill."

Stratford won the next game as well, but not before more cardiac anxiety for the interim coach. Stratford jumped to a 4–0 first period lead, and were up 6–2 going into the third period before a couple of stupid penalties hurt them. The Rapids tied it up 6–6

41

with Father Bill almost in tears. But Erle Burdett scored from brother Bruce in the last minute of the game and Stratford won the provincial Junior B championship.

A number of the players involved in that series, including Cupolo, Bruce Burdett, Klukay, and Howie, went on to the big leagues, as did rookie referee George Hayes from Ingersoll, Ontario, and sportswriter Milt Dunnell from the *Stratford Beacon Herald*, who became Canada's premier sportswriter at the *Toronto Star*.

"Your first championship has many benefits. You usually make a very good friend or two for life; you learn what it takes to win the tough games — hard work and the ability to get along as a group — and hopefully you also learn how to handle success in everyday life. We were sixteen- and seventeen-year-old kids with our pictures in the newspapers and programs, being interviewed on radio along with two big parades, including bands, fire trucks, and thousands of fans at the rallies. Jeez, it wouldn't be hard to think you were a 'somebody.' However, if for a moment you did have a few thoughts like that, they came crashing down to earth on Monday morning when you left the boarding house, walked ten minutes to the CNR shops, clocked in, and then thought, 'Shit, I am five minutes early. I should have stayed outside.' I can still hear that damn bell going ding, ding, ding. Then I'd climb into my dirty, greasy overalls and head off to find my partner and spend the next eight hours in grease up to my armpits dismantling a 6400 locomotive in for a refit — all for 18 cents an hour."

Howie says he didn't learn anything about hockey that year, about discipline, defensive or offensive systems, or improving his mental or physical skills. "Billy and I both had very good individual skills which complemented each other. The skills made it easy for us to be superstar kids during the schedule. But as the competition became tougher in the playoffs our domination ceased and we became just good hockey players. Sooner or later we were going to have to learn how to play this wonderful game."

After winning the Ontario Junior B championship in Stratford, the club hosted a banquet with Hap Day, the Toronto Maple Leaf coach, as guest speaker. It was the year Toronto lost the first three games of the Stanley Cup finals to Detroit, then came back to win the next four and the Cup — the first and only time it had ever happened in the National Hockey League.

Howie won an award and when he scampered to the front table to receive it from the Leaf coach, Day asked, "Tell me, kid, are you going to play in the NHL?"

Howie looked at him and said, "You're darn right I am, sir, and I'm going to play for the Toronto Maple Leafs and nobody else."

Y

Soon after the Junior B championship, Howie was invited to play Intermediate hockey for Milverton, just north of Stratford. The team was in the provincial final game and were allowed to pick up three players. Though just eighteen at the time, Meeker was asked to join for the final match. The game was played on natural ice in Milverton and another pick-up player, Mickey McQuade, proved to be a Billy Cupolo clone — a gifted centre, skater, and playmaker for Howie. "He knew what the game was all about. I kept breaking into the open and he kept feeding me pucks. I must have had three or four goals and a couple of assists."

In the third period, though, the party ended abruptly.

"I must have gotten cocky or something; I don't know how it started but all of a sudden here was this huge guy coming at me with his stick above his head. I panicked, turned, and skated as fast as I could to get away from there." Finally there was peace and quiet and the game resumed.

"Going home in the car, it was probably Mickey who said, 'Kid, you played a real good game but you can't turn turtle and run when someone's coming at ya.' I knew the minute I turtled and ran that it was the wrong thing to do. Both guys in the car mentioned it to me nicely and told me what I should have done. But the stick above my head scared me. If he'd dropped the stick, sure I didn't mind taking a beating — I went on to take how many in the NHL? But the stick, that scared me. It was the first and only time in hockey I turned and ran. I learned that you don't run and if they are coming at you, whether it is hockey or anything else and you're really in trouble, you've got to stand and fight, or put on a hell of a brave show."

The next winter, Howie moved up to the 1942–43 Stratford Kroehlers Junior A club, put together by general manager Harold Wyatt. The team brought in Klukay and others, but for Howie it started off as a rough year.

Cupolo, Howie, and friends were on their way to spend the Labour Day weekend in Niagara Falls just before the season started; Howie was driving and suddenly experienced a terrible pain in his stomach. He finally asked Billy to drive, crawled into the back seat, and doubled up in agony.

When they arrived in Hamilton, halfway to Niagara Falls, Billy decided to find a doctor or hospital. Luck was with them as a doctor was on duty at the first medical facility they located. When Billy came back to the car, Howie said, "It's no problem now, Billy; most of the pain has gone away." However, when the boys did not quickly return to the office the doctor came outside to the curb where they were parked. He took one look at Howie and hustled him inside where he took his temperature, felt Howie's appendix area, and called an ambulance.

"I guess I damn near died that night; my appendix had ruptured, spilling infection all through my body. When I awoke some hours later there were Grace and Mom, both looking somewhat relieved." Three weeks later, with the small portion of the incision still open and draining, Howie was back at hockey practice.

Early 1943 saw him play some fine hockey; however the Stratford Kroehlers were eliminated in the playoffs by a good Brantford club coached by ex-NHL defenceman Al Murray. When Brantford was allowed to pick up a replacement for an injured player, once again Howie was chosen. "What a shock that first practice was, with Mr. Murray teaching discipline and systems of how to play the game of hockey. Brantford had the narrowest rink that was ever built anywhere, and size, strength, and toughness dominated speed, skill, and finesse. After three years of literally no coaching I couldn't grasp or even understand what the hell Murray was talking about."

In the finals Brantford was outgunned by the powerful Oshawa Generals. "We were in over our heads and beat them once in Brantford, that's all. I really didn't help Brantford's cause very much. Oshawa had two stars that year in future Leaf Bill Ezinicki and Red Tilson. Red died overseas a few years later in the war. He would have been a hockey hero, a superstar, great player.

"At the end of the season I was a very disillusioned young man. The coach was drawing pictures on the blackboard, demonstrating plays on the ice and I didn't know or understand what the hell he was talking about. I realized after playing Oshawa and Sault Ste. Marie that there was more to the game than an individual's natural ability. I realized that in reality hockey was a team game and a mental game as well, not just simply based on one player's skills. I realized just how much I still needed to learn about the game and how I'd failed to learn anything up to that point."

The 1942–43 season held another special event for Howie. In mid-February, general manager Dave Pinkney entered the dressing room after a practice and asked Howie, "Do you think you can take off work tomorrow?"

"Why?"

"Well," Pinkney smiled, "the Toronto Maple Leafs have invited you and Klukay to attend their practice at 11 a.m."

Howie responded quickly, "What time are you going to pick me up? I'll be there."

At 7 a.m. the next day Howie was outside the boarding house, kit bag full of equipment, sitting on the curb waiting for Pinkney. At 10 o'clock they arrived at Maple Leaf Gardens. Their names were on the security list, so there was no problem getting in. The usual route for Howie when he was going down to watch a hockey game was to go in the main foyer of Maple Leaf Gardens and immediately turn to the right or left and go up the stairs to the blues or the greens, but that was not where they went this time. "We went through the swinging doors on the ground floor to the ice-level seats and, zowie, the place looked even bigger from there. The greys, the top seats, seemed light years away. We had to walk halfway around the ice surface to the dressing rooms on the other side and as I went behind the net I remember looking at the goal at the other end and thinking it seemed at least a mile away. The ice surface seemed almost as big as Peterson's Flats after a flood and freeze; acres of room."

Soon Dave was knocking on the Maple Leaf dressing-room door while Joe and Howie stood there shaking and fidgeting in anticipation. The door flew open and a round-faced, tobacco-chewing, fat old geezer answered and Howie thought, "It's trainer Tim Daly." When Pinkney asked for Hap Day, Daly left the door open and hollered, "Hap," then left. A moment later there stood "Mr. Hockey." After shaking hands with Dave he turned and stuck out his paw and said, "Hi, Howie. Hi, Joe. I'm Hap Day. Come on in."

Day and Daly had prepared two lockers side by side for the kids and before sitting down, Hap introduced them to the Maple Leaf players, saying, "This is Joe Klukay and Howie Meeker. They play Junior A in Stratford. Both of these guys belong to the Toronto Maple Leafs, or their hockey rights do, and so we've asked them to come down for a practice." Trainer Tim Daly, after spying the boys' battered shin pads and gloves, brought them NHL equipment and insisted they pick out two new hockey sticks from the stockpile to take home. "It was the only time in his life, and I was with the guy for eight years, that Tim Daly was generous with a hockey stick. Ho ho, was he a miser, but with a heart as big as all outdoors.

"Anyways, as I got undressed I turned and looked around the room, shook my head, pinched myself, and said, 'Ah jeez, this can't be true, I gotta be dreaming. Here I am sitting with Billy Taylor,

Bucko McDonald, Dave 'Sweeney' Schriner, Bob Davidson, Babe Pratt, Lorne Carr, the great Turk Broda, and Gaye Stewart. Hah, what a country.' "

If being among the Maple Leaf players was not thrill enough, the ambiance of that already historic Leaf dressing room would become a lifelong memory. There were plaques on the wall honouring Leafs who had won special awards — all-star Leafs, rookies-of-the-year, and other individual trophy winners — and very large plaques honouring the players who'd helped win Stanley Cups for Toronto.

"Little did I dream at that time that years later I would get my name on that wall five times. But after practice, two hours later, I knew I'd be back in that room again as a player.

"One big slogan that impressed me was very huge and right above my locker. It filled up half the wall on one side of the room and read, 'The Toronto Maple Leafs — Defeat Does Not Rest Lightly On Their Shoulders.' Now, looking back, I think that says it all for the many players and teams who have been successful over time in Toronto."

During the practice the players had the usual warm-up and then a series of routine drills; one-on-one, two-on-one, three-on-two line rushes. "Pete Langelle played centre for Joe and me on the first three-on-two and we did okay. What a relief when I found out that I could keep up with and, if I tried, pass Langelle. When we started scrimmages as a line first shift against Taylor, Schriner, and Carr, no contest, they had the puck all the time. But slowly I realized, shift after shift, that without the puck I could skate with them and maybe even a little bit faster than some of them. But I wasn't doing much with the puck, we never had it. I was just chasing the puck and checking.

"About the third or fourth shift, I took Carr's place on the Taylor line and Joe played left wing with Syl Apps. Talk about thinking you'd died and gone to heaven — one day we were playing hockey with a bunch of Humpty-Dumpties, including ourselves, in Stratford, and the next day Syl Apps is playing centre for Joe Klukay and I'm playing right wing with Billy Taylor. Nah, that kind of thing just doesn't happen in real life. Anyway, it was a different game. We had the puck for short periods of time and to make it a very, very special event, Billy Taylor took a pass from Schriner that put him home free. Taylor put a move on Turk, took him down and out, and gave me the puck for an easy goal. Five years later I had a hell of a fight with Taylor, but I'll never forget that goal."

As is standard among hockey players, every Leaf regular razzed the hell out of Turk at the end of practice for letting Howie score. "Shame on ya, Turk, lettin' this kid score a goal on ya," or "Jeez, you were terrible today." The routine carried on right through the showers, dressing, and even as players went out the dressing-room door.

Before leaving that day, Howie gained personal respect for the big, tough, hard-hitting defencemen at the NHL level. Late in the scrimmage, flying out of his own end, he forced a hurried pass from Taylor which wound up in his feet. Howie looked down to kick the puck up to his stick and when he looked up it was into Bucko McDonald's chest. "He clobbered me. Well, Bucko had just been called back up from Syracuse and he too took quite a ribbing from the rest of the players in the shower room afterwards: 'There you are, you big clout, picking on a kid. You can't get any of us, you gotta get these young snot-nosed guys coming down here.'

"As we showered and dressed almost every player took the time to come and introduce themselves and sign our sticks. We didn't even have to go asking for them. Frank Selke, the general manager at the time, came in to thank us for coming down to the practice. Thank us? Ahh, come on. Anyways, it was great fun, Joe and I survived and had the time of our lives, and we returned home thinking, 'They're a great bunch of guys. Someday we're going to be there to join 'em.'

"Before it came time to go, I felt at home in that room and knew if I survived long enough, I'd be back. Joe got there before I did. During the playoffs that year the Leafs had some injured left wingers, and Joe went down to Toronto and practised with the Leafs just to be ready in case he was needed. When Billy and I found out Joe got paid $125 a game, we both made the NHL our number-one priority."

With two years of Junior B hockey, one year of Junior A, a dash of Intermediate hockey, and a Maple Leaf practice behind him, life was Howie's oyster. Except . . . all of a sudden the war was coming on.

Howie and Billy were approaching nineteen, and some tough decisions had to be made.

Three

A Call to Arms

"Then some wisenheimer decided it was time to train us in the art of warfare. What a laugh. They imported fifteen young Canadian hotshots who were going to train us and get us in shape for Jerry."

Billy Cupolo and Howie were both nineteen in 1943 and everybody at that age was going to join either the army, navy, or air force. Howie picked the air force. After his medical, the administration officer said, "Sorry, son — you've got something wrong with your heart. It isn't a 'chicken-heart' but there's something minor wrong with it and we're not going to let you in." Howie had two reactions: "Oh great — maybe I won't have to go to war," and, "Oh shit, everybody is going to war — I want to go, too."

Billy's luck was worse. X rays showed he had tuberculosis and he spent the next six months lying in bed, recuperating. Even after he recovered no branch of the military would accept him, which proved fortunate; Billy went on to play that season with the Boston Bruins while Howie was overseas.

When Dave Pinkney recruited Howie to play junior hockey in Stratford the plum he offered had been an apprenticeship in the CNR shops. Howie soon hated the job, but after being denied entry into the air force, he jumped at the chance to join the army's Engineers' Corps. "I figured it was a bonus that my time served in the army would count towards my apprenticeship, and maybe, just maybe, I'd come to like engineering work."

The Engineers' role was to repair and make operable European rolling stock, if and when the Allied forces liberated Europe. Rolling stock was composed mainly of train engines, passenger cars, and freight cars; as for members of the Corps, the army recruited and transferred any boilermaker, machinist, electrician, tinsmith who had any experience whatsoever from Canadian National, Canadian Pacific, or any other railway line.

So it was that in the early spring of 1943, after some fanfare and fond farewells to family and friends, Howie ventured to London, Ontario, and joined the Engineers' Number One Canadian Railway Workshop Company. A few days later, feeling somewhat embarrassed, he found himself back in Stratford with a sad-sack outfit of rookie warriors. "They were the most motley-looking crew you ever saw," Howie recalls. "Most of the men were between 35 and 50 years of age and soldiers they were not, nor ever would be; but tradesmen with years and years of experience they were. I was the baby of the outfit."

Just three months later in July, shortly after giving Grace an engagement ring, nineteen-year-old Howard William Meeker boarded the *Queen Mary* and headed overseas, accompanied by his cohorts in the #1 CRWC. With the exception of Howie, few of them knew one end of a gun from another. "We had no formal training at all except for some totally useless parade square work to keep us busy while they collected more tradesmen from all over the country. Some of the guys had been in the army for some time and transferred into the Engineers, but most of us had only been in for a short six- or eight-week stint before we were loaded onto the boats and sailed across the ocean, scared all to hell. We kept thinking about the fact that the Atlantic was loaded with German submarines."

The officers repeatedly told the seasick Canucks crammed into the gigantic vessel that they could outrun any German sub, but their assurances did little to console. As promised, the *Queen Mary* arrived without incident near Greenock, Scotland. With little chance to gain their land legs, the Engineers embarked on an eighteen-hour train ride to the large army base at Colchester, England. Just an hour northeast of London, born out of military need, the city had harboured armies since Roman legions pounded its first roadways. Howie's stay in the famed city seemed much more mundane. They killed time there for three or four months, did a lot of drills and useless parades, but nothing to prepare them for mending and repairing railway stock.

"Then we were dispatched to the Midlands, and why they ever sent us there we never did figure out. We arrived in this godforsaken place with one great big house in the middle of it and about twenty Nissen huts scattered around the place; no food, no heat, nothing and it was the day before Christmas."

The officers told the troops, "Look boys, we're here, but nobody knows we're here, and it's going to be tough to get food. It's going to be a dull, dreary Christmas." But Howie and comrades were not about to be done out of a Christmas dinner so easily. It was wet and cold but the ingenuity of the "Canadian army guy" kicked into gear.

"We pooled what little money we had and one of the guys 'borrowed' an officer's jeep and drove to a Canadian air force base about ten miles away. He was given coffee, tea, bread and butter, jam . . . they were very sympathetic to our cause and generous but they didn't have much more than we did. So four or five of us went out 'scouting' the farms in the area and ended up with a dozen chickens and two sheep. On Christmas Day, no one in the army, air force, or navy ate any better than we did. The guys managed to get some beer, all kinds of it in fact, and we ended up inviting the officers down to our Christmas dinner.

"As soon as we possibly could — and at the advice of our officers — we apologized to the people we stole the chickens and sheep from and generously reimbursed them. Like most courteous British farmers, they all said, 'Gentlemen, why didn't you just ask us?' "

After a couple of weeks, the company transferred to Darlington, the centre of rail transportation and home to the biggest repair shops in Britain. The corps went straight to work for three or four months solid, learning the differences between various engines made in different countries.

"Then some wisenheimer decided it was time to train us in the art of warfare. What a laugh. They imported fifteen young Canadian hotshots who were going to train us and get us in shape for Jerry."

The enemy had little to fear from Howie's crew.

Platoons of twelve to fifteen rookies at a time ventured to the hand-grenade range. The young instructors handed out the grenades — plastic practice ones that looked, weighed, and were almost as deadly as the real ones. The instructors took them apart, explained how to throw them and what the dangers were. The idea was to pull the pin, lob the grenade, and then dive into the foxhole surrounded by sandbags.

The very first guy they handed one to screwed up. When the instructor handed him the grenade the soldier froze, saying, "I can't throw that thing." The officer responded gruffly, "Yes, you can. You may have to throw it some day and you better know how."

"Well, when I have to throw it, maybe I will, but right now I can't move," the engineer replied defiantly.

At this insubordination, the corporal puffed himself up and said, "Now pull the pin, put your arm back, lob it at the target, and dive behind your sandbag pit."

The tinsmith never moved.

"Pull the pin," the corporal barked yet again, and still the soldier didn't move. Finally, in obvious frustration, the instructor reached over and pulled the pin out of the grenade. "Throw it," he barked at the shaking recruit, who was one of the oldest in the unit.

"Here, sir, you throw it yourself," the soldier said, tossing the grenade underhand back to the corporal.

Twenty guys never moved so fast in their lives.

The rest of the grenade training day did not go terribly well for the young instructors either, with three or four more grenades falling out of hands and some terribly misdirected lobs. Finally the young officers called it a day, and at the next session grenades were conspicuously absent from the training agenda. However, the highly lethal, rapid-fire Sten gun was not.

It was a similar scenario to the previous day: lecture, dismantling and assembling the gun, practice range. The routine was for instructor and soldier to go into an area with sandbags stacked up three feet high in a twenty-foot circle, stand behind the sandbags, put in the bullet magazine, and fire at the targets. Not terribly complicated.

"We had a jolly, fat French-Canadian fella in our unit," Howie recalls. "He always looked like he had a black beard, like he needed a shave even right after he had one, and his uniform always looked like he slept in it. I played a lot of cribbage with him and we got along fine. 'Frenchie' is in there with the instructor and he slaps in the magazine and the instructor tells him to set the clip on single-shot instead of automatic. We were supposed to aim and fire, aim and fire, aim and fire with single rounds from the hip. Frenchie put the gun to his hip, pulled the trigger and 'thut, thut, thut, thut, thut, thut' the thing starts spewing bullets everywhere. He turns around with the gun as it's still spitting out bullets and says, 'Sir, 'ow do you stop dis t'ing, any'ow?'

"I'm in the next target area and see him start turning with the gun still firing, so I dive behind the sandbags and the next thing you know everyone is diving for their lives. There had to be twenty-five guys just hitting the ground like nobody's business. He never did get the thing stopped until all the bullets in the magazine were gone."

The Keystone Cops go to war scenario continued the next day; in the late afternoon, however, the humour diminished dramatically.

In the afternoon it was time for military maneuvers and the zone of operation was two huge farms and the soldiers had to traverse some 250 yards, much of it crawling through grass, before supposedly taking the hill about a quarter-mile away

"The 'enemy' is on the hill and they're shooting blanks at us, at least we hoped they were blanks. Our guys were advancing through the field and I saw this great big rock fence. In England a lot of the farms were separated by eight- or ten-foot-high rock fences, so I got beside the wall and crept along until *blam*, there was a terrible explosion and I was blown about eight feet straight up in the air. While I was up in the air I remember feeling, for a split second, suspended in time and space. As I looked down, I saw this corporal crouched on the other side of the fence."

It is a strange and powerful thing what fear and the will to live can do for an individual under the most excruciating circumstances. Landing on the ground posed a whole other terror which instantly registered in Howie's mind on the brief descent — land mines.

His mind quickly willed the body a tough command, "Land on your feet," even though the pain from his shattered legs racked his body. Howie quickly yet methodically picked his way across the field to an area he thought safe before finally collapsing, writhing in agony.

Investigation later revealed that the "enemy" corporal behind the wall had tossed a live grenade over the fence in front of Howie. It exploded between his legs.

"The pain was unbelievable and I wound up in hospital with my legs blown all to rat shit. I had metal and Bakelite all through my body, especially my legs and groin area. I had quite a problem getting it repaired because gangrene set in. I was scared to death."

Four significant chunks of metal went into the inside area of

Howie's right leg. About forty small pieces of Bakelite ripped into his legs from just above the knees down to his toes, while at least six pieces entered his testicle sack. The initial pain left Howie struggling for air.

The Bakelite wounds proved no problem over the years, pieces eventually working their way out of the body by themselves, but the metal in Howie's legs had to be cut out. To promote healing, the doctor put Howie's leg in a plastic bag and blew oxygen in twice a day.

"I questioned the nurse about the two open wounds always being wet from condensation in the plastic bag, but nothing was done. About the third day, my wounds started to turn green and fester, so to finally get attention — nurses and doctors were very scarce in the 1,200-bed hospital — I cut the plastic bag off my leg, borrowed a pair of crutches, and hobbled down to admitting. It wasn't long before I had a nurse, doctor, penicillin, and was back in bed with a hot fan trying to dry out the wounds. I refused to put on the plastic bag again."

An anguished, heartbroken Howie took pen to paper in his hospital bed a few nights after the explosion and wrote Toronto Maple Leaf coach Hap Day a letter suggesting Day take his name off the club's player list. For a short while after that, another sort of numbness settled over him.

"I didn't think I'd be playing hockey any more. I didn't think I'd be doing much of anything for a while."

Ⅴ

For eight long weeks Howie lay in his hospital bed wondering what his future held. Slowly the possibilities began to improve. Thanks to a combination of skilled surgeons, a miraculous lack of crippling injuries from the grenade explosion, Howie's strong leg muscles, and his determination to recover, he healed quickly.

An officer from the Workshop Company visited and Howie told him, "Sir, when I get back to camp if you still have that corporal there, I will kill him, stone dead. That idiot threw a live hand grenade over the fence without knowing what was on the other side. It was me! If that grenade had been another foot higher it would have blown my head off. He better not be there when I get back, or I'll kill the son of a bitch." Luckily for both parties involved, Howie never returned to Darlington.

Eventually Howie's legs healed with no long-term ill effects, except the largest wound on his lower right leg was still tender. Even today, if knocked or hit on the inside of the leg just above the ankle, the entire bottom portion of his foot goes dead and then throbs for several hours.

After the two months in hospital Howie was shipped to the Number One Canadian Engineers' Re-assignment Unit located at Farnborough, England. It was there that Howie would find out whether or not his legs could respond to the challenge of conditioning. "I wasn't in too good a shape and needed to start working out, slow but steady. They had a softball team and naturally I went out to watch. Well, the next thing I know I'm hobbling around playing shortstop, then I'm hitting home runs out of the park. They asked me if I wanted to hang around the unit and, of course, play softball for them. I said, 'Sure, but I want to be part of the physical-education staff,' and that I'd take a course for that."

It was another key decision in Howie's life. Howie was sent to the physical-education course in Shorncliffe, Kent, near Folkestone in the Bognor Regis area on the south coast of England.

"I took the three-week Physical Education Instructor's course and it damn near killed me. Those Limey instructors were all five foot six, 140 pounds, and in superb physical condition. They kept us going twelve hours a day, seven days a week, nonstop.

"The last day was a fifteen-mile run with full battle kit and ten pounds of sand in the backpack. I had tears in my eyes more than once. Every muscle in my body ached. We also had to carry our helmet and a Lee-Enfield rifle." The rolling terrain added to the excruciating task with steep, almost vertical, hills pouncing out of the sandy beaches. For some eight miles a narrow road traversed the undulating stretch between Shorncliffe and Folkestone with the route made up of nonstop gruelling cliffs from start to finish.

"As soon as we arrived at Folkestone we'd turn around and run straight back. Going down the hills wasn't half bad but going up was murder. I actually had little problem with my legs; they responded very well and I could run all day on them. The problem was my upper body, which had to carry the packsack, steel helmet, and rifle — I couldn't find any spot comfortable for that bloody rifle. It was a very, very punishing day but you were quite proud when you finished; dead, but proud.

"I admired and hated those Limey S.O.B.s like you wouldn't believe. They laughed their way through every day and then they went out drinking at night. The last day I vowed, 'I'm coming back, you guys, and I will be front and centre and make every one of you guys do everything a step quicker. And I'll laugh through the three weeks and enjoy every minute of it.'"

Running with full gear was a new kind of physical hell for Howie, but gymnastics proved the ultimate endurance test. Because the Canadian soldiers had no training as youngsters, getting any of them to participate in gymnastics in anything more than pommel horse and tumbling was like pulling teeth. Parallel bars, high bars, and rings not only looked foreboding — they were. "That stuff just kills you. We did a lot of exercise on the parallel bars, which is murder, incredibly demanding on the body." It was especially tough in the beginning, but Howie actually grew to like it, or at least the challenge.

At Shorncliffe, the gym and the buildings where they housed and fed the soldiers were high up on the cliffs of the southeast coast, providing a spectacular view of the Channel. One evening at dusk, with the boys back at their barracks, a strange drone came from over the Channel. The sound was much deeper than normal and sputtered, not like the steady drone of most airplanes, and it became louder and louder until suddenly a plane passed overhead at 1,500 to 2,000 feet.

"As it passed over we saw this huge flame coming out of what we thought was a single motor. We remarked, 'Gosh, that's a new one. Never saw that silhouette before.'"

For the next half-hour the occasional strange plane passed by very close. After the fourth or fifth plane, all hell broke loose and every friendly antiaircraft gun in the area (and there were hundreds), opened up on the planes. "Only then did we realize, jeez, they're German planes — not ours. They continued to come about every fifteen minutes all night long and we all agreed that the Nazi pilots had balls; they flew their planes at 1,500 feet straight as a die through this terrible wall of steel being thrown up at them. Some had to have been shot down because the earth shook several times during the night when they hit the ground and exploded a mile or so from us."

All the talk the next day, while the soldiers slogged through their torturous fitness routine, was about the German pilots and strange planes of the night before. "About 2 p.m., just before tea — yes, even then everything stopped for tea — we heard this familiar drone. Finally it was overhead, and we looked for the cockpit and couldn't find one. The motor was sitting on the tail, with a big hole in the front and flames spewing out the back, and the craft was motoring right along. That night and the next day, more of the same air traffic."

Friday night was often pub night and the soldiers would hit the village for dinner and a couple of mugs of beer. All of a sudden there were strangers in the bar: U.S. pilots and ground crew, who challenged the Canucks and Brits for the local girls. In conversation with the Americans it was learned that the German flying machines were pilotless jet bombers called buzz bombs, programmed to fly straight to London, run out of fuel, then crash and explode. The American pilots' job was to help shoot down the bombs.

The Yanks flew their very powerful and fast planes as the first line of defence for England. "Radar will tell us when they are coming and we'll fly out or already be there to greet them, and hopefully shoot them down," an American pilot explained. "We've got all the Channel and three miles of land to make contact and shoot down these planes. At three miles we disengage and the anti-aircraft takes over for the next ten or twelve miles." Then the bombs met a wall of balloons and more antiaircraft.

As Howie remembers, "The last week I was there we had a ball watching the show. Twice we got damn near killed, but we saw some of the greatest flying and super acts of bravery pulled off, I think, in the war." The students and instructors spent more time looking up than any other direction, and a good thing, too. "One day we were on the obstacle course where we had a pretty good view of the Channel and here comes this buzz bomb with a U.S. plane, guns a-blazing, right on its tail. All of a sudden, the bomb changed course and headed for the ground. Someone yelled, 'Christ, boys, it's coming right at us.' You never saw thirty-five guys scramble for cover so quick. The obstacle course was a great place to be because there were all kinds of holes to hide in. The bomb cleared us by about fifty feet and landed a quarter-mile down the road just on the edge of the parade square. The explosion took the corner off our gym maybe 200 feet away."

Later that night at the pub, everybody was buying one young U.S. pilot drinks; he had more than a dozen lined up. Howie asked why and was informed that on a dare from another pilot the celebrity had caught up to a buzz bomb, sidled in beside it, put his wing tip under the bomb's wing tip and did a tight roll to the right. His wing tip lifted the bomb's wing and it rolled over in the air and crashed. He had a witness to this.

Bomb-tipping soon became the rage among other pilots until headquarters heard about it and put a stop to the dangerous game. "We saw a few of the pilots side by side with the buzz bombs but never saw the actual tipping of one," Howie says, still in awe. "However, it was quite common to see a U.S. plane follow the buzz bombs right into the antiaircraft area. Some of the guys had to be shot down and jeepers, those pilots had balls."

Shorncliffe proved significant for Howie. "I went there in terrible physical condition for a nineteen-year-old and came out in pretty good condition — not great, but pretty good. I also came out a much smarter person. It was a great three weeks, but a very punishing three weeks.

"When I got back to CERU from the phys-ed course, I said, 'Boys, where are the pommel horse, parallel bars, high bars, and rings?' They had put away all that gear because you couldn't get a Canadian within ten miles of gymnastic equipment. So I dug out the gear, set it all up, and worked on them constantly until I was in good shape. You knew you were getting there when you could work the parallel bars and it didn't hurt any of the muscles in your shoulders, your side, or your arms. Form didn't really matter in the formula, just the elimination of pain."

At CERU many of Howie's fellow physical education crew were boxers, some of them highly skilled, including the Royal Canadian Army champions. Howie soon became involved as a corner man. "They kept in top shape because they were fighting in London for expenses and 25 quid if they won, 15 quid if they lost. I often assisted not only to get the weekend off but also to pocket the 5 pounds they'd pay corner men." Howie also worked out regularly on the speed bag and the heavy bag in the gyms and often got in the ring with the guys "until they hit too hard."

Y

The tragic reality of war never fully escaped him, even during his quieter postings. One of the places it made itself known was in the mail room where Howie occasionally worked at night. All of the lost mail for Canadian Engineers went through the CERU mail clearing room, so literally tons of lost parcels went through Howie's hands to their rightful owners. It was a solid night's work from 7 p.m. to 7 a.m., readdressing lost parcels from families and friends back home. Once in a while, and far too often for Howie, he'd pull up a soldier's card and it would say KILLED IN ACTION. "That meant you had to return the mail, and usually we would put a personal note on it if we could. It hurt, it hurt an awful lot, but you just did it."

As a physical-education instructor Howie's main job was to keep all the engineers in transit in shape — which was both a challenge and a laugh. A lot of soldiers were also sent to Farnborough for bridge dismantling and construction work and the clearing or laying of mines, so there were usually 1,200 to 1,500 men in camp along with about 300 staff members.

"Our physical fitness classes were usually very slow jogs out of camp to a nearby shaded area close to a pub, where we would disperse for forty-five minutes," he grins. Despite the antics, the physical-education staff spent lots of time getting into shape and no one worked harder than Howie. He still had a dream he wanted to chase again, and now he could almost taste it: the numbness was gone.

"I ran hundreds of miles with Boogey Butler — Canadian Army lightweight boxing champion — and we ran them all in army boots with those big double soles. We played darts for push-ups, double if you were skunked. We had a couple of guys who were great dart players and it took me a while to catch on to the game. If you lost by 301 and were skunked, which I often was, well, that meant you did 602 push-ups. I eventually got to the point where I could do 250 at a time. You had to knock off the push-ups, pay off your debt, that day. We played cribbage for 10 push-ups a point — payable immediately."

One day the phys-ed officers asked Howie to organize a softball team from their base as well as the communications camp a couple of miles down the road. There was a big tournament in London which a number of American and a couple of Canadian softball teams had entered. The Signal Corps had two of the best softball pitchers in the army, both from the old Tip Top team from Toronto. Howie jumped on a bike that night and talked to the boys there, who leapt at the chance for some fun and time off in London.

When Howie returned that evening he told his officer he'd

organize a ball team and play, but wanted to return to Shorncliffe for the next phys-ed course and a 21-day leave after that. To his surprise, the officer agreed. After some tough competition, Howie's club lost out in the final game to an American squad. "We got robbed by the umpire, an American," Howie contends.

When Meeker returned to Shorncliffe he was in as good shape, or better, than any of the British instructors. "I had one of the best three weeks of my life. I learned a lot of skills in gymnastics and actually got to the point where I could start to perform routines."

Most importantly, Howie knew what kind of whiskey the chief cook favoured, and after three days was invited to go drinking with the instructors. "In the army there are three key people one should get to know: the master sergeant running the kitchen, the quarter-master running the quartermaster stores, and the regimental sergeant major. If you were in favour with any two of the three then army life as a sapper or a lance corporal drastically improved. The RSM was usually a hard drinker and tough to break for a lance corporal or corporal. The other two, with good timing, and a bottle here or there, could be reached most of the time."

When Howie had left Canada for overseas, he'd snuck his skates into his personal baggage. Once his recovery was well under way, he needed to test his skating legs. Happily, he discovered he could cut the ice with the same skill and agility as before.

Whenever possible he'd go to London, often with the boxers, and try to skate at the Richmond Arena. Howie also played some hockey with the Signallers team stationed there and occasionally went to Brighton on the south coast, where the pros had pickup games. "Once in a while if they were short some players, I'd get to play. Naturally I was an unknown kid, but I found out I could skate with them. I couldn't play the game with them but I could skate with them. Eventually I got to play on a regular basis anytime I showed up."

When the war ended all kinds of "repat depots" sprung up in Europe to sort soldiers out for home or reassignment. Some signed up to go to the Japanese Zone, but most with enough points were going home as soon as possible. Processing the soldiers took four or five days and it was the phys-ed instructors' job to keep the lads busy — and out of trouble — during the time they were there. The instructors took the soldiers swimming, golfing, walking, playing tennis, baseball . . .

Howie was assigned to a repat depot in Vilvorde, Holland, a suburb of Amsterdam. "I never had a better four months in my life," Howie says. "I had access to an unlimited supply of sporting equipment, and bartered that with the Dutch people who for years had not seen a tennis racquet or ball, running shoe, golf club, or the rest of it. I lived like a king. I didn't get involved in the black market but easily could have."

Howie was then transferred to a Signal Corps and Transportation depot in Germany, deep in the Black Forest. It was a gorgeous place with lush trees and hills that reminded him of Ontario. His stay in the Black Forest would prove to be very brief, though, as fate played him yet another interesting card.

"The first guy I met coming off the truck at the Black Forest was Terry Reardon, a former NHL player who'd temporarily left in order to join the army. I didn't know him but one of my buddies knew Reardon and told him how I'd been on the Maple Leaf negotiation list. Unbeknownst to me, Reardon was in the process of rounding up some hockey players and sending a team back to London to represent headquarters against various clubs, including a touring Russian team. He asked me if I'd be interested in playing for his team while finishing my tour of duty and of course I jumped at the chance."

After just three weeks in the Black Forest, Howie transferred back to London to play hockey. It was there he received his first glimpse of how quickly the Russians would learn the skills of ice hockey.

"While we were putting together our hockey team, a touring Soviet soccer team, which also featured four or five of their star hockey players, arrived. We stayed in the same barracks area as the Soviets and soon became friends with some of them. We outfitted

64

them with skates and other hockey gear and they came out on the ice and practised with us a few times. Even in those days it was amazing to me how well they handled the puck. We skated better than they did and shot the puck much better, but they handled the puck better than 90 percent of our players did — and some players on our team were ex-pros. If I'd have had any foresight or hockey brains at all I'd have known then that although the most important part of the game is skating, anybody can learn to skate; it's how you handle the puck and give and take a pass that really counts. They were so galdarn good at it and that was in September or October of 1945. They were not bad soccer players, either."

After three months of hockey and service in London, Howie's tour of duty came to a close and he gleefully headed for home late in December 1945 on the *Queen Elizabeth*, spending Christmas at sea just outside of New York City.

Like many men, Howie does not discuss the grim side of his war experience, preferring to focus on the rest. "I learned a lot from the army. When they first get you in there they try and reduce you to the lowest denominator, they run the pants off you, they curse you, shout at you, jump all over you, and feed you lousy food. You stand in line for hours upon hours; they like to have you hurry up and wait. They scream at you to get up at 5 a.m., then you stand around and do nothing until 7:30 when they feed you a bowl of porridge, if you are lucky. If it's warm you're happy, especially if there is some cream and maybe a bit of sugar.

"If you get down to a defeated level in your mind then you're a goner. You have to stay brave and not let them get you down; tell yourself it's not really that bad, it just seems like it. You can't let them dominate your mind. Then you can bounce back. The whole key is don't let them get to you. The second they do, the second you become as physically and mentally inefficient as they are, then you are in deep, deep trouble.

"I would think things have changed considerably in the army since then. Killing wasn't too complicated an art in the 1940s.

Today, if you're part of the army, I guess you have to be very well educated and a very smart person in the main. But the army did me good; it made me a much better person and far more prepared for life. There wasn't anything in life at that time that I felt I couldn't do. All it would take was hard work and a little bit of courage."

Howie attributes his disciplined hockey habits to his army training. "Most of all the army taught me how to survive and that to get ahead you need an education more than anything else. I also learned an education didn't guarantee a person could always do the job; however an education did put them first in line."

When Howie returned home he immediately signed up for the government-sponsored educational upgrading program for war vets. The plan was to get his senior matriculation and go to Michigan State University on a scholarship. However, the Toronto Maple Leafs again offered him a professional hockey career.

"Sometimes I look back and wonder what would have happened had I passed those grades and gone to Michigan State? I wanted to take physical education because I'd fallen in love with that way of life, thanks to the army. But when I signed with the Maple Leafs in the spring of 1946, education went out the window. Maybe I should have gone to university but things have worked out pretty good since."

Four

A Dream Comes True

"Nobody was going to stop me from making the club.
I had got this far and I was going to make the
Toronto Maple Leafs or die trying."

On December 27, 1945, in the heart of winter, Howie finally set his feet on North American soil again, feet that just a short time before he thought might never hold him up so well. Despite the fact that Christmas Day was spent rolling about on the sea, the twenty-two-year-old soldier was exhilarated as he sailed into New York harbour on the *Queen Elizabeth*. He was finally going home to his family, friends, and best of all — his sweet love Grace.

While the separation had been hell, Howie was humbled in the realization that for many a young Canadian fiancée, wife, or sweetheart, their loved one's ship would never come in.

The trip from the New York harbour frontage to London, Ontario, was only a day by train, but it seemed an eternity. But Howie managed to be home in New Hamburg and in Grace's embrace for his New Year's Eve kiss as 1946 was rung in.

Grace noticed a few lumps and small bruises on Howie's dashing mug which were not yet completely healed. When asked, Howie smirked, then sheepishly admitted to taking a severe pounding in the boxing ring just before leaving England.

Boogey Butler and the other boxing boys at CERU had put on a match for returning soldiers and one of the entrants was a Canadian army champion. The champ's opponent never showed up so the boys prodded Howie into going a few rounds. Like a fool, Howie took the challenge.

When he entered the change room before the match, he knew he was in trouble.

"I don't remember his name, but he was five foot ten, 180 pounds, with a bent nose and cauliflower ears and he looked mean. He looked at me and said, 'Sure hope the guy I'm fighting isn't too tough and takes it easy on me. I'm coming back from an injury and I'm not up to snuff.' I took one look at the brute and said, 'Don't worry about him, he ain't worth a pinch of coonshit. I know 'cause I'm the guy.'

"He got me in the ring and beat the shit out of me. He gave me a vicious left hook and I went down. Then, like an idiot, I got up again — so he did it again. This went on for a bit and finally the referee just couldn't stand it anymore and stopped the fight in the second round. Good thing he had more brains than me, or I'd have none right now."

Once home in New Hamburg it didn't take Howie long to don his skates and grab a hockey stick. He played just a dozen regular-season and playoff games with the Stratford Kroehlers, a Senior team, before the club was easily eliminated by the Toronto Staffords. But the games had been enough to tell a few trained and interested sets of eyes what they needed to know: the feisty, pugnacious Meeker could still skate in spite of the grenade blast.

Impressed with Howie's full recovery from the accident, and his obvious grit, the Toronto Maple Leafs had a hunch the kid from New Hamburg would be National Hockey League material. In April that year, Howie received a telephone call from Maple Leaf manager Conn Smythe asking him to visit Maple Leaf Gardens and discuss signing a contract.

Howie couldn't believe it when Smythe called. First thing he went to David Pinkney, the Stratford general manager, and said, "David, this is what's happening. What do I do? What do I ask for?"

"Well, son, you have got to ask for and you will get $10,000 a year for three years, plus a signing bonus of $10,000," Pinkney stated.

"What? Hey Dave, I hope so, but I don't think so."

An excited but confident Howie Meeker made his way to Maple Leaf Gardens that day, but this time, instead of entering the seats or the dressing room, he found his way to Smythe's personal office. In later years it would be a trip that reminded him of journeys to school principal War Ruthig's office. Conn Smythe had that effect on people.

After brief salutations and introductions to scout Squib Walker and his secretary, Mrs. McDonald, Smythe cut right to the point. "How much do you want, kid?" he barked.

When Howie responded that he was looking for $7,000 a year for two years and a $5,000 signing bonus, Smythe nearly blew a fuse. "Kid, that's all-star money. Our best players don't get that kind of money, or if they do they're proven stars. If you make any all-star team, or win any award, the Toronto Maple Leafs will give you a $1,000 bonus."

Howie wound up agreeing to $4,500 a year for two years and a $1,000 signing bonus, along with the all-star or trophy bonus offer. "Eventually we shook hands on the deal and as I was leaving Smythe asked me if I wanted two tickets to that Saturday night's Memorial Cup final game between Winnipeg and St. Mike's. I said,

'Sorry, sir, but I'm going to be very, very busy that day — I'm getting married.' Smythe looked at Mrs. McDonald and said, 'Give Howie an extra $1,000 bonus; the kid's going to need it.'

"All the way home to New Hamburg, I knew Dave Pinkney had been closer to my net worth than I was, or what Smythe had given me. Over the years I've kicked my rear end for not sticking to my $7,000 longer. I'd never have gotten it but I should have held out longer. Boy, did we need agents back then."

Ɣ

That signing day marked the beginning of an eleven-year relationship with the Maple Leaf organization. At the Leaf training camp prior to the 1946–47 NHL season, however, Howie Meeker was just another no-name rookie who would get no respect from other players until it was well earned. There would be a battle for jobs and no one would give an inch without a price being paid.

Even though Howie had signed a contract, his chances of cracking the full-time Leaf lineup were slim. Despite the purging of several veterans following the dismal 1945–46 season, a strong cast of experienced Leafs remained on the club, while a crowd of promising rookies waited in the wings.

Indeed, the 1945–46 version of the team had certainly not been up to snuff. The club had plummeted from stardom to near cellar dwellers and neither the management nor the fans were impressed. After finishing third and winning the coveted Stanley Cup four games to three over Detroit in 1944–45, the 1945–46 version, missing superstar Ted Kennedy for several games, failed to even make the playoffs. In 50 games the club managed only 19 wins and 7 ties for a meagre 45 points and fifth place in the six-team league. Only those perennial bums the New York Rangers would fare worse that season.

During the summer, the Leafs had retired, let go, or traded several players, including Lorne Carr, Dave "Sweeney" Schriner, Bob Davidson, Walter "Babe" Pratt, and Billy Taylor. While such players were difficult to replace, the Maple Leaf organization had built a strong farm system in the mid-1940s, including pro clubs in Tulsa and Pittsburgh and three Junior teams: the Winnipeg Monarchs, Toronto Marlboros, and Toronto's St. Mike's Majors. Several players from those clubs were also pencilled in as possible Leafs and had signed contracts. Meeker was in thick.

That early autumn of 1946, when the Maple Leafs held a rookie camp in St. Catharines, Ontario, Howie was among the score or so of prospects invited. Only a few players from the rookie session were invited to the main camp a week later. When the ice chips settled, Howie was among the selected few.

In the rookie camp Howie was immediately placed with Pete Langelle at centre and Vic Lynn on left wing. "I got very, very lucky playing with Pete, who had some Leaf and minor-pro experience — in Syracuse — and was a great hockey player. He only lacked maybe half a step in skating and needed a bit more mental toughness to have made it big, but he had all the hockey skills to play the game." Lynn had been unsuccessful in two previous NHL team try-outs as a defenceman, yet the Toronto coaching staff saw potential in the youngster and suggested he try left wing during camp. A week later, bodies bruised and battered, the majority of fledgling pros were packing up and heading home, or off to minor-league camps. Meeker, Lynn, defenceman Gus Mortson, and a couple of others happily stayed right where they were in St. Catharines and waited for the big-league camp to begin.

"I'll never forget that Sunday morning when Syl Apps, Bob Goldham, Wally Stanowski, Turk Broda, Gus Bodnar, Bud Poile, Gaye Stewart, Ted 'Teeder' Kennedy, and others arrived at the same hotel that I was in. These were people I had listened to and watched play all my life; they had been my heroes. The next day we were all going on the ice together. For a twenty-two-year-old guy just back from overseas, it was a hell of a thrill."

The rookies battled through two workouts and scrimmages a day, one in the morning and the second in midafternoon. On the first morning, Maple Leaf history was created. Coach Hap Day kept Meeker and Lynn together and placed classy centre Ted Kennedy between them. The new Kid Line was born. "If you couldn't play hockey with Kennedy," Howie says, "you couldn't play hockey with anybody. He was probably as great a competitor as has ever played the game, and certainly by far the toughest competitor on our team. He had great hockey sense and great puck-handling and passing skills." The trio instantly clicked and played very well during the three weeks of camp, intersquad scrimmages, and exhibition games.

The St. Catharines rink was smaller than the ice surface at Maple Leaf Gardens. Management, feeling the need to test their rookies on the big sheet, bused players to Maple Leaf Gardens for twice-a-day scrimmages during the last few days of camp. The speed and intensity levels increased as players sensed their fight for a job was entering its final round. Howie's robust, gritty style of play not only caught the attention of management, it also drew the ire of some veterans and rookies who were seeking employment.

"Our line was regularly facing Gus Bodnar, Bud Poile, and Gaye Stewart. Normally I would check Poile, but this day it was Stewart I wound up facing. Stewart had a reputation for occasionally being mean. Well, I was going to do what I had to do to make the team. There was no way in the world I was giving up a chance of making $4,500 that year, although I didn't really think about the money at the time. Nobody was going to stop me from making the club. I had gotten this far and I was going to make the Toronto Maple Leafs or die trying."

That morning's scrimmage started feisty and fast paced with Howie's unit playing well throughout. Stewart and Meeker collided numerous times, and near the end of the session the inevitable happened: a stick fight with Stewart. "While we were flailing away at each other my mind flashed to a picture, which I'd looked at since I was a kid, of Stewart in that infamous stick fight where he cut Jimmy Orlando with two or three swipes across the head. Orlando got him once, too, but it was quite the scrap."

Howie also quickly flashed back to another time when he'd "turtled" from a bully. He remembered the advice from his older teammates afterwards. "Never again," he vowed, countering Stewart's attack.

"We never cut each other. Actually all the shots were below the shoulders, but we whacked each other pretty good. So then in the afternoon scrimmage when I ran him off the puck two or three times, he gave me a slash across the ankles, I gave him an elbow, next thing you know the gloves are off and we were fighting. Gaye couldn't fight worth a lick, nor could I really."

Howie's determined approach to the game not only helped him make the club and have a successful season, it also catapulted the entire Maple Leaf squad to a higher level of play. One of the keys to the rookie-laden 1946–47 Leafs and their domination of the NHL over the next five years was their ability to combine skill with grit.

When coach Hap Day finally pencilled in his team's roster for the start of the season, on defence he had Wally Stanowski, Bob Goldham, Garth Boesch, and the "Gold Dust Twins" Gus Mortson and Jimmy Thomson, all playing solidly. They would be joined later that year by another youngster, Bill Barilko.

"Over the years I don't think anybody played defence as a unit better than Thomson and Mortson did," Howie says. "You can go through the records for the next five years on those guys and their plus-minus rating, won-lost season and playoffs, and won-lost Stanley Cup records would be better than anyone's in the league.

"Thomson was mean with his stick while Mortson was tough and mean. If you went into the corner with him it was lights out. Garth Boesch was as mentally tough as anyone I ever saw. He was good with the stick and would fight anyone. He didn't win many fights, but he would always show up; he played the body all the time and would just punish you.

"Goldham and Stanowski were a great combination. Wally was a great skater and puck-handler. A fun guy to be with. Goldham broke his arm that season. It didn't heal right, or the Leafs didn't give it time to heal, and he wound up in Chicago. He played well there, then went to Detroit and was a standout player there for many years. But certainly the defensive backbone of our team was Turk Broda in goal with Mortson, Thomson, Boesch, and Barilko on defence."

Up front the Leafs looked hot with the new Kid Line, or KLM Line, of Kennedy, Lynn, and Meeker. The unit of Syl Apps, Bill Ezinicki, and Harry Watson was always impressive. The Poile-Stewart-Bodnar trio played exceptionally, as they had the past couple of seasons. Those three were popular with Leaf fans, having all hailed from the Port Arthur–Fort William area. The team was further enhanced by veteran NHL brothers Nick and Don Metz and strong utility forward, rookie Joe Klukay.

"The lines were very strong, with depth down the centre," Howie remembers. "Apps centred Ezinicki and Watson. Apps and Watson were great players. Watson averaged maybe 22 goals a year but had all the ability to get at least 32 a year. Ezinicki was a hitter and checker and what a presence he had on the ice. Watson was big and strong, but gentle most of the time. Kennedy centring Meeker and Lynn, well . . . Kennedy was the hockey player. Lynn and I could both skate and check and occasionally score goals, but we weren't great goal scorers at all. Kennedy was tough and mean, and Lynn and I both liked to play tough, hit hard, and scoot around pretty quick.

"Bodnar, Poile, and Stewart were all great hockey players. They were mainly finesse, not really physical, but no slouches. Stewart could put pucks in the net from anywhere, Poile had a heck of a shot, and Bodnar was a very good playmaker. The two extra forwards, Nick Metz and Klukay, were very valuable; Metz could play any position on the team and Klukay was great defensively yet also had offensive skills. He was big, strong, and a great guy, and I think one of the most underrated players on the team over the years. He could play the game anyway you wanted, tough or with skill. It was pretty special to have Joe as part of my first year in the NHL. Somehow it seemed right."

Between the pipes was the phenomenal goaltending talent of Turk Broda, who Howie claims is the greatest playoff goaltender of all time. "He was a bloody marvel sometimes, stood on his head, especially in those clutch games, key moments. What a goalie!"

Of the team's seven rookies that year, four played on defence. Besides Howie, the rookies were Boesch, Mortson, Thomson, Barilko, Klukay, and Lynn.

"When we played tough we won, when we tried to play with speed, skill, and finesse, the other teams would usually beat us. Detroit was a big team then, but the biggest was Montreal, who'd won the Stanley Cup the year before. They were loaded with all-stars, jammed with talent, and should have won everything in 1946–47. They should have won the Stanley Cup, but we took care of that for them."

Most of the Leaf players, especially rookies, had signed their contracts during the summer. Prior to the start of the regular season, however, the league announced it was increasing the schedule by 10 games, from 50 games to 60.

"Once we had a feeling we'd made the team, a group of rookies and other players went to Day and said we wanted to discuss contracts with Conn Smythe. We wanted to be compensated for the extra 10 games. So we sent in our negotiator, Garth Boesch. Garth was a man among men. He came from Saskatchewan, his family owned a couple sections of land, he drove a Cadillac, had a beautiful wife, was free with his money . . . Anyway, he knew more about money than we did and was definitely the best negotiator of the bunch, so we sent him in, sort of fed him to Smythe.

"We figured it would take about fifteen minutes, but an hour or so later he came out and told us he'd negotiated only $500 each for the extra 10 games. So it worked out that my salary went down to only getting $83.33 a game. We generated a lot of cash flow at that time but no one fully realized how important that cash flow was for the community, the province, or especially for the owner's pockets; and no one seemed to think that we, the players, should have got paid part of that."

Howie points out, though, that back then the game program was just 15 cents, grey seats sold for 60 cents, and the best seats, the reds, were $3.00. That year he was paid $5,000 for playing 60 games, $1,000 for winning the first round of playoffs, $1,000 for the Stanley Cup, and $500 for the team's second-place finish in the regular season: $7,500 for playing on a second-place team and winning the Stanley Cup. Good money at the time — especially considering he had just come out of the army at $1.35 a day.

A day or two after the double dustup with Stewart, the Maple Leafs broke their training camp in St. Catharines. Instead of heading to Toronto, the team bus turned south for Detroit — and the first game of the 1946–47 National Hockey League season. Howie was on the bus.

Five

The Calder Kid

*"The red sweater touched the puck and you knocked
him on his ass, and when he got up
ya knocked him down again."*

When it comes to good years it's hard to imagine one as wonderful as Howie Meeker's rookie season in the National Hockey League. Fairy tales don't come any better than this.

The transition from training camp to the regular season was so fast he barely had time to enjoy the dream coming true. It was Wednesday, October 16, 1946, and Howie was about to play his first NHL game. He shook slightly with anticipation and pride as he pulled on the sacred blue and white game sweater, the number 15 emblazoned on the back, and prepared to step onto the ice at the famed Olympia in Detroit.

Howie failed to hit the score sheet in his inaugural NHL encounter, yet its significance will remain with him forever. When the sweating was done, the game ended in a 3–3 draw. The Leafs allowed the Wings back into the game when Sid Abel scored at 19:49 with the Detroit netminder pulled for an extra skater.

A tall, impressive Detroit rookie named Gordie Howe stole the limelight that night, scoring his first NHL goal against Turk Broda in the second period, and flattening Leaf forward Syl Apps. It would be the first evening of many encounters Howe and Meeker would share in an intertwined, sometimes tumultuous relationship.

"We fought all the time over the years," Howie recalls. "Oddly enough, we got along fine, but somehow we always wound up fighting. I'd always start scrapping with somebody else like Ted Lindsay, and then Howe would step in and we'd go at it. Gordie was a big, tough boy and very, very strong. People always talked about how much we fought and I thought it was an exaggeration. But I never really fought with Gordie; *Gordie* fought — I just took the shit-kickings."

While his NHL debut was a thrill, his second game, three nights later, was a dream come true. This time Howie would play in Maple Leaf Gardens before the hometown fans on a Saturday night. Despite the significance of the event, he felt a sense of calm and belonging. In the dressing room prior to the game he felt his pleasant predicament to be simply one of natural evolution. Ever since that first visit inside the Maple Leaf dressing room as a wide-eyed young Junior player, Howie knew that one day he would be back. A small stall in the legendary room was now his and he grinned as he methodically laced on his skates.

Halfway through the second period, Howie scored his first NHL goal.

"It was on a line change; I jumped on the ice and the play was in Detroit's zone on the far side of the rink, on my wing, so

I just cruised through centre ice. Kennedy intercepted a pass, spied me at the top of the circle, and his pass went through several players, hit a stick, and changed direction slightly. I had to reach way out to stop the puck at the left wing face-off location. I spun around and accidentally invented the slap shot. I raised the stick over my shoulders in an effort to keep my balance, hit the puck a whack, and the darn thing went straight in. Bad goal, bad angle; in those days you hardly ever got goals from there. Anyhow, I took it quite happily. My first goal scored was in Maple Leaf Gardens and we won 6–3."

There were plenty of lessons to be learned for a rookie. It was bad enough that guys on other teams wouldn't hesitate to run you over like a penny on a railroad track, but some *teammates* felt the same way on the ice. "Off the ice we were a pretty close bunch, but in scrimmages it could get pretty wild. Jobs were scarce in the six-team NHL."

If a rookie player wanted to survive, let alone excel in the pros, it behooved him to learn as much as he could, as fast as he could. Inevitably there were plenty of veterans, greatly concerned with their own job security, who were more than willing to play teacher — physically. But sometimes the same fellows prepared to steam-roll your tiny torso turned out to be good friends as well as impressive instructors — like Leaf defenceman Bob Goldham.

"One night early in the year we were playing in Boston. Milt Schmidt used to wind up in his own end with the puck and, just like Bobby Orr, he'd come out from behind the net on an angle, take two crossover steps into high speed, and would be gone like a jet. He'd beat our centre man early and would fly down the middle. Well, this night he did the same thing and I cut into the centre and all of a sudden defencemen Goldham and Stanowski were there and I was in the way. The pass went to my now-vacant wing and Boston's Woody Dumart picked up the puck — *bang* — it was in the net. So I'm on the way back to the bench with my head down, and as Goldham skates by he says, 'Kid, you ever cut into the centre again when you're backchecking and I will cut your head off.' He probably would have, too."

Another early-season match, in Chicago, provided two lessons in one. Lesson one was about self-control and avoiding spontaneous, dumb penalties. The Leafs were up 3–1 halfway through the second period, when someone lobbed the puck out of the Black Hawks' end. Howie impulsively raised his stick over his head and whacked at the puck, which in those years was a high-sticking penalty. Referee Bill Chadwick sent him to the penalty box. No sooner did he sit down than the Bentley brothers, Max and Doug, and Bill Mosienko (the famed Pony Line) jumped on the ice. "I remember thinking 'Oh boy, now I'm in trouble.' Chadwick dropped the puck and it was Max to Doug, back to Max, over to Mosienko, and in the net — 3–2."

Penalties didn't end on a power-play goal back then, so Howie could only sit and shake his head while the Chicago crowd went wild. "Chadwick drops the puck again and all of a sudden it's Mosie to Doug, back to Max, who takes a shot and it's 3–3. I'm trying to hide; I don't want to go on the ice. They face off again: Doug to Mosie, Mosie to Max, Max back to Doug, and — *boom* — it's in the net and they're leading 4–3."

His sentence in the sin bin finally over, Howie slunk over to the team bench under the punishing glare of coach Hap Day. Howie figured he was in the doghouse and would never get back on the ice.

Lesson two followed soon after, compliments of a veteran Leaf teammate. "I finally got back on the ice with Nick and Don Metz, and I went out to the point and knocked Chicago's Johnny Mariucci off the puck. Nick picked it up and gave me a hell of a pass in the air, onto my stick, and I was home free. I walked in, pulled the goaltender out, and passed it back. I was waiting for Nick to put it in and suddenly he was not there. 'Oh, jeez, I blew it again,' I thought, but Nick went around behind the net, picked up the puck, and put it in."

Back at the bench, Nick lectured the rookie. "Kid, any time you are home free like the birds, ya don't pass the puck to your mother. You make the play. I'll come in later if there's a rebound and I'll put it in, but you shoot the puck."

His first couple of weeks as a Leaf provided several eye-opening, memorable experiences, including regular visits to the NHL cities of Boston, Chicago, Detroit, New York, and Montreal. Players who were once just faces on the Bee Hive Golden Corn Syrup photos plastered on his bedroom wall now sat in the same dressing room, or across the ice.

Howie also found himself slightly in awe of the legendary names he recognized from radio and newspaper. As a young boy he had listened to hockey on the radio and consumed everything written about the Leafs. He listened faithfully to CFRB's Wes McKnight with his nightly sports show and Saturday-night interviews with Toronto stars. Howie read or listened to Joe Chrysdale, Foster Hewitt, Jim Vipond, Ted "The Moaner" Reeve, and members of the Hot Stove League such as McKnight, Bobby Hewitson, and Basil O'Mara. There was also Mike Rodden, Jim Coleman, Trent Frayne, Bobbie Rosenfield — "an Olympic woman athlete who could run like a deer and was a great sports person" — Al Nickleson, Red Burnett, Elmer Ferguson, H. H. Roxborough . . .

"I grew up admiring these people and all of a sudden they were coming to talk to me! Golly gee, it was such an unbelievable feeling."

Three other characters at the Gardens stand out in Howie's memories of that first year: publicity director and promoter Ed Fitkin, game program editor Spiff Evans, and strong team supporter/businessman Sammy Taft, the man who Howie remembers originated the "hat-trick" tradition in hockey. Sammy sold hats on Spadina Avenue and one night he gave a new hat to Ted Kennedy for his three goals; it was the beginning of the tradition. From then on you got a new hat from Sammy if you scored three goals in an evening.

Right next to Sammy's on Spadina was Shopsy's delicatessen. "Big ol' Shopsy had the best corned beef in the world and the guys would go there regularly after practice. We paid a nickel or maybe 10 cents for a sandwich, but back then a pack of cigarettes was 25 cents, and a quart of milk was 11 cents.

"Toronto wasn't a very big city in those days compared to today. Everybody in the city knew you. There wasn't television back then, just the newspapers and radio, but there wasn't anybody anywhere in Canada that didn't know you."

Klukay and Howie became good friends and for the first few months, until Grace and Howie found a place to stay in Toronto, Joe and Howie boarded together. At eight o'clock one morning the telephone rang and Howie's landlady woke the boys, announcing, "Coach Day is on the phone."

"Where were you last night?" Day barked.

"Why?"

"Never mind. Where were you?"

"Joe and I went out to a movie."

"What time did you get in?"

"Oh, 10:30 p.m., at the very latest."

"What movie?" Howie told him the name of the show.

"Whereabouts? Put on your landlady." Howie gave her the telephone and Day asked her a couple of questions and then she handed Howie the phone back. Day said, "Well, you'll be expecting a call from the police in a few minutes. It's a good thing you got the right answers to the right questions."

It turned out someone had hot-wired Howie's brand new 1947 Ford Coupe and zipped around town. The thieves were drinking somewhere and the police wound up chasing them down a road. The culprits drove the car into the ditch and ran away.

"Maple Leaf management knew exactly where you were and what was going on all the time. They knew we usually played Thursday at home or on the road, Saturday at home, and Sunday wherever. If it was in Boston or Chicago we were always late getting back the next day, three or four in the afternoon. We'd have a party planned for somewhere — usually at Ernie Shumande's hotel on

Elizabeth Street, where we'd get some privacy, although we didn't have enough sense in the early years to do that. But we'd also go out and have dinner at the Old Mill, a big, famous restaurant in the west end of Toronto, and then get a private room and do our drinking. Nobody drank excessively, but there were three or four who drank enough that their wives probably had to drive them home."

The Leafs practised every Tuesday morning and Day would know who'd been drinking. After the scrimmage was over, he'd keep the four or five guys out who had the most to drink the night before and would skate the pants off them. Jimmy Thomson was usually one of them. One night Thomson announced, "Boys, I'm not having a drink tonight and if that Day skates me tomorrow morning, I'm going to really give it to him."

Tuesday practice was tough because the players usually had Monday off. Day skated the daylights out of them and then held a tough scrimmage.

At the end of practice the next day, Hap named five or six players to stay for extra duty, but this time Thomson was not among them. However, he remained standing on the ice.

"Jimmy, you are not to be here today; get in the dressing room," Day ordered.

"No sir, I'm skating," Thomson balked. "Suit yourself," Day shrugged.

The amazing thing was that Hap knew Jimmy had not been drinking the night before, Howie says. "It didn't matter where we were, at the Old Mill, Schumande's, wherever — he had people all around town. He had his connections and he had that kind of control over us. If any one of us had been out on the town or out doing anything we shouldn't have, he'd know about it. Almost always."

Y

On January 8, 1947, things would get even better for Howie.

"If you're a run-of-the-mill NHL player, as I developed into, you wish for a couple of cracks at the Stanley Cup, perhaps an overtime goal or two, and maybe, just maybe, a very lucky night — one that might get you in the record books."

As he donned his equipment that evening Howie never imagined that in the years ahead he would see all three of these dreams come to fruition. Nor did he anticipate that one of his wishes would occur that very evening.

It was another miserable winter night in Toronto. Most sensible people were staying put, snuggled warmly inside their homes. However, 12,059 die-hard Leaf fans bundled up and made the trek to 60 Carlton Street and the lively confines of Maple Leaf Gardens. The weather might have been frigid but their Maple Leafs were on fire, burning up the league, led by the plethora of hot-shot rookies. If fans needed any further incentive to attend that evening, their Leafs were playing host to the Chicago Black Hawks, a team that had been a patsy for Toronto all year long.

It was the eighth clash of the season against the Hawks and the Leafs had won six of the previous seven games. "That was probably the reason we were in first place then. Chicago was actually loaded with great offensive talent. They had the two Bentleys and Mosienko, and my goodness gracious, could they fly. Adam Brown was a real good hockey player and so was Alex Kaleta. Kaleta was always home free, every time you looked up he had a breakaway or something. He was like me, though — if he could have put the puck into the ocean off a wharf he'd have been a hell of a goal scorer."

Meeker and Kennedy were joined on left wing that night by Joe Klukay. Howie's longtime buddy and former Junior A teammate replaced the injured Lynn, sidelined with severe scalp lacerations from a stick fight with Chicago's Red Hamill.

"The team went out that night and didn't play very well, especially in the first period. Right from the start Mosienko put Max Bentley in home free and Max put the puck between Broda's legs — we were down 1–0. I tied it up a little later in the first period, but didn't get credit for the goal. The pass went from Boesch over to Stanowski at the point. I was facing Stanowski with my back to the net, and not afraid to stand there because his shot wouldn't break a pane of glass. He did shoot the puck, and it hit me, fell in front of me, and my legs were open so I just gave it a whack back towards the net. The next thing I knew the red light was on. They credited the goal to Stanowski, which didn't bother me at all, because I didn't know if it had hit anybody else in the pileup of players in front of me on the way to the net."

Clint Smith made it 2–1 for Chicago. Early in the second period the Leafs were putting the pressure on again. As Wally Stanowski wound up for a shot from the Hawks' blueline, Howie cut to the net, hoping to scoop up a rebound or deflect the shot. "Like I said, I wasn't afraid to cut in front, because even if Wally hit you right between the eyes it wouldn't hurt you. Just as I'm cutting in front Johnny Mariucci cross-checked me, caught me with a dandy and took my feet out from under me; I went up in the air. All of a sudden something nailed me on the ass, I heard the crowd roar, and the red light went on." It was Stanowski's second goal, but again Howie didn't protest. "What the hell, it didn't matter to me as long as we had tied the game. It turned out later that I had scored two goals, but I really didn't do a thing on either of them."

Howie earned his next goal, however, putting the Leafs ahead 4–2. "Deep in our own end I gave the puck to Klukay, Joe gave it to Kennedy, who gave it back to me. I handled the puck about three or four times before Klukay finally put it right on my stick. I'm standing beside Chicago goalie Paul Bibeault and Klukay took him out to lunch, gave the puck to me, and I put it into the net. It was a well-earned goal; I participated in that one."

Hap Day made a line change and as Howie sat down on the bench next to Klukay he said, "Well, that's the third one I scored tonight." Day, passing behind them, stopped and said, "What do you mean?"

"So I told him, 'Well, I think I put the first one in; I whacked it between my legs and if a teammate didn't touch it after I hit it, then I scored that one. The one that Wally shot in this period hit me dead centre in the arse while I was up in the air, with both feet off the ground, before it went into the galdarn net.'"

Unbeknownst to Howie, Day went to the officials between periods and explained the goals. After talking to other players, referee George Gravel changed the goals appropriately. Suddenly Howie had a hat trick.

At the start of the third period the Kid Line was immediately buzzing and Bibeault made two great saves. "Klukay fired the puck and I'm standing beside the net, the puck hits Paul and bounces back to Kennedy, and I'm still standing there waiting — nobody within half a mile of me, and now Bibeault is gone to lunch again. Kennedy slips it over to me and I knock it in to the open net. I basically did nothing and had my fourth of the night."

Goals were coming thick and fast. Howie thinks his team got six goals that period. "Nick got one, Mosienko finally got one for Chicago, then Nick Metz got his second of the night, Poile got a goal, Stewart got a goal, and in between all that, I got my fifth. It was Kennedy and Klukay who did all the blessed work on it. I think I helped get the puck out of our end and then came up late on the play. By that time Kennedy and Klukay had everybody beaten, had everyone taken over on the other side of the ice, including Bibeault, and Kennedy slid it across to me. I said 'thank you' and put it in the open net and that was number five."

It was a relieved Black Hawk team that greeted the game-ending buzzer. When the smoke had cleared, the red-hot Leafs had recorded a lopsided 10–4 win, and Meeker was in the record book.

"At that time a five-goal game was really something special. A hat-trick was great — heck, just to score a goal meant something back in those days when 20 goals (in a season) got you an all-star rating. Twenty goals, you were a heck of a hockey player, 30 goals and you were a superstar. So to get five in one night certainly helped my career. I had some rough games later that year, when I wasn't playing so well, but I had quite a few goals and that helped to keep me on the team.

"It's a night very few players have, particularly as a rookie. It's a rookie record that has been tied once — by Don Murdoch — but no one has broken it. Quite a few established players have scored five goals in a game, Darryl Sittler has and others, but not a lot of rookies — so I was lucky."

Ɣ

Some events and associations in life seem meant to be, no matter what. Circumstances have a way of insisting on the formation of certain bonds. For Howie those bonds seemed to include Grace, hockey, the outdoors, a propensity for trouble, and — much to Grace's chagrin — pigeons. She had cherished the move to Toronto in various unspoken ways, and one of them had been her flight from those damned pigeons. Her freedom was not to last long.

By coincidence one morning the Maple Leafs and Montreal Canadiens wound up travelling on the same train to Toronto, and as Hab coach Dick Irvin Sr. passed by Day's special berth he invited the Leaf coach back to his room. Day agreed and invited Howie to join him, suggesting it might "prove to be an interesting experience."

Howie felt a little out of sorts making the trip with his coach through the Canadiens' car, past all the players, to Irvin's private room at the back of the car. The three men were no sooner seated in the small room than he heard a familiar cooing. Howie tried to pay attention to conversation at hand, but finally, unable to contain himself, he said, "Excuse me, Mr. Irvin, do I hear pigeons?"

"Why, yes, boy, you hear pigeons. How'd you know they were pigeons?"

"I used to raise them as a youngster, sir; I had all kinds of pigeons, homers mostly," Howie confessed.

At that, Irvin opened the door to his washroom. Inside were two large coops with four homing pigeons in each. Irvin informed Howie that he'd been involved in the homer racing business for years. For the next twenty minutes Howie and Dick ignored Hap, babbling on about different breeds of pigeons, shows, flight times, and species. Finally, Irvin said, "Would you like to start raising pigeons again, then? Here, take four with you." Howie politely protested, but that day his arms were full as he left the train with his suitcase and four homer pigeons.

Grace was less than thrilled.

"The minute she saw me she said, 'Oh-oh, not again, looks like we're back in the pigeon business.' Before I knew it I was up to about 100 to 150 pigeons, with about fifteen or twenty different kinds again."

About two-thirds of the way through that first season the team's number-one line — Bodnar, Poile, and Stewart — had somehow become the number-three unit. Day never started the same line twice: one night it would be Apps's line starting, then the next game Kennedy's, and the next night Bodnar's. "He would just roll them over. Our line most often played against the other team's best line, to check, but also to occasionally threaten. We got lots of playing time, as did Apps, Wild Bill Ezinicki, and Harry Watson, but less and less was going to Bodnar, Poile, and Stewart. That treatment went on into the playoffs, too."

"Bashing Bill" Barilko arrived in early February and immediately helped jump start some of the sleeping giants on the blueline. "The powers that be had obviously decided we had to be even tougher on defence," Howie says. "Boesch was tough and mean, no doubt about it, and Stanowski and Goldham were rugged, but not really mean or tough."

Barilko, a five-foot eleven-inch, 184-pound bruiser, had been playing for the Hollywood Wolves in the minor Pacific Coast League, creating quite a stir. His first NHL game was Feburary 6, 1947, in Montreal against the Canadiens, and he wasted no time introducing himself. "Holy jumpin' Jehoshaphat, the guy could hit and hit like a ton," Howie laughs. "We lost that game 8–2, but did he ever toughen up our defence. The addition of Barilko gave us four mentally and physically tough defencemen whom you didn't want to go into the corner with. If you got any of them mad or came out of the corner with the puck, you were dead. At that time I just did not realize the value of the four tough guys on defence. Barilko was something else, a hard rock from the north."

By the time the 60-game regular season was finished Howie had managed to set a new record for total goals by a rookie in one season. "I wound up scoring 27, which probably helped me win the Calder Trophy. I should have scored 37 that year because Kennedy and Lynn set me up home free time and time again." Howie's 27 goals and 18 assists for 45 points placed him third in team scoring and fifteenth overall in the league. "I didn't think 27 goals was that big of a deal but then I never got close to that number again, so there you go."

Howie demonstrated more than just a scoring knack. He let the entire league know his diminutive size would not impede him or his feisty style of play. Indeed, he tossed his 160-pound frame around with reckless abandon, took on all challengers, and by year-end had amassed 76 penalty minutes, tenth highest in the league.

Howie dropped his gloves a number of times that first year, sometimes standing up to a challenge, other times just being an obnoxious, pugnacious pest. The latter behaviour embroiled him in one of his wildest scraps that season. Former Maple Leaf Billy Taylor, a player Howie actually admired, was the target of his bad attitude that night.

"Billy was a hell of a nice guy, didn't fight a lot. I guess I was on him most of the night and he finally gave me a whack with his stick. I popped him back, he punched me with his glove, and away we went. It just escalated from there. Next thing we were really flailing away on the ice. They split us up and sent us to the penalty box. Taylor was just yapping at me and I was steaming mad.

"Next thing I know I feel this hard thump on my shoulder — he'd reached over the timekeeper and gate and punched me. Luckily I'd moved and he nailed my shoulder. If he'd hit me with that punch he'd have taken my head off. Well, I wasn't taking that nonsense and I went after him. Next thing you know the bench is flooded with players, linesmen, ushers, a couple of fans, and finally about a dozen cops. It was wild, just simply wild. Poor Billy, I don't know what I did to make him so pissed off . . ."

Y

The regular season ended well for the Leafs, even though they slipped into second place, six points behind the Montreal Canadiens. The Leafs' 31 wins, 19 losses, and 10 ties for 72 points that season were a healthy jump from the dismal year before. Toronto led the league in goals scored with 209 while allowing 172 — second-best in the league. The club's grit showed statistically with the Leafs well ahead of other teams in total penalty minutes — 669 minutes, 108 more than their nearest rivals, Montreal.

"We had twelve more wins than losses, and in goals for and against we were plus-37. At the time that didn't mean anything to me at all, but later on when you go back and look at the records, and you understand what should happen and what does happen in a hockey game, and why it happens — those two figures are extremely good. The other good one was just 172 goals against. For five rookies on defence, seven on the team, that was just a 2.85 goals against per game and we scored maybe 3.50 goals a game — that's quite a bit of difference and means a lot more wins than losses."

In the opening round of playoffs the Leafs faced the potent Detroit Red Wings. The Wings were powered by veteran stars Sid Abel, Ted Lindsay, and club-leading sniper Billy Taylor. The former Leaf finished third overall in league scoring. Fresh-faced rookies Howe and Jimmy Conacher were still making noise around the league as well.

Howie's dream-come-true NHL season continued in the opening game as he scored the overtime winning goal — against Johnny Mowers, the only overtime goal in his career — leading Toronto to a 3–2 victory.

Going into the Stanley Cup finals the Leafs were the well-deserved underdogs. The Canadiens had the sensational Bill Durnan in goal and wingers Toe Blake and the great Rocket Richard, who'd scored 45 goals that year. On defence Montreal had the biggest guy in the league, Emile "Butch" Bouchard.

Star centre Elmer Lach was injured, but the Habs had two other talented centres: Buddy O'Connor, "who could do anything with the puck," and Billy Reay. A familiar face also patrolled the Montreal blueline — Ken Reardon. "Kenny was not a skilled hockey player, but he was a great leader, a tough, mean guy; he would do absolutely anything he had to in order to win. Johnny Quilty was very, very good with the puck. The meanest guy they had by far was Murph Chamberlain. Murph and I had some real battles."

The Leafs went into Montreal for the first game of the finals, star-struck. "No one really knew what to expect. We knew we were in trouble; no one was expecting us to win. The first game we played terrible, absolutely terrible. Before we knew it Montreal led 3–0 after the second period and we ended up losing 6–0. No contest at all. We didn't play tough, we didn't play smart, we didn't play. Montreal just smothered us the last half of the game.

"After the game, Bill Durnan apparently said, 'How did those guys get in the league?' Later on he would deny making such a statement, but a lot of hockey fans left the building that night thinking exactly the same thing."

Normally, the Leafs would first go on the ice at 7:45 for the warm-up, with the game starting at 8 p.m. "We'd just drop the puck and away we'd go. We were dumb and not warming up properly like they have the last twenty to twenty-five years."

Just before the start of the second game, Conn Smythe walked into the dressing room, something he'd done previously only once that year. Behind him walked Day.

Smythe burst through the door, physically claimed his spot in the room in front of the players, pushed back his coat, placed his hands on his hips, and stared around the room. Then he fixed Syl Apps with a stare — eyes shooting sparks like Rocket Richard's when enraged. Smythe spent thirty seconds tearing a strip off Apps. Then he focused his scathing verbal spanking on Ted Kennedy, another obvious leader. Eventually he went at everybody, up one side and down the other . . . Lynn, Thomson, Meeker.

"Well, when he was done we couldn't get out that door quick enough. If he hadn't stepped aside we would have run him down to get out of there and get started. We got out there, warmed up, and then our line started: Kennedy, Lynn, and me against Bouchard and Reardon. It was their top defensive unit and of course Bill Durnan was in goal. The puck was dropped; it came to me and I headed towards Durnam. I almost got around big Butch Bouchard but at the last second he just bowled me over and took a penalty. For some reason we wound up back at centre ice. Kennedy opened the scoring from Lynn and Barilko. We went back and faced off and Kennedy gave it to Lynn and *boom* — it's 2–0 Toronto and we're not two minutes into the game, we're not one shift finished, before the crowd is even settled in their seats, and it was game over. We finished the first period up 2–0 and scored early in the second for a 3–0 stretch."

Howie remembers Lynn and Richard scrapping. "Richard ran amok that night. You could tell he was thinking, 'How could these young whippersnappers from Toronto come in here and stick it up our arse,' and he got a minor penalty for attacking and cutting Lynn, then I think he went after Ezinicki. Afterwards he got suspended for a game.

"That was a tough, tough, physical hockey game. You took a stride, you touched the puck, and you were gone. It was great fun. I never enjoyed playing in a game as much as I enjoyed that one, particularly when we were up 3–0 in the contest.

"We didn't need any more goals to win the game, all we needed was red sweaters to hit. The red sweater touched the puck and you knocked him on his ass, and when he got up ya knocked him down again."

Years later, Day told Howie that as he and Conn were driving together to the Forum for the third game of that 1947 series, Conn said, "Look, Hap, we should have extra police, because there's going to be a war. I'm afraid this series is going to break out into a war."

But Howie doesn't remember that game or the series as being all that wild. "Maybe being twenty-two years of age was part of it. That Game Two goes down in the minds of many people as the roughest game they'd ever seen. I only remember that Smythe came in and talked to us. We went out and nailed that game with Kennedy winning the game right away. Kennedy scored a beautiful goal and then set up Lynn who went wide, then around Reardon like a hoop around a barrel, pulled Durnan out of the net, and tucked it in. We set the pace right then and there and we dominated that series from then on in, particularly with Broda outplaying Durnan by just a little."

Howie also maintains that the toughness of the Leafs combined with skill gave his club an advantage in the playoffs that year. "We had ten really tough hockey players, most of them of true NHL calibre. The tougher it got — and that is the key — the better the guys played. Ezinicki, Kennedy, Lynn, Bodnar, and I were all like that and on defence we had five guys that were mentally and physically tough. We also had four or five skilled hockey players: Apps, Kennedy, Klukay, Bodnar, Watson, Stanowski, and a couple others backed by the best goaltender in the league. Turk Broda was by far the best goaltender then and as good as any that ever played the game — particularly in big games. Certainly we had the best coach in Hap Day, though we didn't know it at the time."

The Leafs returned to Toronto and won Game Three by a 4–2 score. "I remember the great scene with Frank Selke screaming, hopping up and down, and jumping around trying to pull a Conn Smythe; I don't blame him. Two nights later we won Game Four 2–1 in overtime and Broda was the guy that won that sucker — no doubt about that."

Montreal goalie Durnan stole Game Five back in Montreal. It was 3–0 late in the game and then Poile broke the shutout, 3–1."

In the sixth game back in Toronto, Leaf goalie Broda returned the favour. Late in the game, with the score 2–1 for Toronto, Montreal's Reardon got the puck, flew down the ice around two defencemen, and walked in on Broda at a reasonably good angle. "Had anybody else been going in on Broda I'd have been worried, but Kenny couldn't put the puck in the ocean off the wharf either, and Broda stoned him. We went on to win that game and the Cup in Toronto."

With just a minute and a half to go and a slim one-goal lead, the face-off was set for deep in the Toronto end. Hap Day put Thomson, Mortson, and the Kid Line on the ice to defend against the six best snipers Montreal had.

"I would think that was one of the highlights of my career. At that point, with the Stanley Cup at stake, Day had enough confidence in how I could play without the puck, and how I could play behind the blue line. There were four rookies and Kennedy out there at a key time. We held them off — I don't think they did get a shot on Broda, and there were at least two or three face-offs in our end. It was the ultimate compliment to me. At that time I didn't realize how important it was."

After the Leafs won the sixth game, and the series, in Toronto, there was no presentation of the Stanley Cup. "The reason or excuse I heard was that Conn Smythe had said to leave the Cup in Montreal. He probably expected us to be back there, fighting for a seventh game. I think we surprised him — and the rest of the hockey world — beating the tough Montreal Canadiens who were, at that time, the defending Stanley Cup champions. But we were young, the Canadiens were old. A huge factor was that the Canadiens lost their best centre man, Elmer Lach, so Montreal's offence suffered greatly."

Y

Soon after the Cup victory, Howie and Grace returned to New Hamburg to relax and allow Howie to heal up his numerous bumps and bruises. Early one fine May morning, as Howie sauntered the route into town to Pfaff's Barbershop, a familiar face stopped him on the street and offered congratulations. Howie assumed he meant the Stanley Cup but asked what for?

"You won the Calder Trophy," he was informed.

Sure enough, the story was plastered all over the *London Free Press*. Meeker had beaten out the only other two serious candidates: speedster Leo Gravelle of Montreal and Detroit's Jimmy Conacher.

Years later, Howie's selection would become a trivia question due to the fact that another rookie was beaten that year for the award, Gordie Howe. But Howie contends that too much is made of that issue.

"I was twenty-two years old and Gordie was just seventeen; he was not even in the running at that point. He was really just a kid and you knew he was going to be a great player some day. It's not fair to Gordie to compare us like that. He was a big, tough, talented boy who needed a few years to bloom. I was a man back from a war. Five years later I was getting 7 goals and he was getting 37 a year."

That summer the NHL decided it would start to give all major individual award winners $1,000 each, so Howie received a pleasant bonus to go with the cherished rookie-of-the-year trophy.

"I brought the Calder Trophy home for the summer. It was a fair size and took up a corner of the room. I got a great kick out of telling guys who later sipped champagne out of the trophy that my wife used it more than once as a diaper pail for baby Jane. I came home one day and Grace had put the rinsed diapers in the cup. When I questioned her about it she said, 'Well, what else are we supposed to do with the galdarn thing?'"

Six

All-Star Material

"In 1947–48 we had enough skill on the ice every shift to win any game we all really wanted to win."

The bubble that had been Howie's rookie season burst just before training camp for the 1947–48 season began. The prick came in the form of Conn Smythe with a broken promise and forgotten handshake. It would not be the last of either he would experience during his connection with Smythe.

A few days prior to training camp Howie met with coach Hap Day, who informed him the bonus money the Leafs promised him for winning the Calder Trophy would not be forthcoming. "Mr. Smythe considers the $1,000 paid you by the league sufficient to his personal agreement," Day said. Howie protested vehemently, saying Day *knew* that wasn't the deal.

Howie seethes even today when he remembers the incident. "Smythe didn't have the balls to tell me himself. He got Day to do his dirty work and I could tell Day was very uncomfortable with the task." Howie never did get the $1,000 from the team, and it bothered him considerably. "In those days that was a lot of money. It sort of took the wind out of me. I never forgave Smythe for reneging on his handshake. Anytime I ever shook hands with anybody on anything, I lived up to my end of the deal, even if it killed me."

During that summer back in New Hamburg Howie had put himself through a brutal, self-designed conditioning program in preparation for the new season. Every morning he would run ten miles, often carrying weights. On several such excursions he was joined by his brother Tom. "I'd follow along beside him on my bike and when the run was finished I would be bagged, much more tired than Howie. He was in tremendous shape and so determined."

If running wasn't enough, Howie also went to work on a railroad construction crew to improve his upper-body muscles. The job involved laying new rails on old ties and raising the level of the rails, which involved jacking up the rail, packing all the ties an inch or two, then using a twenty-five-pound, seven-foot-long tamping bar to crunch the rocks under the tie. "Someone with a distorted sense of humour paired me up with Ernie Eichler, a six-foot-six, 220-pound man with shoulders and arms like a sumo wrestler," Howie says. "That twenty-five-pound bar was like a toothpick to Ernie and he'd crunch, crunch, crunch away, up and down, up and down, all day long and it wouldn't bother him. Everyone else would tamp for five minutes and stop for two, but not Ernie."

At 7 a.m. the crew would set to work. Howie and Ernie would start the morning working across from one another on the same rail tie. By 9 a.m. Howie would usually be about twenty ties behind Eichler. "My arms and shoulders would be so sore I'd have trouble raising them to feed myself at lunch time. I can still see the grin on

Ernie's face when I couldn't keep up the pace and fell behind hour after hour."

One day the foreman, a five-foot two-inch, 150-pound man who grew up tamping, stepped in about ten ties ahead of Howie to help him catch up to Ernie. "I remember the look on his face when I told him, 'Sir, you tamp another tie and I'll put you under the damn thing. It's my job; I'll finish it.'"

The daily hard slogging paid off as Howie rediscovered muscles, particularly in his upper body, that he'd allowed to let slip or soften since his days on the gymnastic rings. He was especially glad of the exercise effort when training camp began and the rugged, physical grind of job-hunting in the elite ranks of pro hockey started all over again. Unlike today, few players in those years actually worked their upper chest or strengthened their stomach muscles. For a smaller player such as Howie, every possible advantage was needed in competing for a spot. Thanks to Ernie Eichler, Howie was fit, ready, and in better condition than most of the Leafs.

Despite the rigours of training camp, the forward units remained pretty well unaltered as the regular 1947–48 season began. No one suspected that within a few months an entire line would be permanently disbanded.

At the start of the 1948–49 season Howie switched uniform numbers from his original 15 to 11. The switch had nothing to do with preference or superstition, and everything to do with a better night's sleep. Veteran players had the first choice of sweater numbers. When riding trains players were assigned sleeping berths according to their sweater number with numbers 1 to 12 usually being lower berths, while 13 and higher were upper stalls. Howie preferred ground level.

The NHL held its first annual All-Star game, on October 13, 1947. While all-star teams had been selected since 1931, only three other games involving stars had ever been held, the first being in 1934 as a benefit game for the injured Leaf player Irvine "Ace"

Bailey. In 1947 the league decided it would help establish a players' pension plan. Howie recalls that the players were to put in $900 of their money and the clubs would match it with $900. "There were over 14,000 people that paid to get into that first annual game in 1947, so the league should have made enough money to match all the players' $900 from that game alone." The league decided that each year the all-star affair would be played in the home of the Stanley Cup winners, with the Cup champions playing against the all-star squad. This special unit's lineup was composed of players selected by the hockey writers to the first and second all-star teams at the end of the previous season, with coaches adding players to round out three forward lines, six defencemen, and a couple of goalies.

"I think that formula was head and shoulders the best. There was no way in the world that the Cup champion Maple Leafs wanted to be beaten by anybody in the league, let alone the 'throw-together' all-stars. We played just as hard and tough in that game as we played in any of the regular games, and I don't think the players resented it. Maybe a few stars didn't like the hitting, but no one openly complained. Management and owners feared injuries, but most of the players were used to the thumping and banging that consistently went on if you were going to win. The all-stars adjusted and they eventually beat us."

Despite the Leafs' winning the Cup in 1946–47 and boasting great players such as Kennedy, Apps, Thomson, and Mortson, not one Leaf had been named to the first or second all-star teams, a snub that only motivated the Leafs more. The 1947 NHL squad included the first team of goalie Bill Durnan, defencemen Kenny Reardon and Butch Bouchard, and Rocket Richard, all from Montreal, along with Boston's Milt Schmidt and Chicago's Doug Bentley. On the second team were "Black Jack" Stewart and Bill Quackenbush from Detroit on defence, Chicago's Max Bentley at centre with Boston's Bobby Bauer and Woody Dumart flanking him, and the Bruins' Frankie Brimsek in goal.

"I remember the game was tied 3–3 for the longest time and then the all-stars got the winning goal late in the game. There were a couple of fights as well. Gus Mortson came out of the corner with Gordie Howe; I remember them really scrapping. Later on I took Bobby Bauer into the fence and we came out swinging. It was a heck of a hockey game, tremendously competitive, and the fans got their money's worth. We wanted to win, and certainly the all-stars didn't want to be embarrassed by a bunch of guys that didn't make the all-star team, so they played very well."

During the next few seasons the Leafs continued to be ignored in all-star selections despite winning championships. In 1947–48, Broda was the only Leaf that made it, selected to the first squad. After the 1948–49 season, the Leafs had won three Stanley Cups, but not one member of the team made the first or second all-star team. "Finally in 1949–50 some of our guys got on. Defenceman Gus Mortson was recognized. As good as Gus was, I think the best player was his partner Jimmy Thomson. Mortson and Kenny Reardon made the first team, and if they were picked then Thomson should have been there. Reardon was a great hockey player but he couldn't carry Thomson's stick at any time. Kennedy got the nod for the second all-star team — I mean, whoever picked these teams in those days had to be out of their cotton-picking minds. Kennedy leads us to three straight Stanley Cups and all he deserved was one selection — to the second team? Absolutely mad."

On October 9, 1951, the formula of the Stanley Cup–winning team playing the all-stars was abandoned, because of the problems in the 1949–50 affair. Detroit had won the Cup and placed five players on the first and second all-star teams: Red Kelly, Gordie Howe, Ted Lindsay, Leo Reise, and Sid Abel, all of whom chose to play for Detroit in the 1950 all-star tilt, forcing the all-stars to scramble to find players of similar quality. "That year the Wings beat the all-stars 7–1 and the league said, 'Hey, we can't have that. It has to be a great hockey game.' If it would have been 3–2, no problem, but 7–1 — that's no contest. But the league went to a formula that's been a 'no contest' ever since." Various formulas were used during the next 17 years until the current system of teams selected from each of the two league divisions was adopted in 1969.

V

During the summer of 1947, Leaf star and captain Syl Apps met with Day and announced that the upcoming season would be his last. Apps planned to retire from the game and start his own business. Day immediately went to Smythe and suggested the time to get another quality centre man was "right away." On November 3 they traded Gus Bodnar, Bud Poile, Gaye Stewart, Bob Goldham, and Ernie Dickens to Chicago for superstar Max Bentley and young forward Cy Thomas. Poile, Bodnar, and Stewart formed an entire forward line nicknamed the Flyin' Forts Line. "As a player at that time, and knowing as little as I did about NHL trading, I still wasn't the least bit surprised that three of the five fellows were gone," Howie recalls. "I was surprised that a player of Bentley's quality would be available.

"When the trade was made I remember thinking, 'Well, thank God he's on our side instead of the other team.' It would be a little bit safer to take a penalty against the Hawks. When he was with Chicago, if you tried to play tic-tac-toe hockey with that star line they would kill you. The only way you could stop the Bentley line, or any good hockey line for that matter, was to give them the puck and then run 'em. Actually you really didn't have to give them the puck, the good lines had the damn thing all the time. You let them shoot, let them pass, but would always finish the check and take the man. That was hard work. When you were willing to do that you could beat the good teams; when you weren't willing to, they would beat you."

Boston was one of the better teams in the late 1940s, largely because they had the Kraut Line of Milt Schmidt, Porky Dumart, and Bobby Bauer. "You couldn't run Milt; he ran you. You could tie him but you could never beat him, and Porky was big and strong

— you'd run him and you'd bounce, but he could play tough. The Montreal Canadiens had Elmer Lach, whom you couldn't run because he would cut your throat with his stick, and Maurice 'Rocket' Richard, whom you were half afraid of all the time because you didn't know what he was going to do, whether he was going to take your head off or not. If he played hockey he'd kill you, and if he wasn't playing hockey he could still kill you."

Detroit had the same sort of tough line. Howe was young and tough, Lindsay was young, talented, and mean, and Sid Abel was a veteran, but you couldn't run him or his line. Howie says that's why those clubs hung around the longest at playoff time — they went at each other tooth and nail for the Stanley Cup.

After the big trade Howie remained united with Kennedy and Lynn, while Apps stayed with Watson and Ezinicki. But that still left Bentley. Who was to play with him? It certainly wasn't going to be anyone with the scoring ability he was used to in Chicago in brother Doug or his other linemate, Bill Mosienko.

Chicago had great offensive players then but they had no idea how to win a game, according to Howie. "All of the Chicago lines were totally undisciplined, had no system, no boss, no one made them do what they were supposed to do. Poor Max, if there were fifteen good wingers in the league, he'd left two of them in Chicago in Doug and Mosienko. He arrived in Toronto, and the only quality wingers on the club really were Harry Watson and Joey Klukay. Other than that there was no one else around to play with. Ezinicki, Lynn, and I weren't gifted goal scorers really, we were all hitters. I remember feeling sorry for Bentley, but that was a problem all our centres faced — no real gifted wingers." That talent would come along a year or so later in Sid Smith and Tod Sloan.

Less than a week after that astounding trade, Leaf teammate "Wild" Bill Ezinicki gave his teammates another wake-up call by throwing one of the hardest body checks Howie ever witnessed.

The Leafs were playing the Rangers in Toronto on Saturday night, November 8, 1947, and were not playing well. Late in the first period, Day sent the Apps line, with Ezinicki on right wing, out against Ranger centre Edgar Laprade and his linemates. Laprade took a pass just behind his blue line and picked his way out of his own zone with Syl Apps in hot pursuit. Leaf Harry Watson was in his normal position on left wing, so that route was closed, and "Ezzy," as he often did, was patrolling right wing five or ten feet from the boards.

"Ezzy always reminded me of a vulture lazily circling in the sky, looking for victims. The only open ice was to Edgar's left, towards our right-wing spot, which amongst ourselves we called 'No-Man's-Land' when Ezzy was on the ice. That's where he was heading, into No-Man's-Land, and you could see the collision coming, you could see Ezzy's mind say 'Now!' "

Ezzy took three strides, turned to the middle, and with perfect timing hit the unsuspecting Ranger centre with his left shoulder and hip. Ezinicki was not a big man, maybe five feet nine inches and 170 pounds, but like teammate Bill Barilko he had a knack for making contact with people that really hurt.

"Laprade went to his left and it was literally lights out. Nothing, absolutely nothing, hurts as much as being hit when you don't see it coming. Your body and your mind aren't ready for it and when you come to, you ache all over for days. When Ezzy made his spectacular contact with Edgar he folded like a two-dollar suitcase in a rainstorm. It was like someone had let the air out of the guy — he just collapsed on the ice and didn't move a muscle. I think everybody in the building, especially Ranger teammates and management, were scared of serious injury. Edgar didn't move for a while and we all breathed a sigh of relief when he did."

When the period ended, both teams headed for their dressing rooms through the same walkway, and that's when all hell broke loose. For some twenty feet the two teams were just ten feet apart. Howie was fifth in line off the ice behind Apps, Ezinicki, Watson, and Mortson when one of the Rangers threatened and then challenged Ezinicki.

"With Mortson and Watson present that was very stupid. By the time I got there the brawl was going pretty good and Ranger GM Murray Patrick, who was a former boxer and huge, was standing there getting his licks in. Jeez, I'm next in line and I didn't have a partner. Even though I'm on skates I've still got to reach up to push Patrick's shoulders to get him back out of the fight. Well, he starts to take a swing at me and I'm in trouble — but I got smart, stepped inside close, hung on to his belly, and then ran my skate down his shins to the top of his hundred-dollar Gucci shoes. I cut them all to pieces. Thirty seconds later all's peace and quiet but my, oh, my — what a hit and what a brawl."

A few games later Ezinicki struck again. Struggling Chicago was visiting Toronto and in their lineup they boasted a new hotshot named Metro Prystai. "The newspapers were saying Prystai, a young centre from western Canada, was to be their saviour — 'he could do everything.' Well, we were going to find out."

After a couple of shifts the Leafs agreed that the youngster could play the game, had good wheels, and was going to cause them a problem or two — but as it worked out, not that night. "Prystai was coming out over his blue line, right of centre, about fifteen feet from the boards. He had the puck, made a good move to his left to beat a Leaf checker, which put him on the red line near the centre-ice area. Ezzy was cruising, looking, waiting, and this time the rookie fell into the trap and the trap snapped shut — *boom!* At almost the exact same spot that he nailed Laprade, Ezzy caught this kid and I thought he killed him. But this hit was different. Prystai went up in the air, his stick with him but five feet higher, and his gloves flew off in two different directions. I held my breath, and when he came down I remember thinking, 'If the collision didn't kill him, the fall will.'"

While the trainers were trying to bring the rookie back to the real world, Howie spotted the Hawks' general manager, Bill Tobin, leaning against the boards. "He had the saddest look on his face I'd ever seen, just like the world had come to an end.

"It must have been hard on the nerves of the guys who played against Wild Bill. It took me quite a while to appreciate his contribution to winning; I guess they'd call it 'chemistry' now — reducing the performance of the opposition every shift you're on the ice. In scrimmages I had little or no trouble mentally or physically with Ezzy. However, when he left Toronto to play for Boston and I was on the ice against him, I never went left or shifted to centre ice. I never passed the puck to Cal or Harry unless I was 100 percent sure Ezzy wasn't in that area. I was looking for him all the time. I knew where he was. He made me the best up-and-down winger in the league."

Howie missed just two games during the 1947–48 season, both as a result of a body check by legendary hockey star, and former Leaf, Walter "Babe" Pratt. Toronto was in Boston one Wednesday night and Howie had the misfortune of accepting a pass at the centre-ice area — Babe's hunting ground. The pass wound up in Howie's feet and he foolishly committed the number-one sin in hockey — looking down to find the puck. "When I looked up there was the biggest fat-ass you ever saw in hockey. It was Pratt and I ran into him full-speed." Howie dislocated his right shoulder, which to this day still slopes a half-inch lower than the left. He was finished for the evening, his shoulder iced and put in a sling by trainer Tim Daly. "He put Ikthemal on it, the same stuff he put on almost everything. It was horrible, stinky, and worked 90 percent of the time."

Immediately after the game the wounded Howie headed back to Toronto by train. Pratt's wife lived in Toronto and since they were playing there again Saturday, Pratt got permission from coach Dit Clapper to go home. "As I climbed on the train, Pratt was right behind me with a small shaving bag under one arm, no clothes or suitcase, and a twenty-four case of beer under the other. I sat up all night in pain. I had a couple of Aspirins, but it hurt too much to sleep. Well, Babe sat up with me all night and by 2 or 3 a.m. he was pretty hammered, and if he said it once he said it a hundred times,

'Jeez, kid, I'm sorry. I didn't hit you — you ran into me,' which was true. When we arrived home about noon Babe was in pretty rugged shape. He hadn't slept a wink, but was not too snockered, even though he'd drunk his twenty-four beers — and a few others as well.

"Most amazing, though, was that this happened Thursday morning and Saturday we played them again. Boston tied the game 2–2; Pratt got a goal and an assist, and was the game's first star. Obviously the deal was: let him have his beer, let him play."

The Leafs had a good season. They were a much-improved club even though the goal-scoring numbers plummeted. Despite the individual firepower of Max Bentley, the club scored 27 fewer goals than in 1946–47. Considering the big trade had been five for two, the decline was not shocking, although ex-Leafs Poile and Stewart rubbed salt on Smythe, scoring well in Chicago. Poile finished the season tied with Bentley for fifth place in overall scoring at 54 points, while Stewart finished in fourth place with 56.

The club's defensive game greatly improved, allowing just 143 goals against — 29 better than the previous year — indicating experience on the blueline and two-way hockey by the forwards. The previous year's success had all been accomplished by blood and sweat. Now it was less blood, less sweat, and a little more brainwork.

"If you're going to improve anywhere, it should be in the goals-against category. You can always score goals because with fifteen guys someone will score, everybody gets a shot at it and a chance. If a couple of guys kick them in, and you don't allow too many back against you — that's the secret of winning in hockey."

Howie maintains the key to Toronto's success was sticking to Hap Day's system. "He just let most of us be what we were on the ice, or if we were lax in our duties, he'd encourage us to do what we did best." For a grinder or checker such as Howie, that job was to create an atmosphere in which the talented people on the team could display their skills.

Against Boston, New York, and Chicago at that time, it was no problem. It was hit, hit, hit, and sooner or later — and it was often sooner — they would quit hitting and the Leafs would win. It was tougher against Detroit and the Canadiens. When the Leafs had Thomson, Mortson, Boesch, Barilko, Lynn, Kennedy, Ezzy, Klukay, and occasionally Watson hitting, then four guys were on the ice every shift who would be looking for somebody. A lot of the opposition were ducking, getting out of the way, or hitting the hitters back. While this was going on, it left room for the dancers, like Apps, Watson, Kennedy, Bentley, and Klukay, to move about the dance floor in relative safety.

When the 60-game schedule was complete, the Leafs had tallied 32 victories and 13 ties for 77 points — and first place in the standings. Only the Red Wings, at 72 points, were close. During the regular season Meeker notched 14 goals and added 20 assists for 34 points in 58 games. He accumulated 62 minutes in penalties as well, including another couple of scraps with his regular rivals Gordie Howe and Ranger Tony Leswick. Howie's railroad work came into use in one particular set-to with Leswick. The two started shoving each other and, rather than tossing punches, Howie quickly grabbed Leswick by the shoulder pad with his left arm, and by the crotch with his right, lifted him up above his head and dumped him on the ice. "I was all set to pop him one when I realized he was already in orbit, so I just let him down easy and waved for the trainer."

Despite his fairly decent scoring stats (twenty-fourth overall, fifth on his club), Howie wasn't pleased with his year. "I didn't have a good personal season at all. It started out terrible. Part of the reason, I think, was that I was really counting on the $1,000 bonus from the Leafs. I know I didn't play quite as hard the second year as I did in the first. At the time I thought I did, but years later I realized that with everything going so well teamwise — I cheated a bit. I wasn't quite as hungry as I was in 1946–47."

The 1947–48 Stanley Cup came fairly easy for Day, who could call upon four talented centres in Apps, Kennedy, Bentley, and Nick Metz. "It was just, 'keep them healthy, open the doors and sic 'em!' In the playoffs we didn't have much trouble."

Indeed, in the opening round Toronto eliminated Boston in just five games. Then, in the final round, it was Day's coaching against the Production Line, the best line in hockey at the time — Gordie Howe, Sid Abel, and Ted Lindsay. In the previous series the Red Wing trio had annihilated the Canadiens, scoring 12 of the 17 goals against the *bleu, blanc, et rouge.* The Leafs shut down Production — in four games the threatening threesome were allowed just one goal. Toronto outscored Detroit 18–7 in the sweep.

Howie scored once in the first game of the final series, and in the second renewed his fistic affair with Howe. At the end of that game even Leaf goalie Turk Broda and Red Wing puck-stopper Harry Lumley were given penalties for fighting. The rough-and-tumble final series seemed an appropriate reflection on the wild, physical season throughout the league. The intense, bitter feelings between the Leafs and the Wings had now surpassed even the long-standing feud with the Canadiens.

Still, Toronto had Detroit's number, and now they also had another Stanley Cup. At the end of the championship game, Howie doused Broda with Coke in the dressing room. When the jubilant Leafs returned by train the next day, thousands of fans were on hand to greet them. A cavalcade of open cars, cluttered with Leaf players and management, wound its way from Union Station to the city hall, with thousands of exhilarated fans lining the streets of Toronto to cheer their hockey champions.

"I don't think there has ever been a better hockey team in the league with three or four quality centres like we had. We had Apps, who could fly, then the opposite in Kennedy, who had to work to skate but was as competitive a player as ever played the game — mentally and physically tough and skilled. Max Bentley was a dipsy-doodler who danced on skates, had a good shot, and played the point on the power play. Apps and Bentley were thoroughbred racehorses, and Kennedy was a thoroughbred plow horse who could keep up — but they all had to play with us ordinary plow horses. We were good in many ways but they were the hockey players and we were the workers."

The fourth centre was Nick Metz. Dependable "Metzy" could play any spot, any time. "He could have played second- or third-line centre for any other team in the league. Just a great hockey player offensively and defensively as well. Cool as a cucumber.

"Broda was the key and Day was the guy who turned the key, made everything work. In 1947–48 we had enough skill on the ice every shift to win any game we all really wanted to win."

Ɏ

In 1947, Charlie and Kitty Meeker bought twenty acres of land near Chalk River, Ontario. After the hectic and physical 1947–48 hockey season ended, Grace and Howie made a beeline for the remoter country not only to visit Howie's parents but also to fish for bass and big muskies in Chalk Lake or for pike and pickerel on the Ottawa River.

Another regular visitor to Charlie Meeker's home in Chalk River was Andy Dole, a unique character Howie met as a youth. Andy and brother George were two native brothers legendary for their hunting, fishing, and tracking skills. Howie first met Andy when the brothers had been hired to track German soldiers who escaped from the Ontario PoW camps that Charlie Meeker helped guard during the Second World War. Hearing that Howie wanted to do some fishing, Andy mentioned he knew a lake that had great one- to two-pound trout. The lake was inside camp Petawawa, a major military base, and was off-limits to civilians. The two agreed to give it a try the next day. Howie wondered what was up when Andy included a peavey in his fishing gear. The two drove towards Petawawa and turned down a sandy road. About a hundred yards down, the road was blocked by a steel pole with a log chained to it and stretched across the road. On the pole a sign read, "No Trespassing. Military maneuvers, live ammunition! Stay out."

Andy jumped out of the car, grabbed the peavey, and rolled the huge log out of the way. "They haven't held maneuvers on this side of the road for years," he explained. Five minutes later the duo reached a pristine five-acre lake nestled among the pines.

As Howie tells the story, "It wasn't too long before I waded out about ten to fifteen feet. I looked for a spot with no trees behind me because I didn't want to get the fly hooked up in a tree, as I often do. I laid out about a twenty-five- or thirty-foot cast, waited a second for the fly to sink, pulled once, pulled twice, took in the loose line and all of a sudden — *bang!* Whoa . . . the reel was just humming as that trout reeled off fifteen or twenty feet of line."

Five minutes later Howie had a gorgeous two-pound speckled trout in the creel. Andy had the same success and within a half an hour the two had their fill and settled for some "catch and release" fishing.

The peace and serenity, however, was about to be drastically altered. Howie suddenly became aware of a great roar, like a great big truck changing gears going up hill. The noise got louder and louder and soon sounded like a whole fleet of trucks going up hill. Even the bottom of the lake began to shake. "Then, at the far end of the lake, three Sherman tanks, with guns pointing our way, broke onto the shoreline itself. There I was, twenty feet from shore in a restricted area with tanks coming at me along the shoreline. I turned to head for shore and looked for Andy, but he was gone, just melted into the woods."

Howie slowly wandered ashore, arriving on the beach at the same time as the tanks. A tank hatch opened and a young helmet-covered head popped up and began berating Howie in typical military fashion. "What are you doing here? Don't you know we often use live ammunition, land mines . . ." The lecture went on and on. Soon the second and third tank hatches opened up, the crew climbed down, and joined in the razzing of the hapless civilian. finally, one young officer pointed his finger at Howie and said, "Hey, don't I know you?"

"Maybe. Do you follow the Leafs?"

"Howie Meeker," he yelled. "Christ, man, am I happy to see you." The verbal abuse ended. One crew member hollered "tea time" while the leader told his radio man to summon the rest of the party. A half-hour later Howie was drinking tea with eight tank crews, two jeep crews, and a returned Andy Dole (who snuck back out of the woods), all talking hockey.

Before leaving, they gave Andy and Howie an invitation to their Saturday-night dance at the sergeant's mess and told them to bring their wives. Grace and Howie went to the dinner and Howie answered questions for at least an hour, danced, and ate ice cream all night long. Before leaving, the commanding officer slipped Howie a master key to all locks on the base saying, "Have fun, and don't lose it."

It was only then that Howie began to realize what a wonderful position he was in: twenty-four years old, two Stanley Cups with the Toronto Maple Leafs, and, through radio and newspaper, recognizeable to almost everyone in Canada.

The run-in with the army wasn't the only time Howie would find himself somewhere he wasn't supposed to be — nor was it the only time his hockey fame would save the day.

Leaf teammates such as Joe Klukay and Garth Boesch became regular partners with a rod or gun as well as a hockey stick, and Howie would often take them to Uncle Tom Berner's 150-acre farm near Agincourt to hunt. While Grace and Jane visited with Aunty Mae, the boys would head into the bush with their .22s and a ferret to catch a few cottontail rabbits. Boesch loved hunting pheasant and Uncle Tom's property was full of them because a neighbour raised the birds for his year-round release and shoot business. Very often the paid guests didn't shoot as many pheasants as were released so the Berner farm and other farms in the neighbourhood had all kinds of tasty birds.

"I told Garth we could shoot pheasants as long as we stayed on my aunt's property. 'No problem.' We were out hunting for about an hour and were near the corner of the property, closest to the road, when six to eight cocks ran along the fence, over the road, and onto the railway tracks on the other side. Garth jumped over the fence, across the road, over the other fence, and stood on the railway track pointing at this covey of birds 100 yards up the track. While he went from my aunt's property to private property, I remember thinking, 'Christ, he thinks he's back home in Saskatchewan where he owns two sections of land.' But my other thought was, 'I guess I've got to follow him.' The birds took off towards Garth and boom, boom, boom . . . he had three down. I quickly fired, wounded one, as usual, and he took off like a scalded cat with Garth right behind. I wanted back on the other side of the fence as soon as possible, and figured three out of four birds wasn't half bad, but five minutes later Garth is coming back along the tracks with the fourth one in his hand. I looked the other way just as a police car pulled up."

Howie remembers the exchange to this day.

"You guys hunting?"

"Ahh . . . maybe."

"Any luck?"

"Ahh . . . maybe."

"What's your name?"

"Howie Meeker."

"You got a bird licence?"

"No."

"Got a gun licence?"

Howie gave him his gun licence. The cop looked at it, and said, "Howie Meeker, the Leaf player?"

"Yup, the Leaf player."

The officer pointed at Garth. "And him?" Garth was coming down the tracks with a pheasant dangling from his hand, beaming like he'd just scored a goal.

"That guy is Garth Boesch."

When Garth showed up, the policeman said, "Fellas, I had a

telephone complaint about somebody out here shooting birds so I've got to take your guns and that one pheasant of his. But I tell you what, I'll talk to my boss and see what we can do about this."

The next day a telephone call was received at Maple Leaf Gardens with a message for Howie or Boesch to phone Sergeant Tucker. When Howie called he received a stern lecture. Finally the sergeant said, "Well, I guess you want your guns. It's going to cost you."

"How much?" Howie asked.

"Four tickets to the next Maple Leaf game, two for me and two for the guy who's got your guns," the officer replied.

Howie got him the four tickets, got them into the practice, got them autographed programs, and ended up with two pretty good friends. "We also told them to keep the pheasant, which they did."

𝖸

After two seasons in the league it was time for Howie to renegotiate his contract and, reluctantly, he trundled off to Smythe's office.

"I was still getting $5,000 a year, with two Cups. Back then nobody knew or cared what other guys were getting paid. You were satisfied with what you got, and you were happy to play hockey for a living. You only thought about money when the season was over, or if you had bonuses, which were very rare."

Smythe acted like it was an insult that Meeker had the audacity to ask for a raise. Howie knew it wasn't a personal thing; Smythe felt the same way about everybody who came through his office door.

"I suppose you expect a raise," Smythe growled before Howie was halfway across the room.

"Yes, sir."

"Well, I don't think we can afford to give you one. Our operating costs have gone way up."

The negotiations had begun.

"Well, I can give you $500 a year," Smythe finally succumbed.

Howie stood his ground. "Heck — that's not fair. I've got to be a pretty good hockey player. If not, I wouldn't be part of two Stanley

Cups and you would have got rid of me and found someone to fill my spot. I've seen no sign of that. Hopefully, I'll be on your team again this season looking for three Stanley Cups in a row."

"How much do you expect?"

Howie bluffed, "$1,500."

Steam came out Smythe's ears and his face displayed numerous hues of purple and red. "No way, no way. You're not that good of a hockey player."

"Well, I didn't have a great season but if you average it out over two years I have a pretty good points average for right wingers. It's way above league average."

"Ya, but your plus-minus is terrible."

"My what is where? What's that?" Howie gaped.

"When you're playing six men a side it's the number of goals for your team versus goals against. Your line on the ice is okay, but your personal statistics are terrible. The number of goals you score compared to their left winger is way out of whack, way out of balance.'

"Bull! Prove it!"

So Smythe did. He showed Howie statistics kept by the club outlining every player's record, game by game. Howie could only swallow hard. He quickly noticed that one guy, Chicago's Roy Conacher, was making him look bad. Conacher had good speed and a great shot on the fly. He often caught goalies cold.

Howie finally got a $1,000-per-year raise out of Smythe, and that season he kept his own plus-minus statistics. It was the beginning of his intense study of the game.

Much of his improvement was due to the film work of Shanty Mackenzie. Shanty was another icon of Maple Leaf Gardens in that era. He shot and stored all black-and-white film footage of the Leafs. At Howie's request, Shanty took him into the film projection room where the mounds of 48-mm film reels were kept. "I went through every game and every shift against Chicago and watched when Roy Conacher was on the ice. I noticed when the puck went into their end I would go a couple of steps too deep before making the turn coming back, when they had control of the puck. Conacher would get a step or two on me, the pass would be on his stick, he'd shoot and the puck would be in the cotton-picking net. I said, 'Okay, now I have you right by the short hairs.'"

Howie ended the 1948–49 season plus-5 while his new line was plus-15. "Roy Conacher never did get another goal on us because I learned how to shut him down. I don't think he had more than two good scoring chances the rest of the games he played against the Leafs when I was on the ice against him."

"I went back in next year to sign a contract and got a pretty good raise based on the plus-minus deal."

Y

Despite Howie's improved defensive play, the club had a "bad year" in 1948–49. Howie played with Cal Gardner and Harry Watson, while Tod Sloan joined Kennedy and Lynn. The Kid or KLM Line became the stuff of trivia.

The big blow to the Leafs that year was the retirement, just as he'd promised, of popular and talented Syl Apps. Management had wisely snagged Bentley a year before in anticipation of the move, but now Day needed another substantial centre, and Smythe went hunting. "I think they wanted more toughness at the expense of finesse. They traded Stanowski to the Rangers for defenceman Bill Juzda, and Cal Gardner to fill in the centre gap left by Apps, a very good choice. Cal played extremely well for Toronto the years he was there. We still had the heart of the hockey club left in Thomson, Mortson, Boesch, Barilko, Kennedy, Bentley, Watson, and Nick Metz."

A player who contributed greatly but was rewarded little was winger Don Metz, a fringe player who for years had been spending most of his time in Pittsburgh. "He was an NHLer but the Leaf brass were able to keep him down there. I don't know what salary they paid him, but certainly under today's conditions he'd have been put on waivers and signed by three or four teams in the league. He should have made our team. Whenever we got injuries they called him up and he could play any position — I'd swear he could have played goal, too."

The 1948–49 season also marked the start of a new gang of Leafs coming in. Sid Smith, Fleming MacKell, Tod Sloan, Ray Timgren, and Bobby Dawes, among others, were knocking at the door, and numerous injuries made it an opportune season for them. Howie was among the veterans going down with wounds. He missed the final thirty games of the season as well as the playoffs with back-to-back injuries.

On Boxing Day, during scrimmage, Howie cut in front of the net, stepped on Ezinicki's stick, tripped, and went head-first into the boards. "I busted my shoulder. They had to operate, dig out the marrow, put a wire down through, then wire all the bones back in place. I spoiled Dr. Jim Morrison's Christmas with his family. What he and Dr. Norm Delarue did for us players was far and above the call of duty. Two very talented physicians, and their personalities matched their skills."

In less than ten days Howie was practising. One day just he and injured Joe Klukay were on the ice at the Gardens, 200 feet by 85 feet in size. Hap Day was watching the injured guys work out, as was his practice. "We'd get a puck and have to go back and forth, and around and about, and over and back, from the goal line to the blue line, to the goal line to the red line, to the goal line, to the blue line, to the red line, and oh jeez, just trying to get back in shape.

"Of all things — I'm going all out, Klukay is going all out, I look up and there's Klukay — and I run into him. I still had a piece of the wire sticking out of the back of my shoulder. There was the galdarnedest explosion you ever did see! I meant to turn the injured shoulder, the right one, away from him but I turned and hit him head-on with the right shoulder, got up, lifted my arm and swung it, picked up my stick, and away I went. Day got up and walked away, and when he walked away you knew that was enough, you could go off the ice. Joe and I went in and showered and Hap came in, looked at me, and said, 'Well, I guess you can play Saturday night, Kid.' I said, 'Yes, sir, I guess I can.' The doctor put the kibosh on that but I'll never forget it."

Howie returned to action with three or four games left in the season. His return was short-lived. "We were in Chicago and I took a shot and scored. Just as I turned around, Ralph Nattrass swung his stick, trying to take my head off, missed, came down on the tongue of my skate, and broke my foot. I felt the bone give way. That ruined the season for me — I missed the 1948–49 playoffs."

It was a winter of injuries that Grace Meeker wishes she could forget. Howie missed most of the games in January, February, and March. Gordie Howe had run Vic Lynn into the fence and dislocated his shoulder — putting Vic out for eight games, while at the same time Joe Klukay broke his foot. Vic's wife had gone home to Saskatoon, and Joe wasn't married, so the two players moved in with Howie and Grace, who had a large apartment on Avenue Road in the city, owned by Harry Dowden.

Injury seasons were long seasons for Grace. "I don't ever recall spending a more miserable three weeks in my life than that February," she says. "I had three hurt hockey players moping around the house. They were like a bunch of bad boys. Vic was a growler as it was, Klukay would growl, and Howie, well . . . sheesh . . . it was awful."

In 30 regular-season games, Howie managed 7 goals and 7 assists for 14 points and another 56 minutes in the sin bin.

"With my broken collarbone and then broken foot, and other guys' injuries that year, it was a great chance for the rookies to come into play. Sid Smith had a touch around the net that was unbelievable; I've never seen anything like it before or since. His timing was perfect; someone would shoot it and he would put out his stick, deflect it, slow it down, speed it up, and it would go in. Fleming MacKell was a five-foot-seven, but heavy, 170-pound buzzsaw: never stopped talking, never stopped moving. He was a great Junior and you knew right away he was going to be a great hockey player. Tod Sloan was another goal scorer around the net. The 'old Slinker,' we called him, because that's what he was like. He'd hang around and hang around and all of a sudden, make a dart for the net and *boom* — it was in."

Y

When the 1948–49 season was finished, however, the Maple Leafs looked like they had finally met their Waterloo. With 22 wins, 25 losses, and 13 ties, the club finished 3 games below .500. Almost all of the team stats were down from the previous year: only 147 goals scored, with 161 goals against. Their 57 points gave them a distant fourth-place finish and the final playoff berth. Only Chicago and New York had fared worse. Howie's mug creases with an impish grin when it's suggested the '49 team may have been playing possum in the regular season, waiting until it really counted in the playoffs before turning on the talent.

"Anybody who knew us, knew the Leafs were much better than we showed on paper. We weren't a 'below .500' club really. Anybody who considered us that way was out of their minds. We were exactly the same club, minus Apps, that had won two Stanley Cups in a row — all we needed was something to get going."

On reflection Howie maintains that his study of hockey was fostered during his injuries that winter. He attended many practices and watched the drills, the players, the skills. "I was finally in the process of learning the game of hockey. During the practices Day held before we played the big teams of the era, Detroit and Montreal, we always scrimmaged. Hap turned those scrimmages into minor wars. He always prepared us for battle. And he always started doing it about two weeks before the playoffs."

The 1949 playoffs were almost a carbon copy of the previous year. In the first round the Leafs faced second-place Boston, and the overconfident Bruins were just not prepared for the rejuvenated

Stanley Cup holders. The Leafs, particularly in the first game, whipped them physically.

"Harry Watson got into a fight I'll never forget. Watson was, thank goodness, a very docile, soft player. He was mentally and physically tough but thanks be, the good Lord didn't give him the mentality to be rough and mean, because he'd have been a killer.

"Watson and Murray Henderson collided early in the game; Henderson was not a really tough player but he played the game very hard. Henderson gave Watson a shove; Watson shoved him back; Henderson gave him the stick; Watson responded, so Murray dropped his gloves. Well, he should never have done that because Watson just killed him. After that the team just waltzed to an easy win and we won the series four games to one."

The Leafs then ventured into Detroit and with Broda playing sensationally, snuck the first game 3–2 in overtime. The fired-up Leafs then won Game Two 3–1, destroying any home-ice advantage the Wings might have had. Back in Toronto the formidable defensive play of the blueliners and Broda continued. The Leafs recorded another 3–1 victory in Game Three.

Prior to Game Four in Toronto, Day asked Howie, "Just in case we win, what's happening?" Howie responded that he didn't know of anything.

"Well, keep it that way," Day replied.

Howie was still in a walking cast but it suddenly dawned on him that nothing was planned — again — if the club did win the Cup. "I thought, 'What *are* we going to do, where do we go to celebrate, what are we going to drink, eat?'

"It was 5:30 p.m., so I phoned Grace and she agreed to have the party at our place. Then I had to find something to drink, so I went to the Liquor Control Board and bought a little wine, rum, whiskey, vodka, whatever, and several dozen cases of beer. The boys were mainly beer drinkers, hardly touched the hard stuff — but others did. At one point in the evening I thought to myself,

'Jeez, if we don't win then I'm well stocked for a long time.'

"Of course Toronto won the game, and the Cup, and the party was on."

"Joe and I grabbed ice on the way back to the apartment and stuffed the bathtub full of ice and beer. After the win, word spread like wildfire — party at Meeker's."

Halfway through the party, Howie and Grace realized their new dog was missing. After looking everywhere, Howie eventually phoned the police. About a half-hour later four policemen arrived at the door with the dog. "Come on in, guys, have a beer," Howie hailed them. "Oh, and invite your friends." Later that night every cop on duty in a patrol car was probably at Howie's place at one time or another. "We must have had 150 to 200 people there. There was a crap game going in one big room we weren't using. Baz Bastien and Turk Broda were still playing at 5 a.m. We ran out of beer and the police there said 'no problem' and made a phone call. A few minutes later a police van pulled up and out came some 250 beers, so that kept the party going.

"Around 7 a.m. Grace started cooking breakfast and there must have still been fifty people milling around. By 9 a.m. most everyone had left and we went off to our bedroom, but there was our skate sharpener, Tommy Nayler, fast asleep under the sheets, still in his clothes. Grace and I just laughed and found a bed in the guest room. It was a hell of a party, totally unplanned, and one of the best Stanley Cup bashes anyone probably ever had. Syl Apps showed up, as well as all kinds of arena people, ice makers, friends. We had crowd control and policemen. There are all kinds of ex-policemen my age in Toronto today who remember that night on Avenue Road."

Howie's aforementioned propensity for trouble often involved a sidekick or two, of which there seemed to be no shortage over the years. Of particular nefarious notoriety were his furry ferrets. When Howie went out the morning after Stanley Cup '49 to feed his current ferret, he discovered someone had opened the pen —

and it was gone. His sojourn was a little longer and far more destructive than the wayward dog's.

Howie kept a wary eye out for the ferret. Three or four days later he spotted his neighbour, a big Italian guy named Henry, carrying out a bunch of dead chickens from his barn.

Howie played dumb. "Hey Henry — what the hell you doing killing your chickens?"

"I'm not killing my chickens," Henry huffed. "Something got in my barn last night and killed twelve of them."

"No, you're kidding, what the hell could that be? Jeez, it must be a mink or maybe a skunk," Howie deadpanned, making a hasty retreat. Howie recovered his ferret the next day and took him back to New Hamburg.

"About two years later, just when we were moving, I sent Henry a dozen chickens. He still sends me a Christmas card every year signed 'The Chicken Man.'"

Seven

One Last Sip

"The fingers on one hand were dangerously close to my eyes, and the other hand completed the headlock. But there, like an apple on a stick, sat a nice, big thumb."

During the 1949–50 training camp, Howie lined up regularly with centre Cal Gardner and left wing Harry Watson, forming a solid unit with great potential. Howie had a hot training camp, filling the net and playing solid two-way hockey throughout. *Toronto Star* writer Gordon Campbell wrote of one scrimmage, "Little Howie Meeker operated like a comet at the Leafs' training camp here yesterday, to come up with a hat-trick performance as the Whites slaughtered the Blues 9–1. His first goal was a picture effort . . . The newly formed Gardner-Watson-Meeker trio looked capable of literally setting the league afire as they figured in seven goals."

The new line certainly displayed potential. The only problem was having a chance to play together when it counted. Howie, Watson, and Gardner played fewer than 30 games that season as a unit — Gardner missed 39 games and Watson 10. It seemed Watson and Howie constantly had a new centre, but Watson got 19 goals and Howie got 18, which wasn't half bad. The league expanded to 70 games that year and Howie enjoyed his first and only full NHL season without injury.

Captain Kennedy finally got rewarded with two legitimate goal scorers on his wings, Sid Smith and Tod Sloan. Smith had played just one regular-season Leaf game the season before, but had been brilliant in the playoffs, helping lead the Leafs to the Cup. The talented Max Bentley played with a revolving cast, but no matter who it was, no team had a better third line in the league. Max had his typical, very good, year, scoring 23 goals. The Leafs remained tough and talented on defence as well, but the major bonus that season was that the players remained relatively healthy and injury free.

Joe Klukay, often playing with Bentley, had his best year ever. He scored 15 goals and had 16 helpers while killing off most penalties the Leafs received. Fleming MacKell snagged 20 points in 36 games. "His feet went as fast as his mouth and his mouth went as fast as his feet," Howie says.

The healthy 1949–50 Maple Leafs were a very good young hockey team, and injuries only opened up spots for more youngsters to fill; rookies like Rudy Migay, Phil Samis, Hugh Bolton, and George Armstrong all came up from the minors or Juniors to play a game or two.

A nosedive in November saw the Leafs garner just 8 points out of a possible 26 — during one dismal stretch they picked up 1 point out of a possible 12. Conn Smythe was starting to burn, but Howie remembers Smythe's reaction as mostly a smokescreen. "We had won three Stanley Cups and I think we were all a little complacent, a little fat, thought we were better hockey players than we were, thought we knew more about the game than the coach, and we played like that for most of the year. When you play like that you often get injuries and guys were hurt that year. Either way our play was terrible and Conn blew a fuse."

Goaltender Broda, always a tad roly-poly, became the brunt of Smythe's anger. At the end of the month Smythe benched Broda, saying he wasn't running "a fat man's hockey team," and ordered Broda to lose some pounds. Smythe purchased flyweight goalie Gil Mayer, who weighed maybe 130 pounds soaking wet, from Buffalo of the American Hockey League, and also negotiated a trade, picking up lanky netminder Al Rollins from Cleveland of the AHL. After missing one game, Broda returned, *sans* the poundage, and earned a 2–0 shutout over the Rangers. Maple Leaf fans were delighted to have their popular puck-stopper back, paunchy or not.

Howie says the Battle of the Bulge was mainly aimed at Broda and Harry Watson, but management lumped a number of other guys into the group "more as a publicity stunt than anything else, to get the fans' minds off the lousy hockey we were playing. The kind of hockey club we'd always been relied on hard work, discipline, and system as the winning way. When we got away from that magic formula, we'd suffer."

Howie was briefly in Smythe's Bulge brigade as well. He was in no danger at the beginning, however. When he signed his first contract with Toronto in 1946, Smythe asked him, "How much do you weigh, kid?"

"Oh, 175 pounds," Howie said, straight-faced. First day of training camp that year when Howie stepped on the scales he barely pushed the needle over the 165 mark.

For two years Smythe and Day kept telling him, "Put on some weight, put on some weight." So Howie started drinking a little beer, eating a little too much, and went from 165 to about 175 pounds in two years. "They took a look at that on the scale and said get down to 170. That was no problem, I just cut out the beer and worked a little harder."

By his fourth NHL season, and for the first time in his career, Howie felt reasonably secure in his job. He began to have thoughts about a career in hockey after his playing days were done and began to study systems, style, and business operations, as well as how to build a team and keep it competitive over the years. His study of the game, note-making, and plus-minus record-keeping drew the eye of the newspaper and radio media. Questioned about his green note pad, Howie said he kept statistics of every game, which amazed the reporters. "You can be a student of mistakes as long as you do something about them," he quipped to Al Nickleson of the *Globe and Mail*.

Howie did not record every detail, though. For instance, he can't recall the exact evening when he decided to have a mid-game snack with archrival Tony Leswick of the New York Rangers. Leswick ranked high on the list of those who were regular fistic opponents of "Hurricane" Howie. Gordie Howe and Ted Lindsay were probably the only two above him for frequency. Of the three, Leswick was the only one similar in stature to Howie. "I didn't know much about Tony off the ice, but I heard he was a pretty good guy. On the ice we didn't like each other. We were two 165-pound toughies. Neither of us could punch our way out of a wet paper bag; we just played at fighting."

During the first shift one night in Toronto, Howie and Leswick ran at each other full speed. Later they elbowed one another, then whacked each other with their sticks, "in unprotected areas, so it hurt," and yapped at each other like two chihuahuas. "All the time we knew that sooner or later one of us would have enough, drop his gloves, and we'd make like fighters. What a charade."

In the middle of the second period Tony ran Howie into the fence and he responded with an elbow. Leswick dropped his gloves and the fight was on. "He tattooed me two or three times before I got my gloves off, I threw a few back and we fell; I got to my knees, trying to get back up, and he was on my back with a bear hug around my shoulders and face. The fingers on one hand were dangerously close to my eyes, and the other hand completed the headlock. But there, like an apple on a stick, sat a nice, big thumb. I had one finger stuck in one eye and four more looking for the other one, so I clamped onto the thumb like it was the juiciest of steaks. Did I bite? Did I ever! I never heard a guy scream so loud in my life. He scared the shit out of me and referee George Gravel. But did he let go quick. It was funny to see Leswick chasing Gravel, showing him the teeth marks and hollering for a penalty.

"Gravel was a great guy. When I skated by him on the way to the penalty box he asked, 'Was it tender?' I said, 'No, it was too god-damned bony.' We both laughed."

In the penalty box both players quickly cooled down, and when they simultaneously bent over to tighten their skates, they looked at each other and began to laugh. "We were the greatest of friends for the next five minutes, but when we stepped on the ice we were bitter enemies again for the remainder of the game. I got teased for the next couple of weeks by all the referees and everybody else for biting his thumb."

The Leafs finished the 1949–50 campaign in third place with 74 points, narrowly losing second spot to Montreal, who surged in the late season and tallied 77. The Leafs won 31 games, lost 27, and tied 12. They scored just 176 goals, but allowed only 173. "We were not a great hockey club — good, but not great. I think all that year most of us felt we could make it four Cups in a row if and when we all got healthy."

In his 70 games played, Howie earned 18 goals and 22 assists for 40 points, fourth best on the team and seventeenth in the NHL. He also picked up 35 penalty minutes.

Ƴ

Toronto faced first-place Detroit in the first round of the playoffs and fans anticipated some explosives. The Red Wing–Leaf rivalry had been festering deeper with each encounter, but no one anticipated the incident that would transpire that night at the Olympia in the Motor City.

Toronto grabbed a 3–0 lead early in the game, and as Teeder Kennedy skated out of his end with the puck, Gordie Howe lined him up for a check. The two nearly collided mid-ice along the boards, but Kennedy stepped back just in time to avoid the impact. His judgment of distance now thrown off, Howe hit the boards at full speed and crumpled to the ice.

"They said he severely hurt himself," Howie says. "I've heard since then that it was certainly a serious injury but not nearly as critical as the Detroit press or Red Wing management made it out to be. Either way the propaganda really killed us." For the remainder of the game Kennedy was the target of Detroit players, goaded by an incensed Red Wing coach Tommy Ivan, who suggested Kennedy had caused the injury with his stick.

An operation to relieve a pocket of fluid below the skull, apparently causing pressure on the brain, was successful and Howe made a speedy recovery, though he did not return to playoff action that year.

Game Two was a wild affair filled with fights, stick-swinging, and bodychecks. The Leafs were down 2–1 until late in the game and finally were beaten 3–1, to tie the series. The hacking and attacking by Detroit, especially against Kennedy, and the natural rude response by the Leafs sparked NHL president Clarence Campbell into action. Campbell sternly warned the teams after the game that such violent conduct would not be tolerated in any further matches.

Toronto regained their composure and consistent game plan and won Game Three 2–0 at home. But the pesky Red Wings battled back in Game Four, winning 2–1 in overtime. When the Leafs went back to Detroit for Game Five and shut them down 2–0 in front of Red Wing fans, the players mistakenly figured the series was all but over. The Leafs were leading the series 3–2 with the sixth game at home and, as Howie puts it, "If you can't beat Detroit in two tries, one at home and one away, I guess you're not the best team. We certainly had to be the better club with Detroit not having Howe in the lineup."

Some hockey pundits suggest Howe contributed more to that playoff series by being absent than he might have had he played. Certainly the Red Wing players and management were fired up over the injury and had the momentum, and the papers fed more fuel to the fire. In the eyes of all but the most solid Leaf fans, Toronto was the definite underdog.

A determined Red Wing squad dominated in Maple Leaf Gardens and won Game Six 4–0, forcing a seventh game in Detroit. In the final match the two teams battled back and forth with neither team denting the twine in regulation time. "I'll never forget it. In overtime Leo Reise put one in from deep left centre field and we lost 1–0. We were stunned, it was all over."

Even though the Wings had been favoured, most Leaf fans were shocked by the loss. Things just weren't supposed to happen like that anymore; the Leafs had won three Stanley Cups and were just getting into a groove. What had happened? Howie's analysis is clear.

"Two factors contributed mainly. Our offence was terrible. In the final six games we scored just six goals so obviously our dancers were not allowed to do their thing. The fault had to go to the hitters; we allowed just 10 goals in seven games, so goaltending and defence played exceptionally well. We had great goaltending throughout the series. The guilty ones were Lynn, Ezzy, Gardner, Watson, Klukay, and me. It wasn't our duty or responsibility to carry the team offensively, but we were supposed to create enough havoc to give an edge to our dancers, and we just didn't do that."

The second factor was a blunder by management, Howie says. Between games in the playoffs, Maple Leaf management took the players away from their homes to the club's training camp hotel in St. Catharines. Players stayed there the entire series and commuted to the games. After the sixth game at Toronto the club, for unknown reasons, again went back to St. Catharines. Because the seventh game was in Detroit the next night the Leafs, under normal conditions, would have jumped the train right after Game Six and travelled there, spending the night in the Leland Hotel as usual. They would be fresh and rested to play the next day.

"Someone made the hare-brained decision that we would get up on game day, bus to the closest railroad station, and then catch the train to Detroit. We got to the station at 9 a.m., and at 11 a.m. we were still sitting there waiting for the train. When the train did arrive, more than two hours late, we got on the darn thing and made it to Detroit just in time for our pre-game meal, with no rest or anything, and on to the game. We actually had no right to lose that game, though."

The recently respectable Rangers made it into the finals against the Wings, but because the circus was lodged in their rink at Madison Square Garden, they played two of their home games in Toronto. "Our guys wanted to see the game and the league was great — they gave us standing-room tickets," Howie remembers. "Most of us just kept shaking our heads, wondering, 'How the hell could we not be in the Stanley Cup finals again and winning the Cup?'

"We thought it was a dumb decision to stay in St. Catharines and that someone upstairs didn't want us to win too bad."

Y

Just before the 1949–50 season ended, Ray Timgren suggested that he and Howie "go north this summer and look for Andy's gold," recalling a story Howie had told him about Andy Dole and his prospecting adventures near Springpole Lake, forty miles north of Sioux Lookout in northern Ontario. Dole had told Howie he'd grubstaked in that area twenty years before and found quartz samples that tested high in silver and gold.

At Timgren's urging, an eager Howie mentioned the idea to Grace, suggesting that she and young Jane could join him, Andy, and Ray at Springpole Lake in a couple of months. The men would go up first and get the camp in shape, then she and Jane could come up and stay for a month.

Howie contacted Andy, who was keen for the trip, in Chalk River, and he agreed to come to Toronto and help purchase and pack the giant supply of needed goods. With an Ontario road map spread out before him Ray asked Andy where they were going. Andy pointed to Casummit Lake, a small dot a long way north of Toronto and many inches on the map from the closest road to the nearest community, Red Lake. "Springpole Lake is nearby," he said.

"How do we get from here to there?" Ray asked.

"No problem," Andy shrugged, "there's water all the way, except for the small portage at Swain's Post and maybe a couple of others here and there, including a small one from Springpole Lake to Casummit. It's a piece of cake." He suggested they leave in early May, as soon as the ice was off the lakes, and return home in mid or late August.

The mine and sawmill at Casummit Lake, some twenty miles from their planned base camp, had food, gas, and anything else they might need in a pinch, including contact with the outside world. Still, they needed a plethora of goods: a canoe, small engine, gas cans, tents with flies, sleeping bags, cooking equipment, a gun, a compass, good boots, rainwear, fishing equipment, crosscut saws and blades, axes, backpacks, coal oil, hammers, nails, and a couple of ten-by-fifteen canvasses, amongst other things.

With the hockey season over, Andy and Ray met Howie in New Hamburg and the crew got ready to go. When Ray arrived with his new Chevy, Grace looked at the huge pile of supplies accumulated and said, "Boys, you need a tractor trailer, not a car."

But Andy, who had been through the routine before, said, "Get me that clothesline rope, turn the canoe upside down, then get the hell out of the way." In no time he'd packed everything in the canoe and lashed the rope from rib to rib and across the thwarts so nothing would fall out. When the canoe was flipped over and tied to the roof of the car it worked like a charm.

A day and a half later, with 800 miles of terrible, bumpy, dusty roads behind them, Howie said, "Jeez, Andy, where are we going, to the end of the world?" He looked at the map and discovered that it was another 500 to 600 miles to Red Lake. "No country should be this big, let alone a province."

Once they finally arrived at Red Lake, Andy phoned his brother George. Ten minutes later, Howie recounts, "a half-snockered, five-foot, 100-pound native with jet black hair, fuzzy whiskers, grey eyes, and the broadest Scottish accent I'd ever heard, showed up."

George told Andy that the original assayers from a group he was prospecting for had found something encouraging and were about to set up drills to confirm the same. He suggested they take a few days, go out to Gull Rock Lake, and stake some claims themselves, adding that if the drilling results were favourable they could make some big money.

George escorted them for the first day, leading the way. At day's end, though, rather than camp on the shore beside the road, Andy and George insisted on walking up a quarter-mile to a little path that was 250 yards from the lake. "We carried everything but the boat and motor to the lake. I should have known that my two new friends were never happier than when on a muddy mile-long portage with the first half straight up and the second half straight down, carrying at least 200 pounds each."

In the morning Howie woke up to the wonderful smell of perking coffee and frying bacon on an open campfire. As Howie stepped out of the tent, George handed him a cup of coffee and said, "Sit down and drink this." As if by magic, while Howie and Ray slept, Andy and George had constructed four small stools and a table out of small logs.

"I was shocked. I had a comfortable leg stool, a table to eat off and rest my elbows on, a pile of dried kindling, a roaring fire surrounded by rocks with three flat ones in the middle. A pot of coffee was perking on one rock, a pail of water for George's tea was steaming on another, with George standing over the third with two frying pans, one with simmering bacon, the other cooking huge fluffy pancakes." While Howie took in the sight a second time,

George made toast and put the food on the table. Howie was astounded: syrup, butter, cream, salt and pepper, knives and forks were all sitting on top of a white tablecloth adorned with red cherries. "I will never forget it. I can close my eyes and still see it."

Andy escorted George back to the main road, warning Howie and Ray to stay out of the canoe until he returned. Naturally, Ray and Howie immediately decided to go fishing. "We paddled out far enough to drop the kicker in and I sat on the stern and tried to start the motor — pull, pull, pull, nothing. So I turned around very gently to try a different angle, and still on my knees, on the seat facing the motor, gave a yank. First pull, she started, throttle wide open." Before he could grab the steering handle, the motor turned sideways and Ray and Howie were in the water. Somehow, while turning himself around, Howie had bumped the throttle.

"When I came up amongst the small chunks of ice and the floating gas can, there was Ray, hanging onto the bow. The stern, with the motor, was resting on the bottom in eight feet of water. Ray wasn't much at cussing, but he was very adept that morning, and all of it was directed at me." Quickly, they got the boat ashore, fishing rods still tied in place. They took the motor off, drained the gas, hung it upside down, and prayed. When Andy came back and saw their clothes drying on a line near a roaring fire he said, "Tip the canoe, boys? Hope the motor starts." It did, and fortunately it purred like a kitten for the next six weeks.

That afternoon they set out to find George's corner stakes. Andy had no Department of Mines map or compass; nothing except an axe, a marking pencil, and verbal directions.

"You're heading off into that big wild country with nobody between us and the North Pole, without a map or compass, to find four stakes?" Howie asked.

"No problem," Andy replied.

So off into the wild ventured the two city boys, keeping their fingers crossed that their friend had a built-in compass. "He did, and a half-hour later he was dead on; well, not quite — he was out

440 yards. He got the southwest corner instead of the southeast."

Andy explained he'd looked for blaze marks left by George.

"What are blaze marks?" Howie asked.

"Turn around and look straight back, about three feet up the trees. See the marked trail? Oh sure, plain as day. My brother is short, see how low they are. George always starts cutting a narrow strip with his axe, then goes wide at the bottom. That's opposite to everyone else."

Howie laughs at the memory. "Have you ever tried to follow a trained native guide through the woods, over fallen trees, through growing underbrush, over stumps, through swamps, with mosquitoes and black flies in abundance? Andy was counting steps, blazing trees, and cutting brush, all the while floating along absolutely silent, like he's walking on water. Ray and I are crashing and banging, falling and stumbling, like a bulldozer or an excited male moose."

Ray and Howie had followed Andy for three claims when Andy said, "Why don't you two fellows go due north for 440 yards, put up a corner, then due west for 440 yards and I'll meet you there." Howie looked at Ray, secretly hoping he would say, "Naw, we'll follow you." But he nodded his head and muttered, "Sure, why not?"

The two greenhorns, compasses and axes in hand, started out due north with Howie thinking they might not see Andy again. They blazed everything, dead or alive, that was standing up.

With the job done, the two hollered for Andy. He yelled back, "I'll hit a tree with the back of the axe. I'll keep hitting it; you guys follow the sound and find me." Fifteen minutes later Ray and Howie were still lost, wandering in circles.

"Look boys, find a tree, hit it with an axe, and I'll come and get you," an exasperated Andy yelled to them. Fifteen minutes later Howie was delighted to see Andy come through the bush — and pleased with Andy's suggestion that the next morning they go fishing while he finished staking his claims.

After registering their claims at Red Lake they drove off towards Casummit Lake. George Swain ran a fishing camp, as well as an active trading post for the Hudson's Bay Company, at Swain's Post, about a day's travel from Casummit. To get there, they first drove to Gold Pines, a small village, and paid a fishing-camp operator to take them on his tractor-pulled trailer to Swain's camp. After a two-and-a-half-hour, bone-jarring ride through the woods, they finally arrived at the fishing camp, unloaded the canoe, motor, gas, and other supplies from the tractor, and loaded the canoe again to continue their journey.

George Swain, a stately-looking person, well over six feet tall and 180 pounds, invited them to dinner and to stay the night. In the ensuing conversation someone mentioned that the portage wasn't in too good a shape. Howie had forgotten about that part.

"How far is the portage?"

"About a mile."

"You're kidding — all this stuff, motor and gas included — a mile?" Howie groaned. "Super. Just what I needed."

Next morning Ray and Howie were standing around looking at the sixteen-foot, eighty-five-pound canoe, wondering how they were going to move it, when Andy showed up. Andy laced the paddles to the canoe, lifted the canoe up in the air over his head, and settled it on his shoulders. He shifted one paddle, then the other, to a balanced position, and said, "Meet you boys on the other side," leaving the two sheepish, strong, and fit hockey players floundering in his wake.

Howie was not going to be outdone, so he grabbed the motor and two five-gallon pails of gas. "Have you ever tried carrying an outboard motor on a portage?" he asks now. "Well, don't. There isn't a comfortable spot; they're impossible to balance, and it reminded me of that fifteen-mile obstacle course I ran in England during my physical-education course. Before the trip was over I found out that the easiest thing to carry on the portage was the canoe, wet or dry."

Two portages later, they finally had everything in the Birch and Springpole lakes' watershed and were cruising the shore, looking for the cabin Andy had used fifteen years earlier. They never did find it.

Andy eventually picked a campsite where the group had to climb up a six- to eight-foot bank to get away from the flies. There were very few trees, except for two huge pines close to shore. While Ray and Howie fished for dinner Andy whipped the camp into shape, making three stools, a table with a ten-foot fly over it, and digging a fireplace three to four inches into the ground, lining it with rocks. Within two days they had a full campsite in place with tents up and a cabin started. Andy also guided them in building an outhouse as well as a dry lean-to to store their supplies.

Andy insisted on felling the two trees into the water to make a harbour for boats and a convenient fishing hole. "If we leave the branches on the trees under water, in two days there will be minnows in the branches, then pike and pickerel hunting for the minnows, and then I don't have to leave camp to catch my dinner," he said. Andy felled the trees exactly where he wanted the dock to be, and within no time the area developed into quite a haven for big pike. A few years later, Howie caught one weighing more than twenty-five pounds.

After a couple of days' more work the camp was in great shape, so they headed for the mining camp and fishing lodge six miles away at Casummit Lake to send word for Grace and Jane to fly in. Maggie ran the fishing camp all by herself.

About a mile from Casummit Lake, Ray and Howie passed two young natives in their early twenties, paddling their canoe in the opposite direction. As they passed, about ten feet apart, they said hello to each other. When Howie turned to look, they were paddling back towards Ray and Howie. A minute later, the two natives caught up and the one in the front pointed at Howie and said, "You're Howie Meeker, aren't you?"

The young men were also delighted to find out that Howie's companion was Ray Timgren and invited them back to the reservation, where they met and shook hands with everyone in camp. They signed everything from teepees to beaver pelts to ceremonial headdresses. "This was before television so Ray and I were both amazed at the power of the press, radio, and hockey," Howie says. "We were seventy-five miles from the closest community, Red Lake, and Red Lake was another seventy-five miles from anywhere. That hockey had to be something else."

With the message on its way to Grace, Ray and Howie decided it was time to return to camp and seek their gold treasure. "Five minutes into the woods and I had already used half a bottle of fly dope (bug repellent); I had a tight elastic band around my jacket sleeves, my red chamois shirt buttoned to the neck with the collar turned up, my jacket fully zippered with the collar turned up, my hat pulled down tightly over my head, my pants tied tightly around my ankles with shoelaces, and still the black flies and mosquitoes were crawling up my skin all over me, inside my ears, up my nose, in my mouth and I'm swatting, cursing, and putting on more dope." Howie caught up to Andy, who was in a T-shirt, with bare head, neck, shoulders, and arms, and not a fly on him. After fifteen more minutes of fly bites, Howie asked, "How come you can go in the woods and the flies don't land on you, yet they eat us up?"

"Coal oil," Andy said. "I take a half a teaspoon before breakfast. The rest of the day it comes out through your pores and the flies won't pitch on it."

After a few more forays into the woods with Andy and the flies, Ray and Howie had almost lost their desire to go looking for gold, but Howie decided to continue a few days more with Andy to see how it was done. Eventually, after making sure Andy wasn't pulling his leg — he had watched and made sure Andy actually took it — Howie swallowed the coal oil. "But I'd still bundle up and use the supposedly foolproof fly net hat. They are useless, unless they've improved them immensely in the last thirty years. Every time I'd put the hat on and the veil down over my face and neck I'd trap the galdarned mosquitoes and black flies in there with me. If I did get it on free of flies, they'd climb up my leg, through my underwear, under my belt, up through my chest hair, squeeze through my tightly buttoned collar, and out into the open air. They'd light right on my nose before biting and taking a huge chunk out of it. I'd swear they thought, 'Hi, I had a little problem getting here, but I made it.' Just before the damn thing would dig in I'd swat at it and off would go the hat, the veil, and everything."

So, coal oil and all, Howie headed for the bush, where Andy had staked nine claims. For a couple of days they dug away earth looking for quartz rocks below the surface, with no luck. Eventually, Andy found a small vein of quartz, chipped some out and put it in a little sack, noting its exact location. All Howie found was a pleasant absence of flies. "Sure enough, hundreds were buzzing around but none were landing on me. Yahoo! Good old coal oil. It tastes horrible, even with porridge as a chaser, but it works great."

For the next four or five days Andy went looking for his vein of gold while Ray and Howie hooked and released ten- to twenty-five-pound pike and pickerel and eight- to twelve-pound lake trout.

A week later a small bush plane with pontoons dropped onto Springpole Lake and taxied right to Andy's chopped logs, where it tied up. "Grace was happier to see us than I expected," Howie says. "That night we had a campfire, got into the wine, and when she told us about her trip we shook our heads. We thought it was going to be a piece of cake but it had been quite the ordeal. She had taken Trans-Canada Airlines from Toronto to the Lakehead, then caught a train to Sioux Lookout, before eventually finding the pilot. He was mainly delivering supplies to the network of mines and lumber camps, and took Jane and Grace as a favour. It took a couple of passes over the camp to spot it." Howie and Ray autographed the pilot's work sheet, thanked him, and gave him a $25 tip. "He said he'd fly over camp every time he was in the area and if we ever needed him, to fly a red flag on the wharf and he'd land."

Andy's bannock soon became a popular staple for all concerned. "It's just bush bread, baked in a cast-iron fry pan, but oh my, was it good. Tough to slice but break it off, add butter and jam, or peanut butter, and it was super. We ate a loaf a night."

By August it was time to go home. Howie had been in the woods a couple of times to help Andy, and everywhere he went there were signs of Andy's work: ditches mostly running east to west, one to three feet deep, thirty to fifty feet long. When Ray, Howie, Grace, and Jane decided to head for home, Andy opted to stay with Maggie and help her close camp. I don't blame him, but it was stupid of us not to have andy take us to Swain's Post.

"Our map didn't quite show us the whole route, so Andy drew the last five miles on the edge of the map. If we'd made a wrong turn, we'd still be there. It was stupid to have done it alone. When we ran out of water to paddle on I thought, 'Yahoo, we made it,' but there were times when I wondered if we'd ever get back."

While portaging over Swain's, Howie saw huge wolf tracks. They were fresh and Howie was worried since Grace and Jane were still coming on behind, alone. "Quickly, I found a half-fallen tree, put the bow of the boat on it, climbed out from under, untied the gun, and jeez, did I feel good. For once, I'd paid attention and followed advice. When I reached into my pocket, there were four .30-30 cartridges. Andy once said, 'In our business you're faced with trouble when you least expect it. Always carry a gun with bullets in your pocket.' When I got to Ray, he was fully loaded; he saw the tracks, too. We both ran back a quarter-mile, happy and relieved to see Jane and Grace, hand in hand, coming up the hill."

George Swain, delighted to see a woman and young girl at his camp, proudly showed the crew his garden and flowers, and insisted they stay for supper. He opened a jar of chicken and served it, along with baked new potatoes. "When we ran out of bread, George excused himself, went to the storeroom and came back with a loaf of bread with six to eight inches of hair and mold on it. He cut it off, sliced the bread, and put it on the table. After a glance at each other, Grace and I picked it up, buttered it and ate it. Jeez, was it good. When Grace turned to give Jane a piece, she was sitting in her chair, fast asleep. It had been a long, long day for a three-year-old. George had company, so we turned the canoe three-quarters over, climbed into our sleeping bags, put our heads under the canoe, and fell asleep."

Two days later, back in civilization, things were too easy. When Ray and Howie tried to sleep, their beds felt too soft, so both men wound up sleeping on the floor.

"It was by far the best summer of my life. Andy Dole taught me how to survive, how to live in, enjoy, and respect the woods, and how to manage a canoe. Ray Timgren was the best fellow in the world to share that experience with. Grace and Jane were nothing but a pleasure. I developed a tremendous respect and admiration for Andy, and during the next five summers found many of his native friends to be great people to spend time with."

Y

Hap Day resigned as Leaf coach after the 1949–50 playoff loss to Detroit and accepted the position of assistant general manager. He was replaced by former Maple Leaf star Joe Primeau. Day's coaching demise caught many by surprise.

"After all these years I still can't figure out why he resigned as coach when he did; it wasn't like him to go out a loser," Howie says. "I think he was pushed or shoved. If he would have been made GM, fine, but he was just made 'assistant' GM while Connie retained all the rights to make deals, trades, salaries, and everything else. Hap was just the guy that cleaned up after him. It was very questionable to me. In those days you didn't talk club operations with anyone, you kept your feelings to yourself, but I often remarked to Grace that I couldn't understand what kept Hap Day, the very best coach in the game, in Toronto after 1949–50.

"What I didn't know till four or five years later was that when Hap quit coaching he had a problem with Mr. Smythe. Nothing — philosophy, system, or discipline — changed under Primeau, so you knew Hap was still in control of the team's on-ice performance."

Primeau had coached in the Leaf minor system and led the Toronto Senior Marlboros to the Allan Cup and the St. Mike's Majors to the Memorial Cup.

Primeau was a worrier. His desire for the club to excel was almost painful to watch. Certainly it was tiring. Even when the club was sailing along in second place, winning three times as many games as they lost, Primeau worried. Howie roomed on the road his whole career with team captain Kennedy, and when Primeau worried he'd visit the captain . . . and his veteran roommate. "Sometimes there'd be a close hockey game the next day and it would be tough getting to sleep, then about 2 a.m. there would be a knock on our door. We'd get up because we knew it was Joe Primeau — Mr. Worrywart. Joe would come in and talk hockey, the problems of hockey, and everything else, for an hour or so, and then say goodnight. About an hour later there'd be another knock on the door. I don't think Joe ever slept, and we didn't sleep too much, either."

It was during the 1950–51 season that Smythe started to make wholesale changes to the roster. On November 16, longtime teammates Bill Ezinicki and Vic Lynn were shipped off to Boston. Both men had had very average seasons in 1949–50. Lynn notched just 7 goals and 13 assists in 70 games, not bad for a hitter, but he picked up only 39 penalty minutes, "and that told a story." Ezzy had his usual 10 goals and 100 minutes in penalties, but Howie maintains that for the first time in his life Wild Bill realized he could get hurt.

His hitting sharply declined after a game in Detroit when "Ezzy was in the hardest collision I've ever seen," right in front of the Leaf bench. Hap Day was on the far end of the bench, sitting just about on the Toronto blue line, and Howie was sitting beside him because his line was next to go on the ice. A pass from behind the Leaf net came along the boards, bounced over Harry Watson's stick, and headed for open ice. Detroit's Doug McCaig, a huge man, over six foot one and more than 200 pounds, saw the loose puck and set out full speed to keep it in Toronto's zone. As Ezzy turned in the centre-ice area, top of the circle, expecting a pass or chip along the boards, he too saw the loose puck and started after it. Day leapt up onto the players' bench, anticipating what was about to unfold, and screamed "Yup, Yup, Yup, Yup" to Ezzy — but it was too late. At that point McCaig and Ezzy were less than six feet apart and both under a full head of steam; the explosion was inevitable.

"I've seen some great hits — Ezzy on Edgar Laprade, Ezzy on Metro Prystai, and Bill Barilko on Rocket Richard — but this was by far the greatest — 200 pounds plus against another 180-pounder, both guys giving it their best shot — then *kaboom!* McCaig's stick flies twenty feet in the air and he goes down and lies there like he's been poleaxed, out cold. Ezzy stayed on his feet, but during the five minutes that it took to bring Doug back to the living, Ezzy stood about fifteen feet away and just shivered. He'd be normal for a minute or two and then his whole body would just shake for ten or twenty seconds. He was hurting."

Day never played Ezinicki again the rest of the game, nor did he ask Wild Bill if he was hurt. With Ezzy, somehow that just wasn't done. Howie maintains it was the first time in his hockey career that Ezinicki realized he was vulnerable, that he too could be hurt. "When he recovered it seemed to me he tried to be Ezinicki the hockey player, not Ezzy the hitter. As an occasional hitter he had a huge presence on the ice. As a player he didn't. I was delighted, though, when he was traded to Boston because in 1950–51 Ezzy had a good year there. I'm sure he only played hockey to get money so he could play golf. Golf was his first love, what he was really good at. He had very little skill and finesse in the game of hockey, but in golf he had all that."

In return for Lynn and Ezinicki, Toronto received rugged defenceman Fern Flaman, centre Phil Maloney, Kenny Smith, and highly rated Junior defenceman Leo Boivin. Flaman played 39 games that year with the Leafs, Maloney appeared in one, while Smith never even had a cup of coffee with the team. Two years later, in 1952–53, Boivin would become a regular Leaf rearguard.

Defenceman Hugh Bolton came out of the Marlboros system,

played 13 regular-season matches and then the playoffs. Bolton was a six-foot three-inch native of Toronto and "a gangly guy who could reach a country mile." Another newcomer who contributed significantly that season was left winger Danny Lewicki, a "real smoothey on skates," according to Howie. Lewicki originally hailed from Ontario's Lakehead area and played Junior in Stratford and with the Toronto Marlies. Lewicki played 61 games and picked up 34 points, including 16 goals, in his rookie season with the Leafs. Two other youngsters — centres Bob Hassard and Johnny McCormack — saw spot duty that season. McCormack had already toiled the three previous seasons in the Leaf farm system, seeing sporadic ice time in the big leagues. In 1950–51 he seemed to have finally cracked the NHL lineup full-time. But after 46 Leaf games he was banished to the minors. The reason? McCormack had the unmitigated gall to get married during the regular season without seeking the permission of Conn Smythe. The power-hungry tyrant of Toronto had not been healthy during the 1949–50 season and seemed even more determined to assert his power anew, now that he was back in fighting form. McCormack's insolence simply could not be tolerated and an incensed Smythe sent him back to the Pittsburgh Hornets — the Leafs' affiliate in the American League — leaving more room for young Hassard to show his stuff. "The demotion sort of rocked us all a bit, but it didn't shock us. That was the sort of crap he threw at his players; that was Conn Smythe."

No other regular addition to the club had near the impact that season that goalie Al Rollins and his emergence as a top-rated goaltender did. Rollins was acquired by the team during the Battle of the Bulge episode the previous year but played just two games. In 1950–51, though, Smythe was determined to go with a two-goalie system and Rollins was to be Broda's puck-stopping partner. Smythe's plan later proved to be very prudent, but Rollins's early performances had Howie and teammates wondering what was going on in the minds of management.

"At training camp we looked at each other and said, 'Hey, wait a minute, now. Who traded for this guy? Broda looked, acted, and played like the top goaltender in the game, and Rollins was very average. The difference between Rollins and Broda was like chicken salad and chicken shit. Well, Rollins stayed with us, practised with us, and played some games and just got better and better. Sometime during the season, Turk was hurt and missed two or three weeks of play, so they had to put Rollins in goal. The guy turned out to be sensational! When Broda got hurt he was still twice the goaltender Rollins was; when Broda returned, Rollins was as good as or better than Broda. It was unbelievable the way he improved, and the way that he played. He went from chicken shit to chicken salad."

In 40 games Rollins allowed just 70 goals, for a 1.98 goals against average, and recorded five shutouts. Turk also played well: in 31 games he allowed 68 goals for a 2.19 average, with a sparkling six shutouts. Combined, they had a 1.97 goals against average, the lowest in the league. At year-end Rollins was named winner of the Vezina Trophy as the league's top goalie.

Garth Boesch was retired but the Leafs still had the workhorse bunch of Thomson, Mortson, Barilko, and Billy Juzda on defence. With Flaman and Bolton added to the list they were still a big, tough, and rough blueline brigade.

Up front, Kennedy, Sloan, and Smith had great years. "Teeder had to think that he'd died and gone to heaven. He finally had real skill and talent on his line to match his own. Sid Smith ended up with 30 goals on left wing, Tod Sloan had 31 on right wing, and Kennedy had 18 goals, 43 assists, and 61 points — what a line! Gardner had a super offensive season and the future looked bright with all the youngsters contributing extremely well."

Y

The Leafs came out of the starting gate in 1950–51 with a burst of energy, going 11 straight games without a loss. By early December they dominated the league and were comfortably in first place.

Unfortunately for Howie, he blew his knee out in mid-December and missed 21 games.

During his absence the club slowed from their torrid pace and lost their large lead. In the last few weeks of the season, with Howie back in the lineup, they failed to stop the red-hot Red Wing squad from stealing top spot. Toronto finished second with 95 points, 6 behind Detroit.

Conn Smythe had slowly been integrating his son Stafford into the business and hockey picture at Maple Leaf Gardens. By 1950–51 Stafford certainly had his foot well stuck in the door. It took Stafford and Howie no time to clash, and even less time to dislike one another. Stafford's pompous attitude grated on Howie's nerves; his rude actions, which often parallelled his father's style, only increased the animosity between the two.

One of the earliest incidents to infuriate Howie took place February 10, 1951. Detroit beat Toronto 2–1 that cold winter's evening, and after the game at Maple Leaf Gardens, Grace Meeker, Lill Watson, and Francis Klukay were standing under the stands waiting for their husbands. On evenings when the players left right after home games for road trips out of town, their wives would drive their husbands from the rink to the train station. That car ride was often the only few minutes of privacy a husband and wife might share for a few days. The Leafs were scheduled to grind it out in Chicago the next night and had an 11 p.m. train to catch — so time was tight. Stafford happened along the corridor while the women were waiting. Instead of conversing with them, or even simply tipping his hat, Smythe rudely ordered them "out of the building" and into the snowy night.

"That disregard for wives, and women period, went on the whole time I was with the Leafs when Conn and/or Stafford were involved, but that night I should have found the son of a bitch and popped him. Why I, nor any of the players for that matter, didn't stand up to Conn or Stafford at times like that, I'll never know. I'd gone to war, faced hell, fought many giant men . . . you name it, yet

I took that kind of crap from the little weasel and the old man. I guess it was the fact that they had control and power — that they had us by the short hairs. Either way, I was wrong not to set him straight on that one right then and there."

Certainly things were not always rosy off the ice, but on the ice the Leafs were flying. Despite missing first place overall, the boys in blue and white had a strong season, boasting a twenty-one-point improvement over the previous one. "I think our team realized what damn fools we were the year before and got back on the track of playing hockey. We won 41 games and lost 16, so that's a big plus-25. We scored 212 goals and had 138 against us, so that's a plus-74, and I would think five-against-five (even strength) we were better than that. We easily cruised to second place in the 1950–51 season. I'm sure management thought the boys were ready for anybody."

Complacency and overconfidence can creep up on a team, much like dirt gradually accumulates under a fingernail. Perhaps their cakewalk finish to the season left the Leafs dazed for the first game in the opening round of the 1951 playoffs. The fourth-place Boston Bruins gladly provided a wake-up call in the first game, pawing their opponents 2–0.

Game Two was a Saturday-night match at Maple Leaf Gardens. The robust affair was tied 1–1 after the first period and remained deadlocked there after the first overtime period. During the early 1950s in Toronto, professional sports were not allowed on Sunday, so a late curfew for Saturday-night events was in place to guard against the events extending beyond midnight into Sunday morning. "I think the rule was that you couldn't start any event after 11 p.m. and here we were at maybe 11:05 with a period of sudden-death overtime hockey to play, maybe less than a period, maybe more — no one could say. So they couldn't start the second overtime and the game was called. If you think about it both owners were probably delighted with that call — there might be gate receipts from an extra game to split."

It was a wide-awake and testy Toronto team that travelled to

Boston the very next night, April 1. The Leafs would not be made fools of that evening and showed it in all departments, out hitting and out scoring their hosts. Toronto blanked Boston 3–0. The Leafs had returned to playing Hap Day hockey and went on to defeat the Bruins four games to one, allowing Boston to score five goals in six games. "After that we were just thinking, 'Ha, bring on the Canadiens.' But this time the Canadiens had Elmer Lach."

Meeker had always wondered if the Leafs could have beaten the Canadiens for the Stanley Cup in 1946–47 if Lach had been in their lineup. "He was an all-star, he was the guy that made Richard better, not made him go, but made him better."

Toronto won the opening game of the series thanks to Sid Smith and his linemates Kennedy and Sloan, along with the stalwart netminding of Broda. Smith scored just fifteen seconds into the match, drawing first blood in the game and series for the Leafs, and the trend was set. Sloan sniped another Leaf goal in regulation time and then Smith scored his second of the evening, at 5:51 of overtime.

In Game Two Montreal would have their moment of glory and Howie would be the goat. The Canadiens grabbed a 2–0 lead by the middle of the game, before Toronto rallied and tied the score by the end of regulation play. Near the end of his line's second shift in overtime, Howie was tired and should have gone to the bench. Instead he snagged a pass from Gardner in Toronto's end and took off down the ice. A Hab player pursued him to centre ice and over to the left-wing side, way out of his position. Howie crossed Montreal's blue line and went to go around Kenny Reardon but the wily defenceman performed one of his famous dives, stuck his stick out, and hit the puck. The puck quickly wound up on the stick of Montreal's Maurice Richard and the Rocket was gone. "Richard went around Jimmy Thomson like a hoop around a barrel — Jimmy never even touched him. The Rocket then cut back into centre, behind Mortson, gave Turk the old drop shoulder, went around him and put it in. I felt like a nickel. I came to the bench and took one look at Primeau. I knew I was wrong. I should have dumped the puck in Montreal's end and got the hell off the ice — but no, I was going to win the game by myself. As it turned out I blew it and we went into Montreal tied 1–1 in games."

Despite allowing only five goals in two games, Broda was replaced in goal by Al Rollins. "It was Rollins's big test. Sure he had physical ability, but did he have the mental toughness and ability to function under pressure — two very big ingredients that make a good goaltender a Hall of Famer, a Stanley Cup–winner."

Rocket Richard notched a power-play goal early in the first but Smith blew one past McNeil in the Habs' net, and the clubs were deadlocked 1–1. This time it was Teeder who did the task, taking a nifty pass from Sloan . . . game over. Rollins was the first star of the game, more than passing the first test.

Game Four saw two series trends continue: an early marker in the first period . . . and overtime. Smith and Richard maintained their torrid scoring paces with Smith connecting thirty-eight seconds into the game and Richard tying the event later that period. Early in the second period Howie drilled the puck past McNeil for a 2–1 lead, but with less than seven minutes left in the game Lach scored to force yet another overtime. Big Harry Watson, set up by Max Bentley, enjoyed hero status that night. "I can still see the pass and Watson going wide, and as he cut for the net he let the shot go and it went in the far side, and suddenly we're up three games to one and going home." Once again Rollins was brilliant between the pipes for the Leafs.

In the fifth game, Richard and "Slinker" Sloan drew the teams even in the second period. In the third period the Habs' Doug Harvey made a pass to Paul Meger to give the Canadiens a 2–1 lead and Montreal threw up a defensive shell for nearly fifteen minutes.

In desperation, with less than a minute remaining in regulation time, Leaf coach Primeau put the Kennedy line on the ice with Thomson and Mortson on defence, and sent out Bentley to replace Rollins as a sixth attacker. Montreal fans sensed victory as the Leaf net loomed empty and inviting at the far end of the rink. "Sure as hell, Kennedy won the draw back to the point and Max put a shot in the direction of the net. There were four Canadiens and four or five Leaf players in a fifteen- or twenty-foot square area in front of Gerry McNeil, but the puck danced free onto Slinker's stick and *boom* — with thirty-two seconds left to go it's a 2–2 hockey game." For an amazing and unprecedented fifth straight game the two teams headed into sudden-death overtime.

"We knew right then and there that one of us wearing a blue and white sweater was going to get the overtime winner. The Kennedy line started, with our line next. Early in our shift Watson hit me with a cross-ice pass and I caught the defence standing still — for a change I was flying down the wing. I skated in on the Montreal net, the last ten feet home free, and I could see there was lots of room along the ice on the short side of McNeil for the puck to slip by. I shot and hit the outside of the post, as usual, and the puck bounced against the boards and lay there just behind the net. I headed for it and just as I blindly passed it out in front of the net, big Tom Johnson came charging out of nowhere and ran me into the fence hard."

Johnson put his forearm on the back of Meeker's head and tried to flatten his nose and loosen a few teeth against the boards. "As I turned and was about to try and remove his head from his shoulders with my stick, the red light, not two feet away, went on. I stopped the swing and called that big S.O.B. every curse word in the book, and I knew 'em all. When I finally looked out front to see what had happened, there was Bill Juzda and Cal Gardner with Bill Barilko on their shoulders. 'Christ,' I thought, 'Dumb-Dumb has gotten the winner.'"

There are numerous photographs of Barilko's historic shot from the left faceoff circle that night. In the most famous picture, Barilko is seen falling down while firing the winner, while in the background the familiar #11 uniform of Meeker is seen getting smashed into the fence behind the net by Johnson. "Funny thing, minutes later at centre ice, Johnson and I shook hands and we both laughed about it," Howie recalls.

"Max Bentley had 13 points in the playoffs; Smith, Kennedy, and Sloan scored 10 of the 13 goals in the finals and were incredible, while stars must go to the defence who played exceptionally well: Thomson, Mortson, Barilko, Juzda, and Flaman. Outstanding.

"It was a great, great hockey series, probably the best I ever played in, certainly the most exciting I was ever in."

Toronto fans went delirious with joy over their most recent Cup victory and rightfully so. Within weeks of the victory, though, steps were already being taken to tap the syrup of success out of the Maple Leafs, who seemed poised for a strong future of growth. The club would not see the Stanley Cup final playoffs for eleven years.

Most tragic of all was the snipping away of budding star Bill Barilko, the overtime hero and rollicking defenceman. Bashing Bill set out in late summer for a routine fishing trip in Northern Ontario, but his single-engine airplane crashed. Barilko's body and plane would not be found until the following winter.

While Barilko's demise was accidental, the demise of the Leafs after that victorious year may have been intentional. In Meeker's mind, the fourth Cup in five years for the Leafs, while thrilling for the fans and players, was not making Conn Smythe such a happy man. "Right then and there, in my opinion, the move to get rid of Hap Day started or really escalated. By whom? Obviously Smythe and his son Stafford. I didn't know it then, but I found out later."

Eight

Just Another Game

"The pay was not good, nor did I see a long-term future in politics, but actually I never enjoyed anything as much in my life, not even winning the Stanley Cup."

Howie and Grace wasted little time getting home to New Hamburg following the 1951 Cup victory. For some unknown reason the regular season and playoffs had seemed much longer than in past years.

While the return home was the sort of rest Howie needed, he and Grace were just marking time before heading off on a fishing holiday, and to see Howie's parents at Chalk River. Because it was only late April, the ice was still too thick on the lakes for any reasonable fisherman, so Howie resigned himself to catching up on the chores he'd been absent from over the past six months.

Soldier boy: A dashing young Howie
Meeker heads off to war. *Photo by
Jerome; Meeker Collection*

Wedding bells: Howie and Grace celebrate on
April 20, 1946. *Kitchener Record photo*

All in the family: Rookie Howie enjoys a laugh at practice with his younger brothers Tom
(left), Chuck, and Ken.

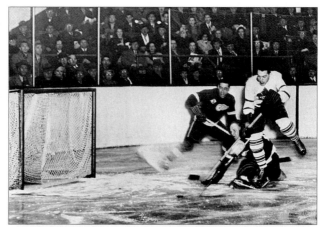

Howie stuffs one into the Detroit net after leaping over Red Wing netminder Harry Lumley as Black Jack Stewart watches. *Meeker Collection*

Enjoying the 1946-47 Stanley Cup win are the Leaf rookies and coach Hap Day. Front row: Jimmy Thomson (left), Day, Howie, and Bill Barilko. Back row: Vic Lynn, Garth Boesch, Gus Mortson, and Joe Klukay.

Howie and linemate Vic Lynn look their sticks over in the dressing room. *Meeker Collection*

Howie as he appeared on Beehive hockey pictures in 1947.

Happy times with Hap: Howie and Hap celebrate Howie's record-setting five-goal game as a rookie, January 8, 1947. Only one other rookie, Don Murdoch of the New York Rangers, has equalled the feat.

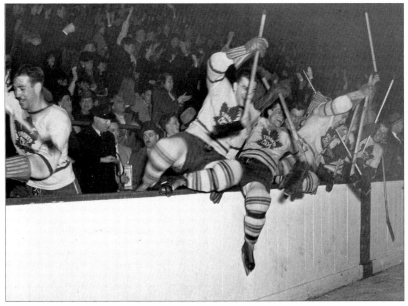

Victory: This classic photo captures the exuberance of winning as the Maple Leafs celebrate their 1946-47 Stanley Cup win. Note the despondent Canadiens' publicist, Charlie DeRoche, in a bowler hat behind the players' bench. *Nat Turofsky photo*

Rookie of the Year
Calder Cup and
silver-engraved
tray are presented
to Howie by
W.A.H. McBrien,
chairman of the
board of Maple
Leaf Gardens.
Meeker Collection

Too late: Howie is caught out of position behind the net on this shot as the Canadiens put pressure on the Leaf net. Maurice "The Rocket" Richard and Elmer Lach watch for a pass in front. *Nat Turofsky photo*

The 1946-47 Stanley Cup champion Leafs. Back row: Howie (left), Vic Lynn, Jimmy Thomson, Garth Boesch, Gus Mortson, Joe Klukay, Bill Barilko. Middle row: Bill Ezinicki, Wally Stanowski, Harry Watson, Turk Broda, Bob Goldham, Bud Poile, Gus Bodnar, Tim Daly. Front row: Gaye Stewart, Ted Kennedy, Conn Smythe, Hap Day, Syl Apps, E.W. Bickle, W.A.H. McBrien, Nick Metz, Don Metz. *Alexandra Studio; Meeker Collection*

Two rookies: Baby Jane Meeker adorns the Calder Cup in the New Hamburg backyard. The cup wound up serving a useful purpose in the Meeker home.

KLM: The Leafs' famous KLM line, also known as the second Kid Line: Howie (left), Ted "Teeder" Kennedy, and Vic Lynn.

Lucky Lynn: Vic Lynn (far right) celebrates his goal while Kennedy (No. 9) joins him. Howie (No. 15) waits for a rebound that never came. Kenny Reardon (No. 17) and Toe Blake, to his left, are not pleased.

On parade: Leafs gather at Toronto City Hall after the 1947-48 Cup win. Howie is fourth from right while team masseur Archie Campbell — "the human rubbing machine" — leans into picture at far right. Apps and Kennedy are between Howie and Campbell. *Nat Turofsky photo*

Howie receives an award in a charity ball-game between members of the Leafs and the Canadiens. *Nat Turofsky photo*

Howie holds a framed cartoon drawn for him. *Capital Press Service; Meeker Collection*

On the campaign trail: Howie's hard work paid off as he was elected the Conservative MP for Waterloo South. *Canada Pictures Limited; Meeker Collection*

This postcard-size picture showing Howie, Grace, and Jane was used in Howie's election campaign. Howie spoke, wherever he went, on the high cost of living and other issues of the day.

Andy Dole holds a fine catch while Ray Timgren looks up from the back of the canoe. Howie's adventures with the pair took him 1,500 miles away from New Hamburg. *Meeker Collection*

Gone fishing: Howie holds a thirty-nine-pound salmon caught in July 1992. Howie's boat, the *Golly Gee III*, is in the background.

Howie chats it up with The Sports Network's on-air duo of Gary Green and Paul Romanuk at the opening of Vancouver's General Motors Place, October 9, 1995. *Charlie Hodge photo*

As he'd done so often as a youngster, Howie also found time for occasional visits to the quaint downtown area. Every community has its unique characters and locations, and in those days the two were often discovered at a local barbershop. New Hamburg was no different. Ed Pfaff's Barbershop was still the main hangout for many folks and it wasn't just because Ed offered the best and cheapest haircut in the country at just two-bits. It was the three pool tables, and the camaraderie. Farmers, businessmen, and occasionally school children would all congregate at Ed's for rousing discussions and an opportunity to smack around some pool balls.

That particular morning Howie decided to head downtown and stop at Ed's for a haircut and maybe a game or two of eight-ball. It was a walk that began a series of escalating events. Howie ambled along the road leading to the large bridge crossing over the Nith River. The spring sunshine added a warmth to both body and soul as it dappled the tree-lined roadway.

Just past the bridge was the rustic home of Earl Katzenmeier. One of the true characters in town, "Katzy" was an insurance agent and, among other things, was responsible for the New Hamburg Derby. In those days the event was the highest-paying horse race in Canada, and the little Ontario village swelled from 1,200 people to 12,000 — sometimes even 15,000 — for the event.

Howie had barely cleared the bridge and set foot onto the road-way again when he noticed Katzenmeier sitting on his front porch, swinging feverishly in a rocking chair. When Katzy spied Howie he came off that rocking chair like he was shot out of a gun.

The spry senior crossed the lawn, scurried up a little hill, through the gate, onto the road, and right up to Howie. Katzenmeier then gently grabbed Howie's jacket and said, "Howie Meeker, you're going to be our next Conservative member."

"Katzy, you've been into the scotch already this morning," Howie laughed.

"No boy, no boy. We're looking for someone to run for the Conservative party and you're the guy."

Howie protested that he had no knowledge, no experience, and little interest in politics. Katzy finally departed and Howie trundled on to Pfaff's, shot a few games of pool, and talked about hockey and farming. When he got home around noon he told Grace about the conversation with Katzy. They both had a good laugh and forgot about it.

But Earl Katzenmeier didn't forget.

Later that evening, just after dinner, Katzy arrived at the Meeker door with two other people in tow: Gordon Chaplin, a former member of provincial parliament for Galt (now part of Cambridge), Ontario, and Norman Hancock, president of the Waterloo South Conservative Riding Association. For the next two hours the trio tried to persuade Howie to let his name stand for nomination as the Conservative party candidate for Parliament.

"We think you can win it and we're in pretty tough. We need somebody to run who can win this election," Hancock said, explaining that the former member, Karl Homuth, had been the sitting member for the previous fifteen years. Homuth had died suddenly, some six months after the recent federal election, and the constituency was holding a by-election.

The two visitors continued to apply the pressure before departing around 9 p.m. Howie and Grace looked at each other, not sure what to think, then both shrugged their shoulders. Howie finally broke the silence. "I've got an idea, let's pack our things, grab Jane, and get out of here. We'll head to my parents' for a couple of days and then go fishing." Grace looked at him for a moment (making sure he wasn't joking), looked at the clock, and then grinned, "Why not?"

Within an hour or so they had packed the car and were headed for Chalk River. Howie drove all night to get there, some 300 miles away on the Ottawa River. Howie says he drank more coffee that night trying to stay awake than any other night of his life.

Charlie Meeker was surprised to see his son a week earlier than planned, so Howie explained that he just needed to get away from it all. Howie talked about the long season and playoffs, and then eventually, and reluctantly, about the political hoopla he was facing. When Howie mentioned he'd turned down the offer, he received exactly the lecture he'd anticipated. Charlie Meeker was a strong, passionate Conservative all of his life and he never strayed from that loyalty.

"Ya won't run? Christ, kid, ya gotta run, and that's it! You've got a chance to be a member of the House of Commons, a federal member of Parliament, and you won't run? You're crazy, son."

"No way, Dad, I won't run," Howie countered. Charlie practically threw him out of the house for that.

The next day Grace and Howie left Jane with her grandparents and set off for a favourite fishing spot just over the Quebec border, a couple hours' drive away. From Chalk River they drove northwest, past the hydroelectric dam at Deswisher, across the dam into Quebec, and up a back road several miles.

They arrived at a secluded little lake the couple had found years before, a place where few folks ventured. It was among their favourite fishing spots even though the lake never yielded any fishing legends. Most of the catches were only one- or two-pound trout, but on a fly rod they were a lot of fun. Most of all it was the simple serenity of the lake, the calm, the peace, that drew Grace and Howie.

After eight months of bone-jarring body checks, fights, screaming crowds, hotels, and seemingly endless travel in two countries, a week or so of wilderness fishing was exactly the therapy Howie needed.

With three days of camping behind him, Howie was starting to unwind. The wind, rain, and ice, however, had kept him off the lake more than he planned. Grace was still fast asleep when Howie rose early in the morning, stoked the fire, and carefully picked the quickest but safest path across the ice to launch his durable rubber dinghy. Breath hung heavy in the cold, crisp, morning air, spiralling and dancing in the beams of early morning light. The blanket of polished white snow and ice around the edges of the lake was enhanced by the clear blue morning sky.

Howie caught a few small trout, nothing of significance, and a few hours later the smell of steaming hot coffee over a wood stove wafted far out from shore as he returned to camp.

Once on shore Howie fired up the Coleman stove and stoked the fire again while Grace started making breakfast. Still damp and cold, the two campers were bundled up in blankets, huddled over the perking coffee and cooking food, when a gigantic white Cadillac pulled up on the roadside above the camp. The large, tinted front passenger window rolled down, and the head of a chauffeur peered out at Howie.

"Excuse me, are you Howie Meeker?"

"Err . . . yes, sir," Howie replied.

"There's someone here to see you," the chauffeur said, and the back door began to swing open. For a few brief seconds Howie was simply bewildered, and a little apprehensive. Out stepped — or rather unfolded — an imposing, majestic man of six feet three inches and 240 pounds, with shoulders like a pro football player. A handsome, immaculately dressed man politely introduced himself as George Drew, leader of the Conservative Party of Canada and the official Opposition.

It was an odd trio that gathered around that campfire in the woods of northern Quebec that morning, chatting away through a breakfast of bacon, eggs, fried trout, and campfire coffee.

"I hear the people of Waterloo South want you to run," Drew eventually said to Howie.

"Yes, sir."

"And you won't run?"

"Nope, not at all."

Howie told Drew he had a list of reasons as long as his arm for not running, including the fact that he neither knew about nor had that much time for politics. Howie also explained that he couldn't afford it. "If I was to run and I lost, who would pay my campaign costs? The nomination fee is $250 and if I don't get a certain percentage of the vote I'll lose the money. Besides, I make $7,000

154

a year playing hockey and you only get $3,000 a session and $2,000 a year tax-free in Parliament. I've got no education, no rich parents, no big business, and no interest. The only thing I know is hockey and I can't take a pay cut."

Drew took in Howie's words for a few seconds, then said, "Would you do me a favour and jump in the car? We'll use the phone at the conservation office down the road and phone Conn Smythe."

Howie knew right then his goose was cooked. Smythe was a stronger Conservative supporter than even his own father was.

Drew, obviously prepared for just such a scenario, dug out Smythe's phone number and in no time had the owner of the Maple Leafs on the phone. After a few minutes' conversation, Drew handed the phone to Howie. Hesitantly, he picked up the telephone and started to say hello, but Smythe wasted no time, cutting to the point.

"Hey, kid, what the hell is this I hear that you won't run for the Conservatives?" the staunch Tory bellowed into Howie's ear. Smythe had donated plenty of money to the Conservatives and was friends with numerous premiers, politicians, and federal officials. Howie was in deep trouble. "Why won't you run, kid?"

Howie listed off the reasons, but Smythe was not to be denied. "You run, kid, and I'll guarantee all the bills are paid," he quickly countered, much to Howie's surprise.

Meeker then pointed out that he made more money playing hockey than he would in politics.

"I'll tell you what, kid, you run, you win, and I'll pay your hockey salary," Smythe said, tightening the knot. "I'll pay whether you can play or not, as long as you sit in the House of Commons."

With no arguments left, Howie told Smythe that he would talk to Grace about the matter and get back to him soon. Back at the campfire, Howie, Grace, and George talked for a long time, then Grace and Howie discussed the offer for a few minutes before Grace grinned in her wise way and resolved the matter. "If you want to do it and you think that it's the right thing, we'll do it."

Howie told Drew he'd give it a try and walked a pleased Leader of the Opposition back to the long white vehicle, shook hands with him, and said he'd return to New Hamburg after a couple more days of fishing. As the huge, somewhat muddy Cadillac ambled back down the old dirt road, Howie's rumbling stomach told him his life was about to take another major shift.

Later that evening around the campfire, Howie and Grace pondered the inevitable question of how Drew knew where to find them. It was Charlie Meeker, of course, who had turned the trick.

No one admitted to anything, but Howie believes Katzenmeier, Chaplin, or someone in Waterloo South, contacted key party members in Ottawa, who in turn got a hold of Drew and told him about Meeker. Ottawa then telephoned Charlie at Chalk River, who was only too pleased to assist his fellow Conservatives. Charlie informed them, however, that Howie and Grace were fishing for at least four or five days. It seems Drew then excused himself from the House of Commons, jumped in his car, and drove for several hours up to Charlie's place. Charlie was honoured to meet Drew and gladly told him where to locate his son.

"Dad was more than happy to help and in fact drove all the way up to Deswisher and got Drew on the right road before he returned home. I gave Dad hell later, but not much. Political life turned out to be a very pleasant experience."

As Meeker found out much later, none of the Conservatives who'd vied for the nomination during the general election wanted to run in the by-election. They had all said no for the simple reason that Norm Moffatt, the former mayor of Galt, was the Liberal candidate in the contest. Moffatt had run against Homuth in the previous election and came within 300 votes of winning. No one was more popular than Karl Homuth, so the other potential candidates all figured Moffatt would be a shoo-in for the by-election. Howie learned only later that he was a distinct underdog.

ᐯ

During the ensuing campaign Howie picked up some impressive

support, with such well-known Conservatives as John Diefenbaker, George Nolan, George Hees, and Don Fleming speaking on his behalf. "I got to know them much better later on and learned a great deal from them."

In Howie's case, being a hockey player certainly did not hinder his political aspirations. As a member of the Leafs he'd made numerous public appearances and speeches. "This is all in hindsight," he says, "but I'm convinced that Howie Meeker the private citizen, businessman, municipal politician, or whatever, would never have made it to the House of Commons, but Howie Meeker the Toronto Maple Leaf hockey player started the campaign with such an advantage over the Liberal mayor of Galt and the other candidates that it was a sin. Absolutely everybody in the riding of Waterloo South had heard of Howie Meeker. Hell, the guy played with the Leafs, who had won four Cups in the last five years. I had been in their homes and living rooms through Foster Hewitt every Saturday night for five years, and was constantly in the *Galt Reporter* and *Kitchener-Waterloo Record*, winter and summer, because I'd played Senior baseball and Intermediate softball in all the cities and villages in the riding for, oh gosh, at least seven years."

If that wasn't help enough, Premier Leslie Frost of Ontario sent Hugh Latimer, his best political organizer (and perhaps the very best in the country). Ontario is full of former Conservative members of provincial parliament and cabinet ministers who owe their electoral success to Latimer.

Howie first met Latimer in early April with the election set for early June, so campaign time was short. They had a lot of ground to make up because, from all indications, everybody expected Mayor Moffatt to win, and win easily. "In fact I had assured Grace that there was no way I was going to win. If I had thought there was a chance, I would not have run."

During their initial conversation Latimer asked Howie how hard he was prepared to work. "Just as hard as you are, and harder," Howie responded. "You're the boss. You fiddle and I'll dance."

And dance they did. Howie maintains he was in and out of every community store on the main streets of Galt, Preston, Hespeler, Elmira . . . Palm-squeezing and baby-kissing in Hespeler alone took two days. "That main street had to be three miles long, with small businesses on both sides of the road. Usually a local councillor, the mayor, or anyone who knew everybody (if he happened to be a Conservative) took me in and out of the stores. But lots of times I just walked in cold turkey and introduced myself to the staff and anyone in the area."

Latimer organized dozens of gatherings at manufacturing plants throughout the riding with plenty of pretzels and beer on hand for the workers. Howie, true to his word, worked day and night meeting people and even shook hands with farmers milking cows at 4 a.m. "I canvassed private homes, I danced at weddings, went to picnics, and I got pretty good reports in the *Galt Reporter*."

In his Junior hockey days in Stratford, Howie had known a defenceman named Bob Marshall, whose best friend Ken Thomson was working at one of his dad's papers in Galt. Naturally, he went to see Ken two or three times during the campaign and they talked about the old times. Thomson saw to it that Howie got his share of press coverage.

Howie also visited most schools in the area at 4 p.m. when the kids got out, and handed out small hockey sticks and blotters inscribed with a political message as well as hockey pictures of him in a Leaf uniform. "I'd sign the things and the kids took the propaganda right home. Mom and Dad had no choice but to listen."

But the biggest draw by far during Howie's two whirlwind months on the stump were appearances by the Toronto Maple Leafs, who played exhibition softball games against teams from Elmira, Galt, Preston, and Hespeler. "All the guys showed up. Hugh Latimer and the local mayor, the provincial members, or the guy who cut the town's hair took me through the crowd. What a country. At one of those games in Elmira we must have had 4,000 people; that was 2,000 kids and 2,000 parents. The one we held in

Preston had over 5,000 people, with almost the full Toronto Maple Leaf team there. You couldn't have a better rally than that.

"My other big plus was that people seemed pretty well dissatisfied with the existing Liberal government. Like all governments that have been in power for any length of time they got arrogant and lost touch with the working people. I know that is true because four of us Conservatives ran in four different parts of the country in by-elections and all four of us got in. My problem was that everyone knew the name and face of Howie Meeker, but what kind of person was he really? All I had to do was be Howie Meeker and if I sold myself, fine, and if I didn't — well tough. If they walked away saying, 'Hey, he's not a bad guy; he might make a pretty good member,' then I'd won. If I was not a good person, or did not come across as being one of the guys, or as someone they'd be happy to have representing them in the House of Commons, then I was dead."

Gordon Chaplin, a former member of provincial parliament, and lawyer John Hancock were on the riding association's executive and they arranged various meetings with business people and service clubs. Howie spoke before the Kiwanis, Junior Chamber of Commerce, and Rotary clubs. "You name it, big or small, Hugh, Gord, and John made sure I got there."

Various unions in Preston arranged for all the area candidates to attend a meeting to hear union views and answer some questions. The idea scared Howie, who knew little about unions or their concerns. "There was no way I could back out of that and I said, 'Well, Hugh, I'm green as grass about union problems, but let's go.'" Preston boasted a couple of huge knitting mills and wood-working factories, among other businesses. Fortunately for Howie, neither the CCF's Peggy Geens nor Mayor Moffatt showed up, so instead of making a big speech and fighting with the other people trying to get elected, Howie spoke for five minutes and then asked the workers what their problems were. He listened to their problems for more than an hour. "You can be sure that the person who introduced me, and the people who thanked everyone for being there, mentioned the fact that neither of the other two had the guts to show up. In most polling areas of Preston we won; I think that meeting had a lot to do with it."

Howie campaigned on a couple of key issues including the high cost of living and adequate old-age pensions. Finally the fiddling and dancing were over and it was time for the audience to decide. When all of the ballots had been counted, Howie Meeker had won the political equivalent of the Stanley Cup. He garnered 9,097 votes, beating Moffatt by 2,553. At twenty-seven years of age he was the youngest member elected to the House of Commons.

V

Howie's unexpected, and sound, victory in the federal by-election was the perfect icing to his fourth Stanley Cup win just a few months earlier. New Hamburg honoured its political son with a victory parade in June that year.

Soon after the election Howie learned that an unexpected fall sitting of the House of Commons would take place, meaning he would be immersed in the political world sooner than anticipated — during the beginning of the next hockey season, in fact. Howie suggested to the press that he might retire from hockey, that such a combined schedule would be too hectic, and that his first commitment would be to the voters. "I'll have to wait and see what happens, though, because I am, after all, still Conn Smythe's boy," he said, referring to his signed contract for that season.

In the final analysis, family and finances dictated that Howie would have to do both. Even if he wanted to (and he didn't), Howie could not afford to hang up his skates. Grace's ever-expanding tummy held the reason: a second child was scheduled to arrive in the world that November.

A rather galling phone call from Conn Smythe added a little fuel to the fire and influenced Howie's decision. Smythe was a man of many faces, moods, and skills. Cold, calculating, manipulative, generous and sometimes even wise, Conn got whatever Conn wanted. On the phone that day with Howie, Smythe deployed a few tried and true weapons, suspecting he could prod the rebellious right winger into playing another season or two. Smythe could certainly use Howie's skills and leadership on the ice, and the positive publicity of having an MP skating for his team would not hurt. Just prior to training camp, Smythe contacted Howie at home in New Hamburg and asked, "Are you going to come down and try out for the hockey team?"

"What do you mean, *try out* for the hockey team?"

"Well, I don't think you can make it."

Howie took the bait. "I'll make your hockey team standing on my head. There is no way, without trading me, that you can keep me off your team." A few days later Howie was in Toronto haggling over yet another contract.

"Well, how much money do you want this time?" Smythe asked begrudgingly.

"*If* I make your hockey team, I want $10,000." Howie was only earning about $8,500 at the time.

"There's no way you're going to get $10,000."

"Well, if I don't get $10,000, that's it, goodbye," Howie said, folding his coat and starting to rise from the chair.

"What the hell do you want $10,000 for? What makes you think you're worth that much?"

"Well, I've been in the league for five years and I've won four Stanley Cups. I'd say that means either I'm a good hockey player or you're pretty dumb for keeping me this long. I think $10,000 would assure me, in my mind, that I'm a pretty good hockey player and that I'm getting paid for it." Even as he spoke the words, Howie had a sneaking hunch there weren't too many guys of his calibre getting that high a wage.

"No, I'm sorry. The best I can do is $9,500."

"If you're going to give me $9,500, you may as well give me $500 more and make it an even $10,000. Then I'll walk out of here thinking the time I spent at Maple Leaf Gardens was worth it —

that I turned myself into a pretty good hockey player and I got a fair salary for one year, my last one."

Howie's persistence paid off. When he walked out of Maple Leaf Gardens that afternoon he had his $10,000 contract in hand. This time he had sense enough to make sure Miss McDonald got it on paper. "I did not shake hands on it," he says.

Howie showed up at training camp and made the hockey team again, despite a major reduction in his normal summer fitness regimen. However, political duty called, and before camp was even complete, Howie was back in Ottawa.

He did not plan on playing a full season, or even close to a full season, when the year started. It was understood by Smythe and coach Primeau that he would play as many games as reasonably possible given his political commitment. With so much to learn about his duties in Ottawa and the new constituency office in Galt, as well as keeping Grace and his growing family in New Hamburg happy, Howie was kept hopping.

Playing politics *and* hockey would demand a lot more work and travel for Howie, while for Grace it meant more time maintaining the home front alone. MPs who lived close to Ottawa often went home on weekends, and it wouldn't be difficult for Howie to catch a Friday-night train to Toronto. Instead of going home, however, Howie would play Saturday-night games with the Leafs. He could play most midweek games in Toronto and Montreal, then occasionally go home for brief visits. On Thursdays the Leafs often played in Montreal, so Howie could catch the 9 a.m. train, play a game there, and take the 11 p.m. train to Ottawa for the next day.

Howie hoped to avoid playing many games early in the season, but once again a telephone call made mockery of intent. Primeau phoned, said he was short of right wingers for Friday night's season opener at home against Chicago, and asked Howie to be there. When the puck was dropped, Howie was on the ice.

That Friday, October 13, night proved bad luck for Toronto as they lost the match 3–1, in front of a full house. No ill fate befell Howie, although his ten days off skates showed. Howie vowed to play better the next night in Detroit. Though he did not score, the Leafs were 3–2 victors, and Howie was clearly the winner in yet another scrap with Ted Lindsay. Wiry, fiery Ted wasted no time throwing the first political shot at Howie on ice, and referred to him just before the set-to as "your honourable asshole."

The political shots weren't all made in the heat of combat. A good chuckle was had by many over Howie's new off-ice profession. One evening he was playing his typical high-energy game and kept jumping into the circle too early during face-offs. After cancelling two face-off attempts due to Meeker's impatience, referee Red Storey admonished Howie by saying, "Would you kindly keep out of the circle, your Honour."

Later that season in Montreal, French-Canadian referee George Gravel tagged Meeker with a minor penalty. After informing Howie of the infraction, he wiggled his finger, and grinned, "Your Honour, please come wiz me to de penaltee box."

Amazingly, Howie managed to play in 54 of the 70 league games that season. Ten of the games he missed were due to yet another injury. In mid-December, in Detroit, Howie was cutting in towards Terry Sawchuk and the Red Wing net from his right-wing position when a Detroit defenceman cut his legs out from under him. Sawchuk jumped out of the way and Howie slid out of control into the goalpost, tearing a knee ligament. When he did return to action it was not without some pain and a lot of tape. In a 1952 *Star Weekly* article, Gordon Campbell quotes Toronto assistant trainer Bill Smith as saying Howie used five yards of tape each game in order to keep his knee mobile. "The 'Senator' needed ten yards of tape daily when his ribs were hurt, too, and that went on for two weeks. But he's had a piece of tape on ever since he started the game, so he should be used to it by now."

When he was healthy he spent most of his time skating

with partners Cal Gardner at centre, and Harry Watson. When he was absent, a promising rookie named George Armstrong often took his spot early in the year.

On January 9, 1952, Smythe traded Fleming MacKell to Boston for Jim Morrison, a bad trade, according to Howie, "because MacKell was a real buzz saw and among the best of the young offensive talent they had coming along."

In early February Howie took part in a Leafs' public relations visit that proved to be a little more unique than the usual schools, hospitals, service groups, and banquets. Howie, Sloan, Thomson, and coach Primeau took part in the opening-season inauguration of the St. Vincent de Paul Penitentiary Hockey League. St. Vincent de Paul was the largest "big house" in Quebec at the time and the league had six fairly competitive teams. The actual opening face-off speech and events had to be held three times, at different locations within the prison, because of security concerns with the large inmate population. Howie and crew had a great afternoon.

Howie received numerous congratulations as well as humorous verbal shots from inmates on his new political career but he was up to the challenge. One inmate asked if it was still difficult to get a ticket to a Leaf game. Howie responded that he would provide the ticket, "If you can get out."

"Swell, I'll be waiting for you at the corner of Church and Carlton in 1955," the inmate replied.

Howie won the game of words, though, when he told the crowds, "I think I know how you guys feel — after all, I'm a Progressive Conservative sitting in the House of Commons run by Liberals."

V

Howie's quick wit also came in handy back in Ottawa. One Thursday night Montreal beat Toronto 4–1 and Howie found himself fending off his Tory colleagues with a hard-luck story explaining why Toronto lost. That particular Friday, the prime minister, after question period, got up and crossed the floor, bowed to the Speaker, went by Conservative Leader George Drew, past all the Tory big shots, up a short flight of stairs and towards Howie. All of a sudden the fellow who shared Howie's desk, Walter Dinsdale, realized the PM was coming to see Howie and moved to a vacant seat behind them. Prime Minister Louis St. Laurent, slid in beside Howie and said, "Mr. Meeker, your team Toronto played in Montreal last night and took a beating; tell me about it."

Howie spent the next five minutes trying to make excuses and trying to get to know the prime minister, and after a joke or two the PM shook his hand, said "thank you," and stepped back across the floor.

After the PM's third trip across the floor to gloat about a Hab victory that first winter, most Liberal members knew what was going on. Those from Quebec took pleasure in watching Howie squirm because Toronto had an average team that year and they never did well in Montreal. The members of his own party started to get an idea of what was going on as well.

Finally, on March 5, 1952, Toronto whipped Montreal 6–2 with Howie getting a goal and an assist. The next morning Howie called C. D. Howe, the minister of trade and commerce and one of the government's biggest movers and shakers. Howie asked if, after question period, he could vacate his seat. Howie explained why, and the minister laughed heartily agreeing to the ruse.

That afternoon the prime minister was present for question period. "St. Laurent very rarely got caught in question period. He was the leader of the band. The guys who hit the drum, the guys who banged the cymbals, those were the guys that usually got into arguments — but old Louis would get away time after time after time."

When the Speaker closed the session to get on with the regular business of the House, Howie got up, walked down the stairs, bowed to the Speaker, and sat down as the honourable C.D. Howe moved out of his seat beside the prime minister. Howie said, "Prime Minister, question period is about to be reopened. The Toronto Maple Leafs played the Montreal Canadiens last night and we whipped their ass 6–2. Could you please explain this for us, sir?"

Unbeknownst to Howie, all the Conservative members knew what was going on and they pounded their desks, and laughed, as did many of the English-Canadian Liberals and members of the CCF. The prime minister chuckled and laughed for several minutes. After that Howie was often invited to his office when he had a few spare moments and they would talk hockey and politics.

Years later, when Howie was coaching the Leafs in Toronto, St. Laurent was at a game in Montreal and sought him out between periods. St. Laurent graciously accepted an invitation to come into the Leafs' dressing room and let Howie introduce him to the team.

Another character Howie came to know and admire was Lester B. Pearson, the minister of foreign affairs at the time. Pearson loved sports and was a big baseball fan. During that first winter in the House Howie often talked sports and hockey with him and mentioned he'd played some competitive ball. Pearson said he had seats at the baseball games and asked Howie if he would like to go sometime.

"Sure," Howie said. "Anytime. Just give me a holler."

One day after question period Howie saw Pearson scribble a note and raise his arm; a page was there like a flash, then headed in Howie's direction and handed him a note which read, "I have an extra seat at the ball game tonight. Would you like to go?" Howie scribbled a "Yes, sir," and two minutes later he had a ticket to Ottawa's Class C professional baseball team.

A ball game to Howie is really the pregame batting and fielding practice — what comes afterwards is considered a bonus. It was a 7:45 game but Howie arrived at 6 p.m. and the usher said, "Oh, Mr. Pearson's box is almost full already." "Yeah, right, don't give me that," Howie thought, but when the usher took him down to the seat there was the Honourable Mr. Pearson with four diplomats from Cuba and two from Mexico, up to their eyes in hot dogs, relish, mustard, beer, and Coke. "I thought right then, 'Gee, what a great way to do business.'" Pearson would later tell Howie about the ball games, "You know, Mr. Meeker, I accomplish more here in one hour with these people than I would in a week in my office in the House." At the end of the game Pearson introduced Howie to his chauffeur, who took him home in the limousine, which became a constant practice after that. At least once a week from then on Howie saw a ball game with Pearson and before the summer was over he was on a first-name basis with diplomats and bureaucrats from every part of the world.

Y

When the 1951–52 season was over Howie had scored just 9 times and added 14 assists for 23 points in his 54 games, not bad for a player used primarily in a checking role. His 50 minutes in penalties proved that none of his feisty, rambunctious attitude towards the game had disappeared. "I'd play pretty well without the puck but not very well with it, the result of missing numerous practices over the winter months. I was practising in Ottawa with the Senators Senior hockey club, but that's not the same. I was not in game condition. My loss of timing, which is everything in offence, was the main reason my goals dropped."

That season the Leafs still had problems, and again, it was lack of offence that did them in. Rollins played exceptionally well with 157 goals against for a strong 2.22 goals-against average, second-best in the NHL. On offence, Smith scored 27 goals and Sloan 25, while Max Bentley notched 24 goals and Kennedy 19. Those numbers were down overall from their normal totals, partly because Primeau placed a greater focus on defence that year to compensate for the lack of scoring punch. "With more defence thrust upon them, their offence was going to suffer. Those four guys scored 95 goals, which was two-thirds of the team's total, or pretty close to it. The rest of us scored just 73." That flaw would prove costly.

Toronto finished third behind a very powerful Detroit club in first, and the Canadiens in second. They finished four games above .500, but were no match for Detroit in the first round of the playoffs.

The red-hot Wings dominated Toronto throughout. In the first two games they shut down all Leaf scoring attempts as netminder Terry Sawchuk continued to demonstrate his outstanding goaltending. Detroit blanked Toronto 3–0 and 1–0 in Detroit, then in Game Three, in Toronto, thumped the Leafs 6–2. The scoring drought continued in the final game with the Red Wings winning 3–1 to sweep the series in four games. Toronto was outscored 13–3 overall.

"Losing that series, especially in four straight games, was probably my greatest disappointment in hockey. It really bothered me and I wasn't much good for a few days. Even though we lacked some scoring ability, we were a better club than that."

During his hockey and political career, Howie was often asked if hockey and politics mixed; could a hockey jock serve his constituents as well as the next guy? At that time he said, "Of course they can," and now adds that "today I know that is so even more. After many years in hockey, and even more in life itself, I believe that one's amount of knowledge of something is not always a factor in either the success of the operation, nor who is chosen to be in charge. In hockey, like in politics, I have seen many an incompetent person, with no knowledge of the game or the business, in the position of control or power. On occasion, I have seen them do superb jobs, but not often. The key is how quickly they learn, adapt, and apply themselves. Politics is a game much like hockey, and the sooner you learn the rules and how to work effectively within them — and perhaps how to improve or change them for the better — the more successful you will be."

When his term in office was complete in August 1953, Howie decided not to seek re-election, primarily because of his lack of time at home, and for financial reasons. "The pay was not good, nor did I see a long-term future in it, but actually I never enjoyed anything as much in my life, not even winning the Stanley Cup. Economically, though, I had to move on.

"Whether I did a good job or not is not for me to judge. Only the people I served can decide that. I hope I did; I certainly tried to."

Not everyone was impressed with Howie's role as an MP. After one session Howie returned home to New Hamburg and asked a local farmer if he'd heard his recent speech.

"Hmmmf, ya, I heard it."

"And what did you think?"

"Well, a damn good rain would have been a hell of a lot better," the farmer shrugged.

Ⅴ

During the summer of 1952 Howie thought a lot about retirement again, and recognized that another hectic season away from home would face him if he should continue to play. "I'd spent all my time between the House of Commons in Ottawa and the Toronto Maple Leafs, and I was never busier in my entire life. It seems I was spending my whole time travelling somewhere." Still, they needed the money, and Howie wanted one more Stanley Cup. He figured the club had potential for the 1952–53 season. They still had tremendous goaltending in Rollins, a solid defence that included youngster Tim Horton, a couple of valuable veteran snipers up front, and several promising youngsters.

If Howie noticed the team's potential, then obviously so did the man who'd largely created it. "Smythe could see that if some of our kids developed, we would have a pretty good hockey team down the road. In my mind, Smythe didn't want that to happen, and escalated his plans to get rid of Hap Day completely.

"Prior to the 1952–53 season, after our disastrous loss to Detroit due mainly to a lack of offence, what did Smythe do? On September 11, the Leafs gave away the best second-line centre in the league, Cal Gardner, along with our champion goalie Al Rollins, Gus Mortson, and Ray Hannigan, all to Chicago for Harry Lumley. That was the most lopsided trade in the history of the game of hockey. Then, on September 16, they gave away our best all-round hockey player, Joe Klukay. They *sold* him to Boston for Dave Creighton. I was stunned, absolutely stunned. Right then and there the Leafs were doomed to failure."

Dumb trades and pure giveaways by the general manager reduced the team's goal production, and despite very good goal-tending by Lumley, increased the goals against. Those trades also kicked some of the wind out of Howie's sails on the ice that season. Between his work in Ottawa, injuries, and the Leafs' plethora of youngsters trying to crack the lineup, Howie played just 25 games during that dismal 1952–53 season. "I spent much more time in Ottawa than in Toronto, and made more trips home."

The Leafs not only felt Howie's absence, they also missed captain Ted Kennedy for 27 games. Without Kennedy, Sloan's and Smith's goal production slipped considerably, and when Max Bentley began to have back problems his production fell off. It was a miserable year for everyone associated with the Leafs.

Near the end of the 1952–53 season, in a rough-and-tumble affair against the Bruins, Howie was checked and fell onto a board running along the fence that stuck up about six inches above ice level and out about an inch and a half. As he fell, he hit the board in the middle of his back and everything went dead from the hips down. Howie's worried teammates helped him onto a stretcher, and the arena crowd quieted as he left the ice. Fortunately, the paralysis was temporary, and though some disc damage was done and nerves pinched, the injury was not as serious as first appeared. "The feeling came back about a half-hour later and it developed into nothing but a bad bruise with some disc damage. But about this time I was thinking, 'I'm 30 years old and it's time to get out.'"

An incident late in the 1952–53 season occurred that would later haunt Howie as being the second time he "turned turtle" in a hockey game. Looking back, he realizes his hockey career should have ended at that moment.

"Montreal's Doug Harvey cut one of my teammates really good with his stick and I was on the ice at the time. Just as I started to step in to give him a stick in the head my brain thought, 'Wait a second, you're a member of Parliament and how would that look on national TV,' so I pulled short. Instead I just gave him a little shove, or something useless like that. As a teammate, I had to give it to Harvey just like he had to my fellow Leaf, but I didn't. I turtled, and I should have quit the game right then and there."

When the regular season ended, not only Howie's year was over early, so was that of his teammates. The club managed just 27 wins and 13 ties for 67 points and fifth place, two heartbreaking points behind Boston and Chicago. For the first time in his pro hockey career, Howie would miss the playoffs.

Some Leaf fans today pontificate that the club's problems in 1953 were largely due to the lack of a true team leader on the team with Kennedy's absence. Howie scoffs at the suggestion. "Funny how things change over the years. I've often wondered how come we won four Stanley Cups in five years without someone who was a 'rah-rah' type leader in the dressing room. I can only remember twice in six years when, before we headed for the opening whistle, somebody made an inspirational or stirring speech, and it was Conn Smythe both times. Hap Day at the noon meeting would sometimes point out the importance of that evening's game, and before going on the ice he would lean over as we were getting dressed and relay a short message, either technical or inspirational, to some of the players.

"Only once do I remember a player standing up. Captain Syl Apps, during the sixth game at home against the Canadiens in 1947, got up first to go on the ice and said, 'By hum, boys, it would be nice to win this one.' And we did.

"Syl was my captain for two years and Ted Kennedy for the next six years, and I can't remember another time anyone stood up and ranted, raved, threatened, or whatever, in an effort to get men ready for battle. There were times when Kennedy kicked my butt, and others as well, when we were on the ice. But along with the coach, the players know who's working and who isn't, and I more than had it coming whenever the captain gave me hell.

"We were hired players, retained for how we performed on the ice, and it was our responsibility to show up mentally prepared. It would have been an insult to every one of us if it was someone else's job to get us up for the game. I'm sure if it was a fellow player we would have pitched the S.O.B. out of the room. Apps, and then Kennedy, set the standards out on the ice, and you weren't part of the team very long if you consistently didn't measure up to their work standards. Big mouths were a dime a dozen. Consistent, all-out effort was, and is, hard to come by, but all that really counts."

No one had to light a match under Howie's butt come game day. In fact, getting near Howie on the day of a game was usually hazardous to one's health. Grace, most of all, paid the price. Howie started to get mentally prepared for a game around 2 p.m. Grace wouldn't talk to him from then until they arrived at Maple Leaf Gardens at 6:30. The half-hour ride was made in total silence and when she dropped him off she would say only, "Good luck." After the game, whether the team won or lost, Grace couldn't win.

"Good game," Grace would offer.

"What d'ya mean, good game?" Howie would bark and then curse, mutter, and grumble about the game. If Grace suggested the guys played terrible that night, it would be the opposite response. "What do you mean we were terrible tonight? *Rarr, rarr, rarr,* grumble, curse." After a while Grace gave up trying to read her husband's postgame moods and simply waited for Howie to speak first.

While recuperating at home under doctor's care near the end of the 1953 season, Howie received an interesting phone call. A good Ontario Hockey Association Senior A rivalry had developed between Kitchener and Stratford. The Kitchener-Waterloo Dutchmen had won the Allan Cup that year and the Stratford Indians' owner and operator Dutch Meier wanted to change that. Meier called Meeker, offered him the coaching job, and told him to visit soon.

Dutch reminded Howie of Heiney Wismer: big, round, fat, very stern-looking, but very jolly when he smiled. Meier had a red face, sparkling eyes, and a hand like a big, thick ham. Meier also had a very active, successful appliance store as well as a reasonably profitable jukebox and pinball machine business operating in a fifty-mile area, mostly west and northwest of Stratford.

After a very short conversation in the back of Meier's store the big man asked Howie, "Well, how am I going to get you here to Stratford?"

"Good question," Howie countered. "My basic salary with the Leafs is $10,000. I need that to survive in Stratford. I also need outside work."

Meier was a clever fellow and likely had the plan figured out long before Howie even walked in the door. "Well, you buy my jukebox business for $25,000 and you'll make at least $10,000 a year, and I'll pay you $5,000 a year to coach my hockey team."

After an unsuccessful search for the funds Howie suggested to Grace that they could get $12,500 or more for their house in New Hamburg, rent a home in Stratford, and purchase half of Dutch's business, with the option to purchase the other half at any time. When Howie approached Dutch with the proposition, he agreed.

"What if my back gets better and I can play for the Toronto Maple Leafs?" Howie asked, not convinced he was done with the game.

"Go play. You'll find someone to run the business and we'll find someone to coach. We'll wait for you." Howie couldn't believe his luck.

Howie worked strenuously at rehabilitating his back all summer. Despite its obvious strength it was still not right. When he moved it up and down it was as strong as a steel chain, but a twisting motion, such as a golf or baseball swing made Howie feel as if someone was sticking a knife in his back. In hopes of playing hockey again Howie even retired from his summer passion of playing senior ball with the Kitchener Legionnaires. When he quit that spring it was not only as the team's third baseman, but also as coach.

By late August even the pinched-nerve pain from gentle twisting had eased somewhat in Howie's back and his desire to play hockey again had returned. When NHL training camp opened in St. Catharines, Howie was ready. "On the Sunday we had our medical Dr. Jim Murray gave my back quite a testing and finally said 'squat.' He put all of his 190 pounds, or as much of it as he could, on my shoulders and said, 'Now get up.' Howie lifted Murray off his feet like he was a feather. Everyone was all smiles — Howie included — but deep down he knew it wasn't the up-and-down movement that was the problem.

Workouts went fine the first week, with no pain, and then Howie and the training staff did a dumb thing. "Normally, first thing in the morning we walked briskly to the park, ran around it a couple of times, and did some upper-body strengthening exercises. We played at getting into condition. What a laugh compared to today's athletes and their rigorous conditioning programs. This day, the instructor brought some medicine balls. The drill was to get four or five guys back-to-back in a circle, hold the ball at arm's length, turn and pass it to the fellow beside you. If I would have had half a brain I'd have refused to do the drill, but no, I reached to get the ball, turned my body, stretched to give it to my partner and *yow*, there was that knife in my back."

Months of work were eliminated in mere seconds as Howie sank to his knees in agony, his season over before it would really start.

Before a dejected Howie emptied his stall in the familiar Maple Leaf dressing room that early fall, Hap Day gave him a $1,000 retainer, just in case he could play a game or two for the Leafs later on in the winter.

Howie sold the wonderful house in New Hamburg, paid Dutch $12,500 for half of his business, which Red and Howie were to run, and moved to a very small house in Stratford.

Doors of opportunity open and close often in life and when Howie's days of playing pro hockey were slammed shut that September afternoon, a career in coaching the game opened up.

Nine

Behind the Bench

"No matter what I've worked on in my life, and very few people have had the variety of jobs I've had, no matter how successful I was at the time, thanks to Eddie Shore I've always tried to make things a little better."

Coaching may be a fascinating, challenging job, but when one shifts from being a player to being the boss, things change. You may still be part of the team, but you're not one of the guys anymore. It was an element of coaching Howie had heard about, and knew he would experience now that he'd decided to coach the Stratford Indians. The OHA Senior A hockey league was a long way from the NHL, but Howie looked forward to teaching and building a winning team.

The September night before the Indians' training camp opened,

Howie lay awake thinking about his next challenge as Howie Meeker, coach. He felt anxious, a sensation he hadn't known since his rookie season. His mind flashed back to his Junior days, when coach Al Murray had scratched play patterns and strategies on the chalkboard. He remembered how so many of Murray's patterns never made any sense until years later in England when, during an army leave, he had attended a soccer game at London's Wembley Stadium. Perched high up in that famous building, looking down at the spider-sized men scurrying over the massive soccer pitch, Howie suddenly saw Murray's play patterns unfold before him. The light bulb came on.

Now it would soon be Howie's turn at the chalkboard. As he drifted off to sleep his final thoughts were, "Tomorrow, I get my first crack at trying to teach game skills, teaching how to play the game of hockey and win."

That summer, Howie had contacted Hap Day and inquired how many graduating Marlboro Juniors he planned to sign. Day said three, maybe four players, and named them. "That leaves Lou Bendo, Ron Ingram, and goaltender Don Head. Can I talk to them?" Howie asked. With the approval given, Howie signed the three, all of whom turned out to be good kids and excellent hockey players. The Indians also picked up two other Juniors: Fred Pletch from Barrie, and walk-on Bobby Mader from Elmira. Pletch was a big, strong, gangly kid while Mader was the opposite — short, slight, and lightning-quick. "Kitchener didn't want him, but he turned out great," Howie says. "He was just 120 pounds soaking wet, but he had a heart that wouldn't quit."

During training camp the feeling in Stratford, and around the league, was that the Indians, led by the great line of Mickey Roth, Billy Flick, and Danny Flanagan, would challenge everybody for the top spot and easily make the playoffs. It didn't work out that way. In fact, Stratford spent most of the year in a life-and-death struggle with Chatham for the fourth and final playoff position. Howie attributes part of that poor showing to his inexperience in coaching.

"For years I've offered the opinion that after the top two or three players in the NHL Junior draft, the rest that graduate know as much about playing the game as I know about flying a spaceship. When I look back, I guess that goes for players who turn into coaches, as well. My, oh my, was I green!"

When the season began Howie had had enough sense to leave the Mickey Roth line alone; the boss loved them, the fans loved them, and the press loved them. For years they had been by far the best and most productive line in the league, and Howie patiently waited for them to strut their stuff. But after fifteen games, with Flanagan twenty-five pounds overweight and not skating, Billy Flick not using his great shot, and Roth not doing much of anything, the team was in fifth spot.

Indians owner Dutch Meier advised, "Leave them alone, they'll come out of it," but they didn't. Howie tinkered with the rest of the lineup and things started to take shape, but the hotshots were still cold, and the team continued to stumble. The young goaltenders, Don Head and Keith Dale, took turns being "either sensational or terrible, not from game to game, but from period to period."

Howie knew Head could eventually be a very good goaltender. "He stood up well. All Don needed to do was improve his stick-work, learn when to attack the shooter, and gain a little experience." He eventually played with the Boston Bruins, as well as in the AHL and WHL.

In February 1954, Stratford was still grinding along, fighting for a playoff spot. Howie figured he'd been patient enough waiting for the Roth trio to turn it around, so he told Dutch it was time they met with the lacklustre line and laid down the law. At the meeting Howie said, "Boys, from now on it's either/or, and the 'or' is that you don't play, as a single person or as a group, unless you perform up to your standards." While he had their attention Howie further explained, "You play behind our blue line my way, or you sit. On offence you can do it your way for now. I'll give you three games to raise your level there as well, and if you don't play well on offence, you sit."

Looking back, Howie says, "I think they resented me getting into their turf and getting some of their attention. It was always *their* town, *their* territory. They were the boss; *they*, not Dutch or the coach, ran the club. Even though their performance was off 40 percent, until that moment they had done things their way."

Coaching Stratford, like most jobs, had both positive and negative attributes. One of the negatives was that it wasn't his home town of Kitchener, and the Kitchener fans never let him forget it. When the Indians visited the Dutchmen, Howie's appearance only fanned the fires of a hot rivalry between the two towns. Bedlam and mayhem accompanied many matches. During that season at least two games turned into knock-'em-down, drag-'em-out affairs. Pugnacious and cantankerous as always, Howie was pitched out of both games. In the second event, Stratford was leading by two goals and just as Mickey Roth, who'd finally come to life and was playing great hockey, came off the ice, a large ball of wet paper hit him right between the eyes. Howie turned in time to see the follow-through of the guy throwing it. Behind the bench was a six-foot wall of cement, with an eighteen-inch railing on top of it, and then the first row of seats. The assailant was three or four rows up, but before he could sit down, Howie was there and got a few licks in before the police arrived. The first officer on the scene grabbed Howie's raised fist and said, "Howie, I'm sorry, we've got to stop this," and pulled him off. When the ruckus was subdued Howie returned to the bench, but referee Hughie McLean said, "Howie, I hope you got him good."

"Yeah, I did."

"Well, I'm glad 'cause, jeez, kid, the rules say I've got to throw you out of the game."

"Okay, no problem," Howie concurred, but McLean grabbed his arm and said, "Look, see that seat on the aisle, up behind your bench? I'll have the police find that guy sitting there another seat and you can sit there and run the team."

Howie had enough sense to know there would have been a riot if he ran the team from the stands, so he said, "Thanks, but no thanks." Mickey Roth took over for the rest of the game, which Stratford won.

Howie finally fired up all three forward lines at the same time and in the final few weeks managed to skim into the playoffs. And what was the reward for such effort? The team once again had to face the K-W Dutchmen, the defending Allan Cup champions, a team loaded with talent.

Against all odds the Stratford players displayed their best hockey all year, and in a wild and woolly session, defeated Kitchener.

In the dressing room after the game, players and close supporters celebrated as if they'd just won the Allan Cup, not the OHA's first round. Howie sensed the celebration would be short-lived. "Sure, we had beaten the Allan Cup champions, but there was a very experienced, talented Owen Sound team still between us and even a crack at that Cup." Although he tried not to show it, he was delighted with the victory over the Dutchmen. A touching moment for Howie, however, was when Uncle Harry Wharmsby, still with the Waterloo Dutchman, came to congratulate him.

In the league finals against the Owen Sound Mercurys, Howie figured his club had a fifty-fifty chance if the Indians played with as much determination and discipline as they had against Kitchener, and received hot goaltending as well. In the first game Stratford was flat, with so-so goaltending. Owen Sound star Tommy Burlington and friends gave Stratford a pretty good hockey lesson, winning the game soundly. The Indians lost the series four straight. Howie insists that Owen Sound "played dirty pool; they wouldn't let us have the puck. The few times we did get near the doorstep their goaltender stoned us. Having me, a greenhorn, behind the bench cost us a lot. Our young, inexperienced kids couldn't carry the extra load of an inexperienced coach. I guess I had as much, or more, to do with our failure as anyone.

"Ten years later, if I had that situation over again I'd have done things differently. First game after the first bad goal, I'd have put Don Head in net for Dale, then on the ensuing face-off I'd have put my five toughest players on the ice with instructions to start a war. In the next face-off, playing three against three, we'd have had another small riot, because unless we got back to that emotional level we had against Kitchener we were dead."

Ｙ

While at Stratford, Howie was so busy teaching game and individual skills during ice time that he didn't keep himself in playing condition. One Monday morning in February, he received a call from Hap Day. "Howie, we're hurting on right wing; we've got games Thursday, Saturday, and Sunday, come on down," Day prodded.

"Hap, my back feels fine, but I'm in terrible condition. Try Pittsburgh, try the Marlies, St. Mikes — heck, even try Stratford," Howie pleaded.

"You'll be the extra forward, the fifteenth man, maybe kill penalties. You probably won't even get on the ice," Day said.

When Howie hung up he started thinking about the payment offered: $150 per game, for three games, was pretty good money. With yet another child on the way he and Grace could use the dollars. Howie phoned the rink, arranged some practice time, and tried to get in game shape in three days.

Forty-three years later Howie can still remember his stomach and legs rebelling, time after time, at what his mind was trying to make them do. "Many times during the previous seven years, when coming off injury, we punished my body in a rush to get back playing. When I look back I wonder why the rush. After the first year I don't think I averaged 15 goals a season. But this torture test was the worst of all."

Howie then discovered his first game was against the Montreal Canadiens. "Just my luck to get really embarrassed tonight," he thought. To make matters even worse, Tod Sloan was hurt and coach Primeau told Howie to start the game playing right wing on the top line with Teeder Kennedy. "Fifteenth man and maybe some penalty killing, my ass," he thought, shaking his head as he skated onto the familiar Maple Leaf Gardens ice. Added to the pressure was the knowledge that many of the Leaf games were now being shown on television. Foster Hewitt and crew had experimented with broadcasting some Leaf games the previous season, Howie's final year of regular play. Now out of condition, Howie was concerned about looking bad in front of the whole nation.

While Howie was obviously out of shape, he still more than held his own, and the Leafs did okay in the three games, collecting a win, a tie, and a loss. "I got lucky and scored a goal, and even made a few good plays and checks. In the first game Lumley saved my ass. Late in the tie game I had the puck just inside the face-off circle, and for some stupid reason I threw it in the middle. I knew the second it went off my stick it would end up on a Canadien stick, which it did, but Harry made a hell of a save. I went over and thanked him and made sure I had a beer for him when he climbed aboard the train."

After the Saturday game, while on the train with the team, Howie talked with Primeau and Day. The trio yapped about the Leafs, about the Stratford team, coaching, and the three Stratford players — Bendo, Ingram, and Head — who belonged to Toronto. Howie suggested all three could someday play professional hockey.

At breakfast the next morning in the dining car, just as Howie was draining his orange juice, Hap asked, "If a coaching position became open in the Leaf system, would you be interested?" Howie nearly spewed juice over a passing waiter.

Howie had some security in Stratford. He and Red Wallace were learning the jukebox business and enjoying it, and Dutch offered

Howie a half-interest in the team and a long-term contract. But Howie had discovered that in most Senior hockey cities the expenses far outnumbered income and even if an owner toughed it out, and covered his yearly losses, there was the risk that his part-ners, or other teams, might go under and the league fold. Howie mentally began making a case for moving. He knew that Grace was tired of Stratford and they now had Jane, Peggy, and baby Kim living in their small house. Other than Red and Betty, they hadn't made many new friends.

Howie told Hap he'd talk to Grace and Dutch about it.

"By all means, let's get out of here," Grace told Howie. Dutch, meanwhile, gave Howie an open-ended contract saying that as long as Dutch was in hockey, Howie could come back, own half the Stratford hockey club, and be involved. A few days later Howie called Hap and said that he would indeed be interested in a coach-ing job somewhere.

After the NHL season Hap called and explained that Primeau was retiring and that King Clancy, who had coached in Pittsburgh for the last two years, was to coach the Leafs. Would Howie be interested in coaching Pittsburgh? Hap explained that since it was a minor-league job Howie would only get a minor-league salary. The top wage he could offer was $7,000 for the season. Howie was already getting $5,000 for coaching at Stratford, not including his thriving business venture and cheap rent just twelve miles from family and friends.

"If I go to Pittsburgh I'm eight hours' drive from home," Howie told Hap. "Jeez, I've got to talk to Grace. Is there no two- or three-year deal? No moving or travel expenses, no team performance bonuses, bonuses for developing talent? Just a flat $7,000?"

"No, I'm sorry, that's it. But I'll talk to the owner, John Harris, and see if he can add something. I'll call you back in a few days."

The next day Hap phoned Howie and said Mr. Harris would add $1,000 if Pittsburgh reached the finals and $500 more if they won it. Howie asked, "How good will we be, Hap? I don't have a clue about the quality of the league or whether Pittsburgh will be competitive or not." Hap assured Howie that with good coaching and a few breaks, Pittsburgh should be able to make the finals.

When Howie talked to Grace again, she said, "Go, at any price."

Howie wanted to talk to Dutch and his banker again before saying yes to the Pittsburgh offer. "The last time I saw my banker I was trying to borrow $12,500 to purchase half of Dutch Meier's jukebox business. At the time, the bank assured me that I was in a very enviable financial position — no debts, some assets — but no, the bank would not lend me $12,500 to purchase Mr. Meier's business. I tried several other people and businesses in New Hamburg without success. So I got to thinking, well, I've got to protect my ass. Even though I have Dutch's guarantee of a hockey job there might not be a team to come back to. If Pittsburgh doesn't work out, what will I do?"

Finally Howie and Grace decided to be bold and gamble on Pittsburgh for the 1954–55 hockey season. "When I did decide to go, Red and I agreed I should sell my half of the business back to Dutch. He gave me $5,000 more than what I paid for it."

Y

In July 1954, Howie flew to Pittsburgh to meet team owner John Harris, his right-hand partner, tobacco-chewing Jim Balmer, and their hockey man, Baz Bastien. John Harris was a successful entrepreneur who, in addition to the Pittsburgh Hornets hockey club, owned the Ice Follies and had married the star of one of his shows. Baz had been a very good goaltender with plenty of NHL potential until he lost his eye to a puck at a Pittsburgh training camp in the 1940s. Howie had actually joined other Maple Leaf players in visiting Baz in the hospital soon after the injury.

After discussing what players they had, and what they might get from Toronto, Baz agreed the team could be very competitive. At lunch, when Howie mentioned he would need a place to live, he was told that Baz had three homes lined up for him to check out, all with reasonable rents.

The Hornets' training camp was held at Niagara Falls, Ontario — just fifteen minutes' drive from the Leafs' camp at St. Catharines, but the two camps might as well have been half a hemisphere apart. If the Leaf camp had reflected a militant, no-nonsense, high pressure atmosphere, the Hornets' camp was just the opposite. A relaxed climate prevailed everywhere: on the ice, in the dressing room, at the hotel, on the street. It was a fun training camp, so much so that the wives, Grace included, often came to camp Friday, went to the game that night (or read a book as Grace would do), stayed Saturday, and left Sunday for home. "They even had their meals with us," Howie says. "After eight years of no wives at training camp or during the playoffs, what a pleasant change. The real boss, Smythe, was fifteen miles down the road and apparently had very little, if any, interest in anything other than what we did on the ice."

Baz was correct in his assessment of the talent in Pittsburgh. Skinny Gil Mayer was a great goalie, small but very quick, stood up, played his angles very well, and hardly ever gave away easy goals. The Hornet defence was led by Frank Mathers, undoubtedly the best defenceman outside of the NHL and actually better than many in it. Mathers was tough, talented, very durable, and taught many a raw rookie how to play the game. For toughness, Pittsburgh had Ray Gariepy and Bill Burega. "My, oh my, when they went headhunting, it was a pleasure to watch," Howie says. "You couldn't play them together, but put either one on the ice with a finesse hockey player and they'd contribute." Out front the Hornets' sting was provided by Willie Marshall, a tiny but talented centre with a big heart; veteran Andy Barbe, "the best up-and-down winger I've ever seen"; Bob Solinger, who, when happy and contented was a great hockey player; and Gerry Foley, a tough kid who skated just well enough to get there and was the best second-line player in the league. Those fellows gave Howie a solid footing to build on. When he analysed the Leaf roster, he was confident he'd get Marc Reaume, Bob Bailey, and Jack Price on defence, and perhaps forwards Ray Timgren, Bob Hassard, Jack Caffery, Earl Balfour, Gord Hannigan, and Hugh Barlow. The Hornets looked to be competitive.

Before camp ended, Day gave Howie his orders. After each game he wanted a written report on the three best Pittsburgh players; the best opposition players; if any could be future NHLers; full records of goals for and goals against, as well as plus-minus stats. Although Howie never received orders for it, he also sent written descriptions to Hap of every goal scored against. "While a Leaf, when things got bad, and goals against were bad, chances were that the coach would go over what players were doing when each goal was scored. I carried that tradition to Pittsburgh to a degree, but unlike in Toronto, I didn't have the help of film footage."

Game scores in the American league on average were much higher than the NHL, so even though Pittsburgh was the best defensive team in the league, they quite often allowed five goals or more. Howie often went on the road with the team alone, and along with all the other chores of directing a team from the bench, had to record all Day's required data. But twenty-five or so letters to Hap and about 100 goals later, he had a much better understanding of team and individual defence. On the road, unless they had a train or a bus to catch immediately after the game, Howie and Baz would disagree over beer as to who was on the ice, and why, or how the goal was scored.

When Howie eventually wound up coaching Toronto, Hap's secretary, Doris Ludlow, told him that both Hap and King howled with laughter when they read his letters from Pittsburgh. "Some of my descriptions must have created a chuckle or two, especially regarding my two toughies, Gariepy and Burega. They ran at everything, every time, everywhere, at any cost. There's a time for aggressive checking and a time for sensible hockey, but not with those two; but God bless them — they were great guys.

"Up front, Caffery, Sabourin, and Barlow would just up and

disappear, like Houdini. I'd be looking everywhere, they're not on the bench; they're not in the penalty box; they're not on the ice — they must have gone out the Zamboni door. After some high-scoring games (and after three beers and a good sandwich) when describing the fifth or sixth goal against, on paper with Baz, even I used to have a laugh."

Ⅴ

In Howie's neighbourhood in Pittsburgh he came to meet several kids and teenagers, a number of whom were tough cases, who really just needed or craved some attention. Howie took a couple of them under his wing, providing them with sticks, pucks, and conversation. In return they provided him with some amusement as well.

"One particular Halloween the kids had had enough with a grumpy old bugger who lived across the street. They placed a whole bunch of dog dung in a paper bag, placed it on the grouchy guy's step, lit it on fire, rang the doorbell, and sat on their bikes on the road to watch. They called me first to watch the show. Naturally the old guy came outside, saw the fire, and stomped on the burning bag. He was so incensed that he ran inside, shoes covered in the stuff, and grabbed his car keys so as to chase the kids. But they were a step ahead of him and had tied the screen door to the car's bumper. You can imagine what happened next," Howie chuckles.

The next day, when a police car showed up, Howie intervened and told the neighbour and the policeman that he would pay for the screen door. "It was worth it just for the laugh," Howie recalls. "Eventually the neighbour saw the humour, too, but it took a while."

Ⅴ

The 1954–55 Pittsburgh Hornets may have been a good club, but so was every other team in the American Hockey League: Hershey, Cleveland, Buffalo, Springfield, and Providence. Springfield was independently owned by the legendary Eddie Shore, while the others were farm clubs of NHL teams.

During the club's first road trip the Hornets played in Springfield and Howie briefly got to meet Eddie Shore, who was often the talk of hockey players over a beer or two around various leagues. There were many funny and fascinating stories told about Eddie's hockey philosophy, his practices, and his handling of men — not to mention his 14-year career in the NHL as a rugged but talented player. At a 7:30 a.m. practice, Baz took Howie into a tiny office and introduced him to Shore, who was lacing on his skates for practice. "Two things flashed through my mind right away: 'Jeez, he's not as big as I thought,' only about five foot ten, 170 pounds; and those eyes — Connie Smythe, Rocket Richard, Ted Lindsay, C. D. Howe had those sort of eyes. You knew that behind those eyes there was something going on — maybe good or maybe bad, but definitely something."

Shore was the sole owner. He also was the general manager, coach, publicity director, stick boy — Eddie did just about everything including run and work the concession stands. Shore often would make the players work the stands and sell game programs. "Did he ever run a different practice," Howie says. "They were light years ahead of the norm. Some things were way, way out, but if you could separate the wheat from the chaff his storage bin was mostly full of wheat." For an hour and a half all the drills were aimed at improving the individual skills, physical and mental, and the next hour was a scrimmage to improve team skills.

It was mid-February before Howie got to talk to Shore again. Springfield had very little trouble beating Pittsburgh through vigorous forechecking and Howie had to leave the bench and watch from the stands to figure out why. He saw that Shore broke the golden rule of defencemen — always have one defenceman in front of the net in your own end. Shore applied that rule when the opposition had the puck, but the second Shore's guys got the puck the rearguard left the front of the net and took part in bringing the puck out of their zone. Under the normal system of the day, four defenders would try to beat three forecheckers, but Shore increased the odds. He involved five people against three, and it worked. It wouldn't be long before teams everywhere adopted the system.

Baz and Howie took Shore to lunch and Howie was full of questions. "Mr. Shore, you are not affiliated with any pro club. How do you get quality players and stay competitive? Your training, practices, and game philosophy are different than everyone's; are we all wrong and you right?" And finally, "Mr. Shore, my team is fighting for first place and yours for fourth, why?"

Eddie grinned and told Howie that "Mr. Shore the general manager is not giving Mr. Shore the coach the offensive skills or tools needed to win. Mr. Shore the coach is mainly responsible for how his team plays without the puck, and with the puck coming out of the defensive zone. Mr. Shore the coach, other than putting the offensive units together, has little or no influence on offence. Mr. Shore the coach can improve skating, puck-handling, passing, and thinking skills, but can't teach goal-scoring skills; it's a gift or is self-taught. Also, physical and mental toughness is a scarce commodity in hockey these days and those with it usually aren't available to an independent operator. So Mr. Shore the owner is angry at Mr. Shore the general manager because of sparse crowds, because of lack of offensive talent and physical toughness, and Mr. Shore the coach is also angry at Mr. Shore the general manager because he is doing his job, which is keeping the goals against respectable, while Mr. Shore the general manager isn't doing his, and that's supplying the offensive skills or the toughness."

Howie would recall that conversation a few years later when the Maple Leafs' general manager gave away gifted offensive talent like MacKell, Lewicki, Nesterenko, and others. Years later when Wayne Gretzky and the Edmonton Oilers were winning Cups while filling the net at a record pace, the conversation among TV crews would eventually turn to the playing of hockey. Howie pontificated a dozen times a year that if he was an owner and his coach couldn't keep the goals against below three, Meeker would fire him. "The young, talented TV pups in the crew would think, 'Ahh gee, old age does strange things to the mind; poor Howie.' But I repeated to anyone over the years who would listen that it was the coach's job to supply defence and the general manager's responsibility to supply offence. Again, they thought, 'Two scotches and he's lost his mind.'

"Shore was a different kind of dude with very different ideas on hockey and life. Day, Primeau, and Clancy taught me a lot about hockey, but so did Eddie Shore. The biggest lesson by far, though, was to take a look at what you are doing and make it better; don't be afraid to change the rules, try new ideas. There is always something better, something smarter. How many times I've heard that sometimes silly statement, 'If it's not broke, don't fix it.' No matter what I've worked at in my life, and very few people have had the variety of jobs I've had, no matter how successful I was at the time, thanks to Eddie Shore I've always tried to make things a little better."

Howie's job for Leaf general manager Hap Day was to develop talent. At the same time, Pittsburgh Hornet owner John Harris relied on him to win games and fill Duquesne Gardens, a rundown, former streetcar barn infested with the biggest rats in the league. It was a juggling act keeping both parties happy: one wanting you to play the kids late in the game to protect the slim lead or earn a tie, the other demanding you play the veterans. "As the season wore on I found out my kids were good enough to do the job at any time, so it made it a fun season."

Howie talked with Hap about every ten days and began to suspect Day was on the phone with Baz regularly. Howie would receive notes from Hap regarding certain prospects and what he should do to help them develop. In Howie's mind that was simple. "If the player was a defenceman, I'd put him with Mathers, and shut up. If he was a winger, I'd put him with Willie Marshall, and shut up. If he was a centre man, I'd put him with Andy Barbe and Bob Solinger, and shut up. If the kid had talent, heart, and was teachable, those guys would do the job. Poor Frank Mathers was partnered regularly with our rawest rookie or least talented defenceman. Willie Marshall put so many kids home free, Balfour and

Sabourin in particular, at least a hundred times each before they learned how to score a goal."

In early January, Howie received a phone call from Hap, just after Pittsburgh had played Springfield on a Sunday and Providence on Monday then headed home. "How'd the game go in Springfield?" Hap asked.

"We won it 7–5. That Eddie Shore and his system of coming out of his own end gives us problems. He's got a couple of guys who can score goals, their goaltending was very good, we were behind most of the game but came back and won it."

Suddenly Howie became suspicious that Hap knew more than what he was letting on. When Howie hung up the telephone he thought, "Jeez, Baz wasn't with me on the last trip. Where did Hap get his firsthand information? Who was he talking to?"

Howie knew Hap and Eddie Shore were pretty good buddies, but Shore wouldn't say much about anything to anybody — he was far too sly for that. Later, Howie looked at the Maple Leafs schedule and they had played in Toronto Saturday, Boston on Sunday, and in New York Wednesday. Howie figured Hap travelled with the Leaf team to Boston, slipped over to Springfield, then to Providence, on to New York, and home Monday. The next time Howie phoned Toronto he asked Doris Ludlow, "What hotel did Hap stay at in Springfield?" With no reason to suspect that Howie didn't know Day was there, Ludlow told him. Years later, Meeker found out from Clancy that Day had done the same with him when Clancy coached in Pittsburgh. "I guess he was just checking our reports to him, but he saw both of those games and didn't let me know he was there."

Ɣ

When the regular season ended, Howie and the Hornets flagged first place and won the first round against Hershey. In the championship round they faced a determined Buffalo club. "We had very little trouble with them during the regular season but playoffs are always different." Buffalo travelled to Pittsburgh for the first game and stoned their hosts, but the Hornets rebounded and won the second game. Buffalo refused to go down easy, only bowing out in the sixth game when Timgren scored the winner for Pittsburgh. Howie hovered in hockey heaven.

Most American Hockey League players, fringe NHLers, were great people, Howie recalls. Their basic pay wasn't very much — $3,500 to $5,000 — but most had contracts with bonus clauses for points, mainly goals. And there was Howie, on behalf of the Toronto Maple Leafs, making it much harder for them to collect their bonuses, which they all needed or deserved to get.

In those days contract talk or even exchanging such information was taboo. Even as a coach it was hard for Howie to obtain any information from Baz or Jim Balmer. When he asked Baz for salary figures Bastien would offer a guess, but wouldn't know for sure. Balmer, when quizzed, would take another bite of his chewing tobacco and say, "Toronto signed him and we just pay a portion of his salary, so I can't answer your question." So Howie would meet with each player and ask them about their bonuses, then he made sure each veteran had an opportunity to earn the bonus.

When the season ended Howie wrote his final report to Hap, then did a strange thing . . . he took a holiday. After past hockey seasons Howie had always immediately begun to play ball or gone to work for at least a month each summer on their fishing lodge at remote Caribou Lake. What with training camps, politics, ball, hunting and fishing trips, and other assorted distractions and commitments, over the years Howie and Grace had never taken a real holiday. So Howie suggested they take a trip to New York, down to Florida, then home to New Hamburg. Howie and Grace were pleased to be managing financially much better on their $7,000 than they had ever done before. But when Howie suggested that they fly in his mom to look after the kids while they were on holidays, Grace thought Howie had lost his marbles. "What? You and me, go on a holiday? We've got the money, and you've got the time? You're kidding, right?"

Grace sputtered in a combination of disbelief and sarcasm.

Howie and Grace set off, making the grievous error of driving their car to the Big Apple. Just getting to the hotel was a miracle. It was a decision Howie never repeated.

That evening Howie noticed the Dodgers were playing the next afternoon, and the Yanks were playing at night. After some fast talking he convinced Grace she wanted to see the games. At 10 a.m. Howie and Grace started for the subway to the ballpark at Ebbetts Field. Four trains later (it should have only been two), they arrived. It was a 1:30 game and there was hardly anyone there. Grace and Howie were into the hot dogs and beer and at about the eighth inning the Dodgers blew the lead; it was a tie game that went into extra innings. The day had started out sunny, but now it was cloudy and cold and they were into the hot coffee instead of the beer. Howie wisely said, "Let's go get dinner somewhere, and then we'll go to Yankee Stadium."

Anyone who has ever been to New York will testify that trying to catch the subway in Brooklyn at 4:30 p.m. is an insane idea. Finally, amidst the rush-hour madness, Howie grabbed Grace, ran upstairs, and after a fifteen-minute search finally landed a cab. But travel by car was even worse. Every street was blocked and a half-hour later, at a cost of $5.50 and a tip, they were back at the hotel.

Over dinner, as they were waiting for dessert, Howie leaned over to Grace and said, "Grace, let's finish the coffee, go upstairs and make love, and go see a movie. In the morning we'll get the hell out of here and head for Florida." Grace looked Howie right in the eye and replied, "Okay, but let's change the order of things. We'll see the movie first."

Howie and Grace spent a wonderful week in a motel on Pompano Beach beside the sea. One day Howie shared the cost of a fishing boat with another motel guest and caught his first saltwater fish, a sixty-five-pound sailfish. "Until then I hadn't seen anything so spectacular in the water. With that big sail you could see him attack the bait, hit it, come out of the water two or three times in what looked like six-foot leaps, then out of the water again the length of his body, sort of sit on his tail and walk along the top of the water with his head thrashing back and forth trying to shake the hook.

"Once the guide realized that he didn't have a complete idiot on the rod, he settled back and enjoyed the fifteen-minute fight as much as I did. His wife was at the helm and I did not realize how great a job she did. Later in my fishing life, with 300- to 500-pound tunas hooked to my line, I discovered that the handling of the boat was every bit as important to success as the handling of the rod."

After a sound battle by all involved, Howie boated the fish. As he was having his picture taken with the catch, the guide assured Howie that it was a very big sailfish and would cost about $125 to have it mounted. "I didn't have that kind of money at the time, so we gave the fish to the crew. Since then I've caught hundreds of what you would call big fish, but nothing has been as beautiful or thrilling as the first three or four minutes after I hooked into that sailfish.

"A couple of years ago, while on holidays with Grace in Kenya, I caught and released nine sailfish in one outing. Their performance in the warm Indian Ocean was almost as thrilling as the one in the Atlantic."

Y

With the holiday complete and another five-week adventure and work period at Caribou Lake over, Howie, Grace, and family returned to Pittsburgh to prepare for the 1955–56 season. For the most part, the club remained intact and most observers anticipated another Calder Cup championship. Of significance to Howie was the $1,000 raise he received, skyrocketing his income to $8,000. Not bad for a coach in the minors.

Any coach or general manager worth their salt would have anticipated possible problems the next season, especially with the quality veteran players if they weren't appeased. The veterans maintained that since they'd finished first and won the Calder Cup they should get a raise, and the $500 offered to some wasn't enough. As Howie puts it now, "Sure, your hot-shot kids, with the NHL in their eyes, will give you a hundred percent — but the results of that in games won is not impressive. It's that core body of nine or ten veterans who determine the outcome of most games, and when individually or collectively unhappy, the team is in trouble, and we were."

The problems began in goal, where Gil Mayer seemed to have lost his touch. Small, very quick, and competitive, Mayer was good enough to deserve a shot at the NHL but was playing for peanuts. Ten games into the season, Baz and Howie knew Mayer's problems in net were a combination of things, including guessing and going down on his knees or body too early in the play. "Weeks later, after Baz, a former goalie, and I tried every known trick in the goal-tending book to get him going, he still wasn't there. On Hap Day's advice I threatened to fine him $100. Well, Gil panicked, packed his bags and went home." Eventually Gil came back, got on track, and the problem was solved.

A handful of new players joined the club, including rugged defencemen Larry Cahan and Jack Bionda. Bionda was a great Canadian lacrosse legend, probably the best the game ever had, but on skates he did not fare as well. Up front, new players included Parker MacDonald and Brian Cullen, a superstar junior out of St. Catharines. The newcomers gave Howie headaches at first. Both Bionda and Cahan were liabilities on the Hornet defence early in the year but by season's end proved to be big pluses. "Cullen had everything necessary except NHL wheels," Howie says. "In Junior his mental and puck-handling skills put him a notch above the rest, however in the pros he just couldn't do it often enough. A lack of mobility really shortened his career."

The best addition of all that season was MacDonald, a great minor league goal scorer when he wanted to be.

Providence had the big team that year, solid and deep in every position. Pittsburgh was six points behind Cleveland, in second place, with five of their last six games on the road. While Howie was collecting his meal money cheques from GM Jim Balmer, owner John Harris came into the office and pointed out how important it was that the team finish in first and that every effort be made to beat Providence, because that meant an extra home game. Howie knew it had to be important for Harris because he sent Baz along on the trip, "and that cost him a couple of bucks." Baz couldn't help. "When the score was close he'd be out walking back and forth in the lobby, or the tunnels of the arena. He never saw the last five minutes of a close hockey game in his life."

Howie then focused on the remaining few games in the regular schedule, top spot, and the extra game. It proved costly. "Like a fool, I treated the road trip like the playoffs. We won four games, tied one, and as I found out in the first round of the playoffs against Cleveland, I had killed my hockey team. We came off the road trip battered, bruised, and bagged. Like an idiot, I'd played my best players the most. A couple of them were chasing bonuses, which they reached. Solinger and MacDonald had no trouble getting theirs, but Hannigan and Foley needed eight good scoring chances to get a single goal, so it took a lot more work. Once MacDonald and Solinger had their bonuses, I'd put them on the power play to set up the other two. They would be in great scoring position, but feed the puck to Hannigan and he'd miss, or to Foley and he'd fan on it. The guys all worked together, to get everyone their bonuses, and we did it. We ran up the score at the other end, but we got their bonuses."

Cleveland had a veteran hockey club, backstopped by excellent netminding, and two very good lines. They also received some good breaks, and Pittsburgh had some bad ones. Either way, Cleveland quickly swatted the Hornets out of the playoffs.

"It's funny, when I left Stratford it was a fairly successful year, but I didn't take very much knowledge with me as a coach, and I probably wasn't worth the $7,000 Toronto was paying me. When we won the Calder Cup in Pittsburgh, I thought I had gotten a little smarter and learned something; but I gained more from losing the following season, than the previous two years of winning. In winning you hardly ever look back, at least I didn't at that time, for reasons *why* you win. In losing, you go back over the entire season, break it down into 20-game packages, compare your talent to the rest of the league, review individual and collective performances, and most of all, do a very thorough research job on your performance. All of that helped me learn a tremendous amount."

Howie's regular reports to Day were supposed to include scouting reports, not just on Leaf products, but on other teams' players, and any unsigned boys out there loose in the great North American hockey abyss.

"Hell, at that time I had enough trouble looking after my own and individual team performances, plus the opposition's game philosophy. The guy had to stand out like a festered thumb, game after game, before I would have recognized his talent. There were a couple of kids in Providence, Zellio Toppazzini was one of them, who had some potential. Camille Henry was great, but he quickly disappeared to New York — Toronto was asleep on that one."

Howie never even thought about a couple of guys who made it, and made it big: Kenny Wharram and Pierre Pilote. "Sure Wharram could shoot, but he never caused us five cents worth of trouble. He was small and we just ran him out of ice and finished the check. Pierre, too, was of average size for a defenceman, not physically tough or mean, not an outstanding skater, but pretty good with a puck. While in Buffalo, both worked on their skills and later had many successful years in Chicago."

V

In late February stories began to appear in the Toronto newspapers that King Clancy was considering retiring at the end of the season, and just prior to the NHL playoffs Day was on the phone. "Well, kid, what do you think? If an opening comes up as coach in Toronto, are you interested?" Howie's heart did a kerthunk.

The adage "it never rains without it pours" could have been crafted with Howie in mind. Less than twenty-four hours after his offer from Day, Hornet owner John Harris invited Howie to his office. When Howie arrived and saw Jim Balmer waiting as well, his first thoughts were, "Oh, shit, what have I done wrong?" After discussing the team's playoff chances, Harris finally said, "Howie, this is very confidential information, but we are getting out of the hockey business. In my contract with Conn Smythe and the Maple Leafs, I have the right to purchase, at a fixed price, up to six players belonging to Toronto presently playing here. We've had discussions with the Hershey ownership and they have agreed to purchase the six from us. They also are interested in having you as a coach."

Howie was speechless. Add Mathers, Gariepy, Marshall, Solinger, Price, and Mayer to the talent Hershey already had and the club was a cinch for the Calder Cup finals for the next three years.

Harris went on, "If you agree, they'd like you to get there as soon as possible and talk contract." The day after Cleveland eliminated Pittsburgh from the playoffs, Grace and Howie were in Hershey. Home of the Hershey chocolate empire, the city was a gorgeous part of the United States: great parks, golf courses, stately homes with large green lawns, wide roads, excellent shopping, good arena, superb company homes on big lots with reasonable rents. Hershey had a quiet, lazy atmosphere, a pleasant step and a half below the city norm for speed and stress. Grace and Howie were impressed. Before leaving, Howie verbally agreed to a three-year contract with the provision he could break it, if and when he received an acceptable offer from the Leafs. He promised to sign the contract in fifteen days if nothing happened with Toronto.

While in Hershey, Howie recommended the six players he thought would help them the most. Meeker knew Harris bought those players from Toronto at a ridiculously low price, and at least doubled his money when he sold them to Hershey. Even then, Hershey got them at a steal.

Speculation was soaring in Toronto as to who would replace King behind the bench. There were three or four candidates, including Turk Broda. One full week after his visit to Hershey, Day phoned and said, "I'd like you to get up here as soon as possible to talk." The next day, Meeker was in Day's office at Maple Leaf Gardens.

"We've decided to offer you the coaching job. Do you want it?" Hap asked.

Howie exploded inside with joy. "Thank you very much. For how long, and how much?" he asked, forcing himself to speak calmly.

"One year starting at $9,000."

"Come on, Hap, that's not much of a raise from the minors to the NHL," Howie pumped. "What about bonuses?"

Day offered $1,000 for making the playoffs, and another $1,000 for every round the club won. But that was akin to betting on the rabbit and not the hare. Only the most loyal or blindest of hockey fans could fail to see the Leafs' future was not bright. Now even goaltender Harry Lumley and captain Ted Kennedy were gone, and so was Flaman. Smith's production had plummeted. The newspapers were predicting at least six new rookies would be in the Leaf lineup, and none of the rookies named were from Pittsburgh. Howie knew the rookies he had in Pittsburgh were better than the rookies they had in mind, so Toronto was up to its ass in rattle-snakes. Boston, New York, and Chicago appeared to be in better shape than Toronto, so the playoffs seemed a long way off.

"I've verbally agreed to a three-year deal with Hershey for more money, with a team that's got a lock on the Calder Cup," Howie told Hap. "I'm going to get medical expenses, medical plan, a pension, a free golf club membership, $200 a month rent for an incredible home, a free car, and access to their hotels in New York and Miami Beach. That's your best offer?"

"Yep, $9,000."

Back in Pittsburgh, when Howie explained the offer to Grace, she was silent for a while and then said, "Well, we both thought leaving Stratford for Pittsburgh was an economic mistake, and it worked out pretty well here. Phone Dave Pinkney and Dutch Meier in Stratford and see what they say. To me, Hershey would be fine; Toronto would be okay, too. At least we'd be close to the family.

You do whatever you'd like to do the most."

The two advisers were a great help. Pinkney suggested Howie take the Hershey offer; Dutch said to go with the Leafs.

The decision was really never a contest. Howie was a die-hard Maple Leaf fan from day one. He was a Leaf player for seven years, never donning any uniform but the famed blue and white, and he was a member of the Leaf organization as coach in Pittsburgh. When the Leaf head-coaching job was dangled, no bait ever looked so sweet. Howie bit.

He phoned Hershey and said, "Make Frank Mathers your playing coach and you'll have an excellent hockey man for the next thirty years." Howie's words proved prophetic. Mathers was part of the Hershey organization until 1991, serving as a player, coaching the Bears to several Calder Cups, then moving to the front office as general manager and president. As a result of his contribution to hockey he was elected to the Hockey Hall of Fame in 1992 in the builders' category.

After signing his contract with the Leafs, Howie asked for, and received, the month of July off. Within days, Howie, Grace, and kids departed for Caribou Lake and a month of fishing camp construction.

Ten

A Leaf Once Again

"We were a small, gentle, inexperienced group masquerading as an NHL team. It was a group that only a man with a purpose could have put together."

It seemed, in many ways, to have happened in the blink of an eye, but it had been thirteen years since he first stepped into the Maple Leaf dressing room as a wide-eyed, starstruck youngster. Now, the familiar room was his domain. At the beginning of the 1956–57 NHL season, Howie Meeker, coach, stood quietly alone in the Maple Leaf dressing room and briefly pondered his life. It seemed he had reached the top of the mountain.

"Coaching is an incredible learning experience," Howie says. "It can be exciting and heartbreaking; it can be extremely challenging, and then all of a sudden you are powerless over a situation. There's also the aspect of the game that gives nothing but pleasure and satisfaction, and that's teaching skills. It is by far the most needed part of the game."

Early in his rookie season of 1947, Howie once disagreed with coach Day about how a particular goal had been scored and his description of Howie's poor performance in preventing it. Day countered, "Well, when this meeting is over, kid, we'll look at the film." Reviewing the film proved that Day was dead-on. Howie had been asleep on the play.

"I was nowhere near where I'd thought I had been. As I discovered over the years, most players really don't know where they are on the ice much of the time. There were others, besides myself, who made mistakes on that goal, but I made the key ones."

Howie saw the value, even then, of reviewing games on film or video and used the process many times over the years for coaching, teaching the game, and improving his own hockey skills. His later use of the telestrator as a television hockey commentator was to him simply an extension of the visual aid he first learned from Day.

Coaching the Maple Leafs gave Howie an opportunity to meet and talk with the coaches, scouts, and general managers for the other teams. During the time he coached the Leafs, Junior teams played Saturday-afternoon games and he rarely missed a game since it was a chance to network with other people in the hockey business. He chatted with ex-leaf Harold "Baldy" Cotton of the Bruins (who seemed to live in Maple Leaf Gardens), Ranger scout Jack Humphries, Montreal's Kenny Reardon and Sammy Pollock, Jimmy Skinner of Detroit, and numerous other experienced hockey people. In true Howie fashion, his passion for learning overshadowed any shyness, and he picked their brains like a starved vulture.

Howie also routinely quizzed Toronto's chief scout, Squib Walker. When he once asked Squib what the top five priorities he looked for in a hockey prospect were, Squib quickly replied, "Skating ability, puck-handling, heart or desire, hockey sense — the ability to think and know what's going on around you — and, a distant fifth, size."

Howie's eyes and hockey sense could tell him four of the five things to watch for in a player, but how could anyone assess the amount of heart and desire? Out of a hundred or so prospects nationwide, picking the top six to ten players is relatively easy — they usually stand out. The problem is figuring out who comes after that. That was the question that burned in his mind as his focus turned to coaching and teaching the game. He comments: "Is there a formula that gives you the edge in picking the best players, or do you guess? It's the people who can pick the potential players out of that remaining large number that are successful, so there has to be some formula, reasoning, or philosophy to it. I kept questioning all the scouts at that time . . . I really couldn't get any solid consensus. When I talked to Squib he'd mention that he often included the boy's status, or reputation in the community, in his reports."

A year later Howie learned Smythe's philosophy as general manager. During the summer of 1957, Howie took two folders of scouting reports to his wilderness fishing lodge at Caribou Lake, but with docks to repair, motors to fix, canoes to patch, cabins to paint, portages to clean, and pickerel, lake trout, and pike to catch, he didn't read a page. On the train from Armstrong to Toronto, he consumed it all.

"Connie loved horses and was a great believer in bloodlines and good breeding and I'm sure to a degree he made picks from numbers eleven to one hundred on breeding. Squib and his scouts rated the hockey skills of the prospects, but they also added verbal and written information about the boy's parents; they talked with the clergy, school principals, bank managers, anyone and everyone who could help determine which lads had the best breeding. Hockey ability many times took second to breeding in Connie's mind."

No one questioned Howie's courage or heart for the game, based on his background. In fact his bloodline was the subject of more than one publication. Newspaper columnist Fred Arnott told his story of meeting Howie's grandmother during the Second World War, after the woman's entire neighbourhood had been flattened by German air raids, but she refused to move. The story was repeated by Miller Stewart in the 1949–50 Toronto Maple Leaf game program.

"When I met his grandmother, I should have known that she would have a grandson that wouldn't back up from anything . . . . So when Hitler died in the flaming pyre of the Reichschancellorie or wherever he finished up, one of the things he hadn't done was make Howie Meeker's gallant old granny move," Fred Arnott wrote.

Ⴟ

Hap Day believed defensive hockey could be learned, and learned well. It was a system Howie knew. Even when Howie was coach of the Leafs, it was Hap Day hockey on the ice, or at least an effort to achieve Hap's system.

Howie points out that Day, as assistant general manager, which he was through the Primeau and Clancy years, was still the coach. "He saw that all three of us lived and taught his philosophy, particularly how you played in your own zone and without the puck. Providing offence was Day's or Smythe's job and the coaches supplied the defence.

"Hap influenced and manipulated in such a way that you didn't know it, so there was absolutely no resentment. In the two years that King Clancy had the team no one ever played defence better."

But no matter who was behind the bench, Smythe never relinquished his hold on power. "Sure, the coaches ran the practices and made most of the speeches at the prep rallies. We helped put the team defence pairs together, the forward lines together, and suggested changes when things weren't working, but in those days, and especially during the Hap Day coaching era, it was Conn Smythe who really controlled the team."

Nearly everyone who was ever benched or injured had to sit with Smythe in Berchtesgaden, Connie's special seating box up in the green seats. Throughout the game Smythe would send players back and forth to tell Day what to do or who to play next. Injured players drew cards to see who would sit closest to Smythe and take the first message down, because the player taking the first message was expected to be back to take another. Day knew the players had no choice but to follow Smythe's orders.

The players knew what a horrendous burden Day, and those coaches who followed him, had to carry. Says Howie: "In those days there was one coach and no assistants, so you had to control three lines, three sets of defencemen, the power play, penalty killers, assess who is playing well and who isn't. You're like an orchestra conductor, you are in control — totally wrapped up in the task at hand — and all of a sudden this snot-nosed, injured player tugs at your coat sleeve and says, 'Excuse me, Mr. Day, but Mr. Smythe says to play Lewicki with Max Bentley, not Joe Blow.' Five minutes later another wounded duck arrives with another message and on it went.

"I'll give Smythe credit as a motivator, as an organizer, and a judge of personalities. He had a fair eye for talent, but, compared to Hap Day, what he knew about playing the game of hockey you could write on the head of a pin."

Smythe's obsession with controlling the bench from his lofty box in the Gardens was such that he would even employ the team's cameraman, Shanty McKenzie (a former star football player with the Toronto Argonauts), to run messages. One game, when Howie was the lone injured Leaf running messages, he dawdled on his way back to Smythe. En route, he ran into Shanty scampering down the seats towards the players' bench. Howie intercepted him, asking where he was going. When Shanty told him, Howie promised to relay the message to Day and sent Shanty back to his camera.

"I never did deliver the message, but I could not believe Smythe would interrupt his cameraman to send messages."

Eventually Smythe realized that either the message he was sending down wasn't getting there, the players weren't delivering the right message, the receiver didn't understand the message, or horrors . . .

the receiver ignored his advice. So one day, near the eighteen clocks Smythe had installed in Berchtesgaden to record the ice time of everyone who played, he installed a telephone at ice level. To do so, Smythe had a hole drilled through the eighteen-inch cement foundation holding up the red seats, right behind the players' bench. Once again, though, Day seldom answered the phone, suggesting, perhaps, that with all the crowd noise he couldn't hear it. Undaunted, Smythe pushed on. At practice one day, a maintenance crew approached the bench with huge drills and jackhammers and set to work.

"Next game, about ten minutes into the first period, the phone starts ringing and then suddenly there is a huge light going on-off-on-off. We turned around and were almost blinded by a twelve-inch strobe light flashing, while the telephone is ringing. I said to Bill Juzda, beside me on the bench, 'Gosh, all we need now is flashing red lights.'"

"The Tank" was a mischievous little guy and he gave Howie a wink and said, "That's okay, I'll fix that next shift — watch me."

At the end of his next shift, Juzda returned to the bench and Howie stayed close, thinking, "I've gotta see this." As Juzda neared the bench at full speed, he yelled to the stick boy, "Give me a new stick; this one's broken," and hurled the stick, javelin-like, into the bench, through the hole, and directly into the light bulb.

Kaboom! There was glass and sparks everywhere, but no more flashing lights. Howie said to Juzda, "Jeez, Bill, if you could shoot the puck like that, you'd make the first all-star team."

During the coaching stints of Joe Primeau and King Clancy, Day was able to act as a buffer between Smythe and his coaches, eliminating the midgame interference.

Ⲩ

Accepting the job as Leaf coach meant yet another move for the Meeker clan, which had increased to four children when Howie Jr. entered the world during the family's second year in Pittsburgh. Grace and Howie found a house in North Toronto, located in Hoggs

Hollow, at the end of the bus route and almost the end of town.

Howie and family were barely settled in Toronto when the Leaf training camp opened, on September 19, 1956, in Sudbury. A total of thirty players showed up at camp, thirteen of them rookies, including four goaltenders. Anyone with any hockey knowledge knew the Maple Leafs were looking thin that year. The season before Ed Fitken and Spiff Evans had tagged the 1955–56 Leaf club to the media as "Goals, Guts, and Glory." Unfortunately the team was severely lacking in all three qualities. Nevertheless, they continued with the snappy slogans. With the emergence of that new fad of rock 'n' roll music, Day pegged Howie's 1956–57 club as "Rock 'n' roll with Howie Meeker and his Crew Cuts." The media ate it up and the fans digested it.

But Howie didn't. Actually, it was making his stomach rumble.

"Rock? Who were we going to rock with? We never had one mean toughie on defence, nobody. Dickie Duff at 165 pounds was our toughest forward. Gerry James, the football whiz, couldn't fight and couldn't get there in time to hit. Ron Stewart on rare occasions could be mean but not tough.

"Roll? Well, Dickie Duff for sure, then I had to hope that Tod Sloan, Sid Smith, and maybe George Armstrong would spark a bit of offence, but after that it was zilch."

The lack of strong skaters was Howie's most burning concern. He tried to teach the forwards how to forecheck, how to take the puck carrier off the puck coming out of their own zone, how to make them pass the puck, and how to run them out of rink. He would put the best Leafs behind the net with a puck and challenge them to skate out either side and past Howie with the puck. But none of them could outskate or deke past Howie and over the blue line. Brian Cullen, then Barry Cullen, and Gary Aldcorn couldn't beat him. Neither could Gerry James, Bobby Baun, Al MacNeil, Mike Nykoluk, Rudy Migay, George Armstrong . . .

"Jeez," Howie thought, "I'm in three-quarters' shape and three years out of playing in the National Hockey League and these guys can't beat me. Here is the heart of their development program, and not an outstanding skater amongst them." If the players couldn't consistently outskate Howie, they were not going to have much success coming out of their own zone against anyone still in the league. "Skating is the number-one priority and we were lead-footed."

All summer long Howie had tried to convince management to take Pittsburgh farmhands Parker MacDonald and Gerry Foley to training camp because they were better than eight of the forwards that the Leafs were counting on. "Parker could play and score goals and Gerry could play tough and play plus. Neither were great hockey players but in my opinion better than what we had." Howie was not successful and the two were sold to the New York Rangers.

After two exhibition games against the Cleveland Barons of the American Hockey League, Howie knew the Leafs were in big, big trouble. "They tied us and beat us, both physically and on the scoreboard. They physically beat on me, too."

The Barons had a small tough centre who skated rings around the Leafs. Late in the third period, just as he touched the puck, Ron Stewart blindsided him and stapled him to the boards. Stewart ran at him for about twenty feet. All hell broke loose when they carried him off the ice.

After the game Howie left the arena through the back door, and just as he was ready to climb into the bus he sensed something about to happen. As he turned he saw a clenched fist coming. It was too late to duck and the fist exploded into his eye.

In the scrap that followed Howie realized it was Cleveland coach Freddy Glover he was fighting. As the players broke them up, Glover accused Howie of deliberately ordering Stewart to attack the kid. "That upset me because there was no way I operated that way. I liked it to be played tough and rough, and sometimes mean, but not that way. For two weeks I carried around the most beautiful shiner you've ever seen. I was a little embarrassed with the galdarned thing. I never did forgive Stewart for running that guy into the fence. I don't blame Glover for taking a run at me, but it should have been face to face."

Y

By the end of camp, Howie figured the Leafs had seven players who, if they had normal or good years, could help get the club into fourth spot, the position management was aiming for. Still, he had one of the youngest teams in Maple Leaf history, and a club designed neither for slick, high-scoring affairs, nor rough, robust games. At one point during training camp his club's lack of enthusiasm for bodychecking caused Howie to blast his players for "checking like a bunch of pantywaists."

The chastisement seemed to work as the Leafs added some fire to their play and started the season hot. Toronto tied their first regular-season match, 4–4, with Boston, lost the home opener to Detroit, 4–1, and then recorded their first win, a 1–0 blanking of the Blackhawks in Chicago. "Slinker" Sloan notched the only goal while Ed Chadwick picked up the shutout. After the first month the Leafs looked fairly respectable with an impressive record of 4 wins, 1 loss, and 4 ties. However, it was the calm before the storm, and the storm proved damaging. On Thursday, October 25, in Montreal, veteran defenceman Hugh Bolton crashed into the boards late in the game, breaking his left leg in two places. It proved to be Bolton's final NHL game.

Less dramatic at the time, but of greater significance later, was another October incident at the Montreal Forum. While 13,095 fans gathered to watch the 1956 All-Star game, another kind of meeting was happening on the ice. Prior to the game, Red Wing star Ted Lindsay approached Montreal all-star Doug Harvey with the idea of forming a players' association. It was not a totally new idea; the various problems players were facing, such as low pay, inadequate pensions, and manipulation of players by team owners or management, had led to discussion of an association. But Lindsay was determined and Harvey responded favourably to the idea. Before the evening was over, Lindsay and Harvey had arranged a secret meeting with many of the top players from around the league, including Bill Gadsby of New York, Fern Flaman of Boston, Gus Mortson in Chicago, and Jimmy Thomson of Toronto. It was a move requiring an impressive amount of courage from all parties concerned, especially since league rules strictly forbid any fraternization between players on opposing teams.

In November, the Toronto Maple Leafs, led by the youngest coach in Leaf history, took a complete nose-dive, winning 1, losing 9, and tying 2 games. It was an indication of things to come.

When Day and Howie talked early in the season about naming team captain, the answer was obvious to Howie — veteran defenceman Thomson. Duff was the only other proven veteran. Armstrong, Stewart, and rookie Bob Pulford were too young and inexperienced and still trying to prove themselves in the NHL.

"On the ice Jimmy set a great example. But Conn Smythe let everybody know he strongly disagreed with our selection of him as captain. It broke Jim's heart because he'd lived and died for seven or eight years with the Toronto Maple Leafs. So he came to me one day and said, 'Howie, give the "C" to someone else,' but I talked him out of it."

Halfway through the season the announced formation of the NHL Players' Association surprised fans and team owners. On February 12, Lindsay and a handful of representatives broke the news in New York, informing the press they had the full support of almost every player in the NHL, a fact supported by the lofty $100 dues paid by each player. Lindsay announced he was president of the association with Harvey as vice president. Thomson was appointed secretary, while two former Leaf teammates, Flaman of Boston and Mortson of Chicago, were named second and third vice presidents accordingly. The players were quick to deny the association was a union, claiming it was not intended to be confrontational.

The announcement was an absolute shock to all team owners

and media, and has to rank as one of the all-time best-kept secrets in pro sports. Amazingly, for four months, while the association was formed and dues collected, not one player leaked a word.

Smythe, who had long ruled his team and the league like a power-hungry tyrant, and treated his players much like livestock whose value was short-lived and based on production, went ballistic. When Thomson returned to Toronto he was immediately summoned by Smythe, who verbally beat on the rearguard, calling him a traitor as well as a disloyal, thankless scum. For the remainder of the year Thomson was ostracized by Smythe.

After Smythe's attack, Jimmy's play fell off by 50 percent. He'd lost his heart, or jump, and seemed a crushed man. Certainly Thomson did not appear happy, and played much like he had back in 1952 when he lost his defence partner, Gus Mortson, to Chicago.

Some of the pressure was removed from Thomson with the return of Ted Kennedy. A month before the association announcement, with the Leafs plummeting in the standings, Kennedy ambled into a Leaf practice at one of the new midtown arenas, skates in hand. Kennedy had retired in March 1955.

"Teeder, what are you doing here?" Howie asked, thinking maybe he'd lost his job and Kennedy was coming in to coach.

"Can you use me, Howie? I'd like to give it a whirl," Kennedy replied. Howie nodded and in a half hour Kennedy was dressed and on the ice. He looked terrible, which was nothing new because he always looked terrible at training camp. Howie soon discovered that Kennedy's return had been arranged. Day, knowing the club was down the tube unless he did something, called Teeder and asked for help and the player said he'd try. It was a few days before it occurred to Howie that trainer Tim Daly had an extra set of equipment and sticks already at the rink for the player. Day knew Kennedy was going to show up, and so did Daly, but Howie didn't.

When it became common knowledge that Kennedy was making a comeback and might help the team get into the playoffs, Conn Smythe exploded. He claimed that by playing Kennedy, Toronto would be taking a backward step, stopping development and taking time away from the rookies. Howie was in the middle, again.

Before Kennedy signed and played, Hap requested that Howie write a letter to Connie, saying he believed Kennedy would help the hockey team. Ted got into reasonable shape, was given the captaincy, and played 30 games. "He still had the spirit, toughness, and work ethic; the puck and head skills were there, but he had absolutely no skating legs. Throughout his career, if Kennedy's skating had matched any other of his skills, he would have set records even Gretzky would have found tough to beat.

"I tried playing Kennedy with Smith and Sloan, but when it became their turn to help Teeder a little bit, they couldn't or wouldn't do it. When that didn't work I gave him the kids and he did okay."

One night in Detroit, in a pivotal match, the teams were tied late in the third period. The Leafs had been barely hanging on all game and near the end Tim Horton took a stupid penalty. Immediately, the most potent power play in the league hit the ice: Gordie Howe, Lindsay, Alex Delvecchio, Red Kelly, and Metro Prystai (now with the Wings). "Kennedy hadn't been on the bench for thirty seconds, but he looked at me and his eyes were saying, 'I want to go; I want to go help kill this penalty — please?' So I think, 'If I say yes, he's going to climb over the bench and be up to his ass in all-star hockey players.'" Howie had younger, better-conditioned players on the bench who, except for Rudy Migay, were trying to make themselves smaller so he wouldn't tap their shoulders. Meanwhile the old-timer, who could and should be excused from such duty, was standing there asking to go.

"I couldn't say no to such a class guy. It was a good decision that he made — I didn't make it, he made it — because we escaped out of there with a single point. Over the long haul we might have made the playoffs with Kennedy as a regular, but I think even that's iffy."

Y

When times were looking desperate during the year, Hap Day talked over possible trades with Howie. In the sports business, as legendary baseball executive Branch Rickey said, "sometimes the trades you don't make turn out to be the best." Step up, Tim Horton.

After three years in the league, between 1952 and 1955, Horton was very slowly learning his trade. Near the end of the 1954–55 season, he crashed into Bill Gadsby in Chicago and the check broke his leg and jaw. The leg didn't heal properly and had to be reset, so the rearguard sat out the second half of the 1955–56 season. Thirty games into 1956–57, Howie was still recording how goals against his team were scored, and they consistently seemed to show Horton at fault. In addition, even Horton's offensive play was suffering. Then one day after practice Day asked, "Would you trade Tim Horton?"

"Horton for who?" Howie asked.

"Gus Mortson back from Chicago," was the reply.

"Are you thinking long term or short term?" Hap didn't answer so Howie continued, "Mortson will help this club immensely over the next two years, but Horton is five years younger. If he gets any hockey sense, he'll be a dandy player for eight, nine, or ten years. If your job depends on making the playoffs, get Mortson, but if you want to win three or four or five years down the road, I'd say no."

Howie never knew why the deal wasn't made, but whatever happened it was a good decision. During a Hall of Fame career, Horton would play 1,185 games as a Leaf — second only to George Armstrong on the club's all-time list — was named to five all-star teams, and played for Toronto's four Stanley Cup–winning teams.

George Armstrong, Rudy Migay, and Dick Duff were by far the Leafs' best forwards. Howie had seen enough of Bobby Baun and Bob Pulford to know that in time they would be very good hockey players. Marc Reaume played well, but Howie thought he was just too nice a guy to be a successful defenceman.

During the season, rookie netminder Ed Chadwick played well, considering that every night was a life-or-death struggle to get even a tie or a one-goal win. He didn't win Toronto a of lot games, but neither did he cost them many.

When the season ended, Toronto finished in fifth place with 21 wins, putting them nine points behind the fourth-place New York Rangers. Toronto scored just 174 goals, fifth in the league, and allowed 192 against, the third-highest total.

Howie thinks the club might have had a shot at fourth place, but injuries to a couple of key guys at the wrong time killed them. Late in the season George Armstrong missed eleven games and at the same time Tod Sloan missed eighteen games. "We just weren't good enough in any facet of the game that involved winning. We weren't tough enough physically or mentally; we weren't big enough, experienced enough, fast enough, smart enough, and we weren't deep enough. We were a small, gentle, inexperienced group, masquerading as an NHL team that only a man with a purpose could have put together. There was only one person, at that time, that I knew in hockey could have done a worse job and that was Bill Tobin of the Chicago Blackhawks," whose teams in the late forties and early fifties finished last six times in eight years.

During that winter Howie knew there was something of major importance going on. He could usually tell when players were arranging a poker game, a big party, or whatever, but when he began to see three to six guys huddled in the hallway, gathering in Daly's equipment room, lingering after the game meal, six, seven, or eight guys always with Thomson or Duff, sitting around a table with no cards — they had to be talking about something special. The looks on their faces were game faces; they were clearly not consumed by thoughts about cards, beer, girls, horses, or food.

One day after Kennedy returned, just after a noon team meeting, Howie entered a hallway and saw Thomson, Sloan, Duff, Smith, Mortson (in town because Toronto was hosting Chicago that night), and Ted Kennedy involved in serious conversation. "I started heading over to say hello to Gus, took one step in that direction, but all their faces said, 'Hello. We're busy. Goodbye.' So I stopped in the middle of the step, said, 'Hi, guys,' and turned and walked away." It was a harsh reminder that he was no longer one of the guys.

On the team's next train trip, Howie made a point to have breakfast with Teeder and asked him what was going on.

"Howie, the players in the league are making a move. If I were to tell you, and you didn't go to management with it, you'd be fired when they found out." The two men finished their breakfast with some conversation about horses and hockey. When finished, Howie said, "Good luck, Teeder. I don't know a thing."

Howie fully agrees with the players' need for such an association, and respects the players for the courage they showed. "Everybody in the game now owes a great debt to the originators of the movement."

When Lindsay announced the formation of the NHLPA, Howie's reaction was a joyful "About time," followed quickly by the realization that such news meant Smythe would immediately be on the warpath.

The next morning at nine o'clock, Howie walked into Maple Leaf Gardens and found Day sitting in his little cubicle, feet up on the desk, with a newspaper opened to the sports page. Day pointed to the headline about the association that had been formed and asked Howie, "Did you know anything about this?"

"On or off the record?" Howie replied.

"Off record. I was a player, still am a player, always will be."

So Howie told him exactly what Kennedy had said, and added that he had received additional information from George Meade, who amazingly knew more about what was going on in the NHL than most folks.

"Mr. Smythe wants to see you before breakfast," Hap continued. "I suggest that you tell him that you had no idea what was going on. You've got lots of company — neither did I, or King Clancy." A small smirk creased his lips.

Connie, with Stafford present, tore a strip off of Howie for several minutes. Smythe refused to believe — and it was hard for Howie to believe as well — that someone could form an association between 120 players, in six different cities, get them to pay $100 each in dues, and have no one outside of that select group — owners, management, scouts, media, family members, or even trainers (some of them a direct pipeline to management) — find out. If anyone did, they kept it quiet.

"It really was amazing. Poor Jimmy Thomson followed me into the lion's den, but if anybody on the team could handle what Conn was about to dish out, Jim could. Connie and Stafford set out to destroy the association, ordering solicitor Ian Johnston to do everything possible to bring about its downfall."

Smythe, Johnston, league president Clarence Campbell, and others tried to intimidate and sweet talk members of the Leafs into abandoning the association, but the players would having nothing to do with it. Early in the following season, 1957–58, those same three men barged into the Leaf dressing room and demanded the players vote on the "union" issue, but again the players held firm. Leafs present that day were Tim Horton, Ron Stewart, Tod Sloan, Dick Duff, Barry Cullen, Al MacNeil, Jim Morrison, Sid Smith, Frank Mahovlich, Bob Baun, Marc Reaume, George Armstrong, Brian Cullen, Rudy Migay, Billy Harris, Bob Pulford, Ed Chadwick, and Pete Conacher.

Howie salutes the players' courage: "Many times in the last forty years I have had reason to be proud of my association with the players of the Toronto Maple Leafs, but never more than to the eighteen gentlemen who withstood the challenge of ownership, who put the game and the players before individual persecution."

With a lousy season coming to an end, Howie anticipated a pink slip any day. With a week left in the season, he stayed an extra day in New York after a game in order to discuss a possible job in the Central Hockey League. Ironically, Smythe had also stayed an extra day in New York, and the two men sat together on the airplane back to Toronto.

"I thought I was a dead duck as coach, so when Smythe asked why we missed the playoffs I had nothing to lose and was honest in my answer. I told him we weren't good enough in goal; both Smith and Sloan had had very average years; with one or two exceptions, our defence was terrible; we had no offence past the first line, and we played a defensive game even when we had the puck."

When Smythe asked what changes should be made, Howie advised that the club needed a veteran goaltender to play key games while Chadwick matured; he also recommended an immediate trade for Boston defenceman Allan Stanley, a deal for left-winger Johnny Bucyk from Detroit, and that Smythe grab a goalie in the minors named Johnny Bower. Howie added that the team had to totally change their philosophy with the puck behind the blue line, and especially on the attack once out of their own zone.

The hour-and-fifteen-minute flight seemed to take only ten as Howie talked most of the way. On a couple of occasions, Howie reminded Smythe of poor trades he had made, and even questioned Smythe's game philosophy. When they landed, Smythe asked Howie to meet again with him soon. On March 25, Smythe held a press conference. Smythe refused to show any desire to keep Clancy as assistant GM or Howie as coach, and made no reference to Day at all. The blatant absence of Day's name as well as barbed comments by Smythe indicated the writing was on the wall for Hap. Smythe also took shots at Thomson, the NHLPA, and swore that his club would not be dictated to by outsiders any more.

Day, his pride finally stomped on once too often, beat Smythe to the bloodletting and announced to the media the next day that he would no longer be available to the Leafs.

Smythe summoned Howie to his office within the following few days, and the duo talked hockey for an hour or so. Then, out of the blue, Smythe asked Howie if he would like to be the Leafs' general manager. He suggested a three-year term, starting at Howie's current salary of $10,000 the first year, with a $1,000 raise in each of the second and third years.

"Out of the frying pan and into the fire," Howie thought, and asked Smythe to give him a day to think it over.

"Whoa boy, stop right there!" Howie says now. "At that time I knew about the problems both on and off the ice that Hap Day had had. I also knew that as general manager I'd have advice and interference not only from Connie, but also from Stafford, a young man with an ego as big as all outdoors and not an ounce of class or hockey sense. The thought scared me."

Howie was reflective as he drove home that night. "During that season as coach I knew that at age thirty-two or thirty-three and just three years removed from playing, my decision to coach the Leafs had been a major mistake. Sure, I knew how to teach systems both offensively and defensively, I knew when the player was giving sufficient physical effort, and I knew how to put defensive pairs and forward lines together. My problem was I didn't know how to handle the temperamental NHL men. It was tough to threaten, tougher to whip, and even harder to bench my former buddies. It was Hap Day who, when he realized I wasn't going to play mental games with the players, took over that ugly part of the game."

Howie knew before he got home that his decision would be "Thanks, but no thanks. Make me that offer ten years down the road and I'll take it."

Grace Meeker had firsthand experience with such questions. For about eight years she'd experienced Howie's sleepless nights as a player, then four more with Howie as a coach. At the thought of Howie as GM in Toronto, working with Stafford, whom she despised, she had every right to say, "Howie, take that job and it's grounds for divorce." But once again she left it to Howie to gauge.

Howie phoned Day, told him of the offer, and asked if they could visit that night. After going over pro's and con's, Hap advised Howie to take the job. Grace and Howie were both shocked.

"Well," Day explained, "there's only six jobs like it in the world, and since Conn will sell Maple Leaf Gardens to Stafford, Harold, and others, you won't last very long. However, get your three-year deal and while you're there open up the files — mine, Squib's, Doris Ludlow's, and Conn's — and read, and learn, and learn. You'll also get a chance to meet the other owners, and have a wonderful opportunity to learn how to make trades and deals.

"You'll learn more about NHL hockey operations in a year, if you last that long, than you will in five years anywhere else. Also, Howie, the owners and general managers are always looking for competent help and you'll get first crack at a job if something opens up."

On the way home Grace told Howie, "If you want it, take it."

The next morning Howie saw Smythe and said he'd take the job but needed $11,000, $12,000, and $13,000 instead. Smythe agreed, and once again the two men shook hands on it. Conn asked Miss McDonald to draw up a three-year contract and suggested Howie should come by in a day or two and sign it.

That night Howie phoned his potential boss in the Central League and told him of his decision, which made him unavailable to coach there the next winter. "Congratulations and good luck; you'll need it," Howie was told.

Smythe called a press conference a day or two after shaking hands with Howie. Smythe said a few words of introduction, then Howie took the podium. He told the press his first job was to secure a part-time experienced goaltender, and to actively pursue an experienced defenceman and acquire some scoring punch up front. Howie suggested there were four or five players available that could help the team and that he was looking forward to signing a young, talented giant from the St. Mike's Juniors, Frank Mahovlich.

In the media scrum that followed, Red Burnett from the *Toronto Star* asked Conn Smythe how long Howie's contract was for. Howie turned around and saw that Smythe's face had turned red like a ripe tomato, his eyes black and fiery and shooting those famous stars. "It's for one year, isn't it, kid?" Smythe spouted. "Actually, if you can't get the job done in one year, you can't do it at all."

"I had him by the short hairs, and I didn't have the courage to immediately take him aside and question his memory, and if it wasn't recalled properly, then tell the world. I hesitated, it seemed like five minutes, before looking him right in the eye and saying, 'If that's the way you want it, Connie.'"

While driving home that afternoon, Howie knew he was on a limited schedule. When he told Grace about what happened, she said, "So what's new? Now I know for sure where Stafford got his character from — his father."

Howie recalled April 1946, when he and Smythe shook hands on his rookie deal and Smythe later reneged on his promise of bonus money for winning any trophy.

Howie thinks Smythe had justifiable reasons to have second thoughts about hiring him as general manager. "I caught him at a very emotional time. His long-term plan to discredit Hap Day had just come to a very successful conclusion. He got off the plane from New York after talking with me and thought, 'Now here's a kid who thinks somewhat like I do, who wants to play run-and-gun hockey, who has his eyes on two or three good trades, and who is a Toronto Maple Leaf, true blue and white.' Next morning he offers me a contract and I agree. Then he finally contacted Stafford — which, for whatever reason, he didn't do earlier — and Stafford likely had a fit.

"Before the press conference, all Smythe had to do was call me in and say, 'Kid, I made a mistake. The group of seven directors, led by Stafford, run the club now — so let's make a deal.' I hope I would have been smart enough to say, 'Okay, but let's put it in writing.'"

The next day Howie went to work and for the next six months worked without signing a contract. "I don't think I was ever offered one. So I had what you would call one foot on a banana peel." Howie started with Syl Apps and went through every Leaf contract signed over the previous fifteen years. Later he went through Smythe's files.

"I was shocked at how little we were paying for, even the very big stars — the guys instrumental in winning Stanley Cups. The only exception was Ted Kennedy, who was well paid. He was not paid half of what he was worth, but paid well in relationship to the rest of us.

"Hap had protected his ass on many occasions when he objected to trades that Smythe was making with other clubs. He noted them on paper in his files and I'm sure I saw copies of it in Day's folder, and in Connie's filing system. I got into Connie's filing cabinet and went through it folder by folder. I learned quite a bit about minor-league clubs and the relationship the team had with other sponsors — the people who had the right to use our pictures and/or our endorsements, for which we got basically nothing in return." Once a year the players received a cardboard box half full of Bee Hive syrup and the other half containing corn starch.

Howie's one big signing was Frank Mahovlich, who actually came in all by himself. Howie had talked with Smythe and found out what to offer Mahovlich. The GM and Mahovlich talked Junior hockey for a long time and then Howie offered him an $8,000 signing bonus, and $8,000 for each of three years. While waiting a day or two for the Big M's response, Howie did an interview with *Toronto Star* sportswriter Milt Dunnell. When Dunnell asked if the Leafs were going to sign Mahovlich, Howie responded they were. Howie agreed with Milt that Mahovlich was a great hockey player, had great potential to star in the National Hockey League, and was going to make the Leafs a lot better.

"The story hit the newspaper and I don't think it was on the streets a half an hour before Connie was on the phone. He was steaming mad and he tore a strip off my back. 'You're saying all these complimentary things about this young kid and that's going to cost us money. You can't say anything at all, how bad you want him, how good he is, or anything. Just shut up.'"

Within a few days Frank said he wanted $12,000 a year, Howie countered with $9,000 and finally settled for a $10,000 bonus and $10,000 a year for the next two years.

Howie didn't see much of Conn Smythe that summer. He'd get the odd note from his office. One of them was to sign Hugh Bolton for $1,000 to an agreement that if, and when, his leg healed properly he would play hockey for the Toronto Maple Leafs. Howie couldn't understand why, but didn't question it.

Howie called Hugh on the phone and said, "Look, Hugh, the boss wants me to offer you $1,000 to sign a contract that when your leg heals enough to play, you'll play for the Toronto Maple Leafs."

"I'm from Toronto," Bolton said. "I'd not play for anybody in this league but the Toronto Maple Leafs. That's it. Goodbye." Howie sent a copy of that information to Conn and never heard from him, but Howie got a note from Stafford saying get back to Hugh Bolton and, "make sure you sign him to a contract. We want him protected."

Howie got in touch with Hugh again and asked him to come to Maple Leaf Gardens. The two men talked about everything but hockey and then Howie said, "Hugh, you haven't changed your mind? Stafford is going to blow his cork, and so will the old man, if I don't get your signature, if I don't give you $1,000."

But Bolton didn't operate like that. He said he didn't want any part of anything that he hadn't earned. "If and when I do come back and play, I'll get that $1,000 and a few more."

Howie had three phone meetings with Stafford, never face-to-face, that summer, and sent several notes to Conn, which he knew went directly to Stafford. Howie talked possible trades with different general managers, but received no action or input from the Smythes. He suggested reacquiring Harry Lumley while Chadwick gained experience, and if not Lumley, some other veteran goalie. At least once a month he requested permission to talk trade with somebody and got no response. "I knew then I was on the outside looking in and that sooner or later I was gone," he says.

Howie attended two weekend parties at Stafford's cottage north of Toronto and Harold Ballard was there both times. Howie could get Harold to talk hockey, but not Stafford.

"At that time none of us suspected, even for a moment, that Harold would evolve as the dominant force, but I knew our conversation would get through to Staff, so naturally I talked and advised pursuit of certain players."

Before taking the family on a two-week vacation to their fishing resort at Caribou Lake, Howie sent letters to King Clancy, Conn, and Stafford requesting permission again to go after people he thought would help the Leafs, writing that he would appreciate their thoughts on who the untouchables were on the Leaf roster. In the last three or four years, Staff and Harold had run the business end of the Toronto Junior Marlboros with considerable success, and Staff had informed Howie, through King, that the Leafs' future was assured because of his development plan with the Juniors. Stafford thought youngsters like Gary Aldcorn, the Cullen brothers, Ed Chadwick, Al MacNeil, and Bobby Baun were the answer.

By midsummer 1957, it was clear to Howie that the future of the Toronto Maple Leafs was in the hands of Stafford Smythe and Harold Ballard, not Connie, and that he and Staff did not see eye to eye or have any apparent plan on what to do for 1957–58. Howie happily turned over the coaching reins to Billy Reay, a former Montreal Canadiens centre. "His philosophy, because he was with the Montreal Canadien organization for years, was close to mine, so I gladly left the coaching problem in his hands. I don't think I would have had any influence anyway."

Prior to the training camp Howie attended an NHL-sponsored meeting with hockey people from the National, Quebec, and American hockey leagues regarding sponsorship and other related activities. When Howie walked out of the meeting, the only person to impress him with his presentation, arguments, and advice was Punch Imlach. For years Punch had been coach and general manager of the Quebec Aces in the old Quebec Senior Hockey League. Punch had been around the barn as a player, coach, and general manager for a long time. "I think Stafford Smythe left the meeting with that same feeling and already had him tagged as a replacement for Howie Meeker."

Y

When training camp opened, Howie was frustrated with the lack of input he was receiving as well as the feeling his ideas weren't welcome, and the lack of action in changing player bodies on the roster. Columnist Red Burnett expressed similar concerns in a column that came out at camp's opening:

Toronto's hockey Leafs are gambling that a new front office, a Montreal-trained coach, the addition of star juniors and top players from minor pro farms, plus the best of their holdover crop, will move them back into the Stanley Cup playoff picture.

Going by past performances, it looks like a long-shot gamble. Last season's records indicate that Leafs lack scoring punch, a solid defence and heavy hitters, three "musts" in assembling a title contender. Their change in playing personnel doesn't appear sweeping enough to cure those deficiencies of 1956–57. . . .

Stafford Smythe, chairman of Leafs' new seven-man hockey committee, and the man who will call most of the shots, doesn't go along with that type of reasoning. "You can throw out last season's form. Our fellows were trying to play defensive hockey, something that was entirely foreign to their early training. I'm confident that, under Reay's tuition, they will regain their scoring punch and provide pleasing hockey. I know that once they learn the emphasis is off defensive play, Tod Sloan, Dick Duff, George Armstrong, Bobby Pulford, the Cullens (Brian and Barry) and our other forwards will start finding the target. You can't score goals with one eye on your check and the other on the net. . . . Our young defencemen will benefit by that season's experience and will blossom out once they find out Reay won't bench them for every mistake."

A few days after the players arrived at training camp Stafford called Howie into his suite. He wanted to know what, if anything, he had done to improve the quality of the team. Early in life Howie learned to always try and protect his best interests so he interjected, "Don't leave, I'll be right back," and went to get his Samsonite attaché case with copies of his summer's messages to Connie and Staff. He returned, sat down, and read every one of them to

Stafford and Harold, then he pulled out the folder with messages from the two bosses and read them word for word.

When he'd finished fifteen minutes later, Howie stood up and said, "Stafford, I asked for direction, for permission to trade for players, on three different occasions, and you totally ignored my correspondence. You know why I haven't done anything." Smythe said nothing for about ten seconds, then arrogantly asked, "Well, did you at least get Hugh Bolton to sign the agreement to play for the Leafs when he got better?"

The two men were now about three feet apart and Howie, taking a step closer, said, "No, I didn't. In fact I didn't even try. The second Hugh believes he is 100 percent and can play again, he'll be in our backyard in his uniform at your price, not his."

By this time the two men were almost eyeball-to-eyeball. "Well, that's not good enough," Stafford bellowed. "Your orders were to sign Bolton. I want his name on a contract." Stafford then placed his hands on Howie's chest, preparing to push him, and yelled, "Go do it!"

Bad move. Howie immediately hit him right between the eyes, turned on his heel, and said, as he left the room, "Go sign the big lug yourself."

As he wandered out into the crisp fall air, Howie wondered how long it would take before he received the golden handshake.

Eleven

Leaf Decay

"Getting Day to leave would take some time, but Smythe knew if the team was no longer competitive, Day, being a proud man, would eventually bow out."

It has been said that, "It takes one to know one," and when it comes to characters, Howie Meeker has certainly met his share. Busher Jackson, Dave Pinkney, Billy Cupolo, Syl Apps, Babe Pratt, Rocket Richard, Eddie Shore, King Clancy, and a host of others were introduced to Howie through play with the puck. While varied in their personality and demeanour, all shared a common denominator: a passion for the game.

Two men who made perhaps the greatest impact on Howie's life via the world of hockey, were Hap Day and Conn Smythe. Howie first heard of the two men while he was a youthful Leaf spectator: Day, the talented defenceman and winger who had become coach of the Leafs, and Smythe the team owner, guru of Maple Leaf Gardens, and former Leaf coach. Smythe and Day's lives had been intertwined since 1926, when Smythe bought the Leafs and became coach, and Day was a dazzling player on the team. For the next thirty years Smythe largely controlled Day's career like a puppet on a string — and in the end he would coldly cut the connection.

Over the years Howie's respect and admiration for Day increased, while his esteem for Smythe steadily declined. "Grace, on the other hand, had the two sorted out from day one," Howie grins in hindsight.

Howie has his regrets about Hap Day, for words left unsaid, actions left undone. For more than ten years Howie knew Day as an acquaintance and an associate but never as a close friend.

"I played hockey under him for eight years and coached his game at Pittsburgh and Toronto. I knew his hockey philosophy, his methods, his theories, his teaching techniques. He taught me what's needed on a hockey team, his priorities, and just about everything he knew about hockey that was teachable. I'd dress for practices right beside the guy. I knew Hap Day the hockey man very, very well, but never did get to know Hap Day, the person.

In Howie's mind, Day was the best hockey coach during that era, perhaps ever.

Howie maintains that despite the efforts of a few others — like Al Murray and Dave Pinkney — it was Day who taught him the game of hockey: how to play and coach the game. Day also helped provide Howie with one of his proudest moments.

"In September 1946, at my first training camp, Day put me with Ted Kennedy and Vic Lynn and that year we finished second, challenging Montreal for first place. That surprised even Hap, and what surprised him more was that we blew by Detroit in the first round. Then against the Canadiens, the big, bad, tough, talented Canadiens, well . . . there comes a time in everyone's life . . . and one of them for me was after the final whistle of Game Six at Maple Leaf Gardens, when the players scrambled over the boards, anxious to join their teammates on the ice who had killed the last two minutes for a 2–1 Stanley Cup win over Montreal. Although I never realized it at the time, it was the supreme compliment from Hap Day that I was on the ice with three other rookies, Thomson, Mortson, and Lynn, allowed to kill off those final two minutes.

"Hap Day thoroughly understood the team and the individual talents needed to win, and man, oh man, could he get the three most important ingredients out of his talent: hard work, discipline, and respect."

Howie remembers a rare personal discussion with Day late in the 1956–57 season. Following a Leaf road loss, Day's actions led Howie to believe Hap conceded the Leafs probably weren't going to make the playoffs.

"When I met Hap outside the dressing room in the hallway after the game he just looked terrible. He looked like a beaten man." During the ensuing taxi ride to the train station Day said absolutely nothing, which surprised Howie since that was normally when the two discussed the evening's game. When they climbed aboard the train and into the coach's cubicle they generally shared on the road, Day immediately put on his pyjamas and climbed into bed, again shunning the usual evening chit-chat.

In the morning, Day was still in a funk. Hap would usually wake up at 6 a.m., eat breakfast, and then wake Howie around 7:30. That morning, however, Howie awoke at 8 and Day was still in bed. Convinced that Day held him responsible for the club's failure, a dejected Howie slipped out of the berth and went for breakfast alone. An hour later, back in the berth an ashen-faced Day sat across from Howie. After exchanging morning pleasantries, Day muttered something Howie could not make out.

"Hap, are you okay?" Howie ventured.

"Yeah, errr, I . . . I don't know," Day stuttered. "I guess, Howie, blood is thicker than water." Day stopped, attempting to suppress his shattered emotions. After a few seconds Howie nodded, encouraging Day to continue. Hap sighed; his shoulders heaved in regret as he sadly shook his head and started his story.

"My wife has told me since day one that Harold Ballard wasn't a true friend, that he was using me to gain access to Maple Leaf Gardens people. Year after year I kept telling her she was wrong, but she kept insisting that it was so."

Howie still didn't get the picture. To him, Harold Ballard and Stafford Smythe were merely executives of the Toronto Marlboro Junior hockey team, which belonged to Maple Leaf Gardens. But then Hap continued, "Mr. Smythe has been making moves for years that will eventually force me out and guarantee that Stafford gets control of the team." Howie's attention was piqued. Sure, Stafford had been hanging around more and more, and was obviously being groomed for work of some sort by Daddy, but control of the team? The mere thought was chilling.

Day paused, looked Howie in the eye, and said, "Now I'm on my way out and Harold Ballard and Stafford Smythe will replace Hap Day and Conn Smythe."

Before Howie could say anything, Day revealed the key reason he stayed so long with the Leaf organization, a company called C. Smythe for Sand, controlled by Conn. Day had been a shareholder for many years after connecting with Smythe, and had continued to buy shares at Smythe's encouragement. While Smythe controlled the company, Day spent considerable time running the operation. It was quietly suggested by many that C. Smythe for Sand's success, like the Leafs', was due more to Hap than Conn.

"It's a huge gravel pit in the west end of the city. You probably know about it," Day continued. "When Stafford and Conn force me out of the hockey club, I'll have to leave the sand pit as well. That's how it works." Day talked on while Howie, stunned as much by what he was hearing as by Day's sudden outpouring, said nothing.

"When I first saw this possible scenario coming years ago," Hap said, "I asked to be bought out of the company. My number of shares by then were pretty good . . . it was in the high thirty to forty percent somewhere. But when I asked them to buy me out Conn made a ridiculous offer."

Day told Howie he then hired two different, independent assessors, to advise him on what his shares in the business were worth. Both estimated Day's shares at between $900,000 and $950,000. "The last offer Conn and Stafford made wasn't even for half of that amount. Since then, I agreed to the deal, but they lowered the bid."

Howie thought for a moment, then suggested, "Well, why not just sit tight, or walk away and take your dividends?"

Day grinned sardonically and replied, "That would be fine, but this company is set up in such a way that Stafford votes Connie a $50,000 bonus, Connie votes Staff a $50,000 bonus, and they both vote me a new car. Fifteen thousand, tops."

Y

Many a tale is told about many a character in professional sports, especially unique players and management members. Conn Smythe's name often ranks high on the list.

Certainly there was as well the wise, witty, often generous and highly respected Conn Smythe, the Major, the war veteran, born in Toronto in 1895, who'd more than proven his ability to withstand the harshness that life may deal. Cut loose by the New York Rangers after one year as GM, Smythe convinced the owners of the Toronto St. Pats to sell him the hockey club. He immediately changed the team name to "Maple Leafs" after the World War I fighting unit, the Maple Leaf Regiment. When Smythe bought the club he made himself coach, but in true Smythe spirit fired himself on October 13, 1930, and hired Art Duncan to replace him on the bench.

Conn, ever the entrepreneur, envisioned bigger things for the Leafs than the dimly lit, 8,000-seat Arena Gardens on Mutual Street could provide. On November 12, 1931, Smythe and his fellow investors in Maple Leaf Gardens Limited basked in the spotlight as their brand-new building held a capacity crowd of 12,500 people in the opening night game against Chicago.

The Gardens was built in less than five months in the midst of the Great Depression. According to Andrew Podnieks's Maple Leaf fact book, *The Blue and White Book*, construction of the Gardens required 13,500 cubic yards of concrete, 600 tons of reinforcing steel, 760 tons of structural steel, and 1.5 million bricks and tiles (the former provided by Smythe's sand pits) . . . The total cost was $1.5 million.

Ɣ

Smythe seemed to think Howie Meeker was all right. Howie was not a pet of Connie's, nor was he a confidant, but he was a feisty, pugnacious, gutsy kind of kid, and Smythe liked that. It didn't hurt that the kid from Kitchener had been wounded in the war and had had the guts to overcome it. Smythe liked that, too. Though several of his own acts and deeds over the years have been called cowardly, cold, or untrustworthy, Smythe only respected what he considered to be *real* men. He had little or no time for anyone who did not measure up, or who stood in his way. Certainly he had little time or respect for most women.

During Howie's playing days, hockey teams truly *owned* the players. Often, players were not allowed to hold a summer job without the team's consent, and playing any other sport was frowned upon. Most players were expected to jump when called, show appropriate respect, be damn thankful to be in the NHL, and feel lucky to be getting paid at all.

"They totally dominated our bodies and our minds for seven months of the year and then kept you worried for the other five months; would you be traded, sold . . . We had one Stanley Cup team party given by Maple Leaf Gardens. It was in the press room area and the wives weren't invited. Management invited some women who were major advertisers, directors, and Gardens employees, including usherettes, secretaries, concession workers . . .

but not the wives. That's how much they thought of them."

Why did NHLers of that era take such treatment? Simply put, fear. Not the sort of fear men overcome or stifle in war; instead the no less real, understandable fear of having nothing — no means by which to provide food, shelter, warmth, or security for oneself and loved ones. You learned to keep your head down. It was toe the line or hit the road, and the road was usually one-way, to the minor leagues.

Smythe's fixation with maintaining control and wielding absolute power became evident, according to Howie, when the Major returned from World War II. "While Smythe was overseas the stockholders at Maple Leaf Gardens had been paid tremendous returns, the team had won two Stanley Cups, and every game had sold out, and when Connie returned from overseas, I believe he set about to discredit, or get rid of, Frank Selke."

Howie maintains that eleven years later, Smythe used similar tactics to privately and publicly embarrass and discredit the employee who threatened his or his son's job. That employee was Hap Day.

Howie's theory closely parallels what Day told him that morning on the train: that Smythe set out to destroy Hap Day's credibility as coach, and later GM, by intentionally weakening the team. It was Smythe, after all, and not Day, who made and approved trades, sales, and other such player movements.

"We won three Stanley Cups in a row between 1947 and 1949, and even though we lost that year, Smythe could still clearly see the potential for another two or three Cups directly ahead of us." In 1951, the Leafs appeared set in goal for the next three to four years with Al Rollins and young Ed Chadwick; Jimmy Thomson, Gus Mortson, Bill Barilko, and Fern Flaman led the defence with Hugh Bolton, Marc Reaume, and Tim Horton showing potential. Up front, veterans Teeder Kennedy, Sid Smith, and Tod Sloan formed the top line, with Harry Watson, Cal Gardner, Joe Klukay, and Max Bentley providing backup. Young, promising forwards in the Leafs' system included Fleming MacKell, Danny Lewicki, Dickie Duff, and Eric Nesterenko.

With a lineup like that, Howie reasons, Smythe must have known that, despite Detroit's and Montreal's apparent stranglehold on the league, the Leafs could be Cup finalists for the next four or five years. That success would pose a big problem in eliminating Day: how do you fire or shaft a guy with five Stanley Cups in six years, or maybe six Cups in seven years, without being painted as the villain? Day, always known for his pride, made Smythe's job a step easier by resigning as coach at the end of the 1950 first-round playoff loss. Smythe assigned Day the role of assistant general manager, in effect preventing him from taking another job and so being in a position to demand a fair price for his gravel and sand shares. But Smythe knew Day would have to be out of the Leafs' picture completely by the time Stafford was ready to become GM. So he sped up his plan by dismantling his talented team.

Smythe senior also had to eliminate the obstacle posed by dissenting shareholders and directors, so he began purchasing large blocks of stock from original investors and friends as they died.

Howie says that Smythe knew if the team was no longer competitive, Day's pride would eventually force him to bow out as it had in 1950. Smythe figured once Day had left the Maple Leafs, he would take anything Conn offered for his shares in the sand and gravel business.

That's also when the major dissection of the hockey team began. In 1951–52 Toronto finished third, with the second-best defence in the league — but the second-worst offence. Toronto lost four straight to Detroit in the first round of playoffs, scoring just three goals in four games.

"Defence was fine, offence terrible, so what did they do but get rid of Fleming MacKell, a hell of a prospect at centre. They didn't trade him, they *gave* him to Boston. Could you believe?" Howie asks. In 1952–53, MacKell was tenth in scoring in 65 games with 27 goals for Boston, and was an All-Star. The next year MacKell was ninth in league scoring. The centre played ten years in Boston;

in 536 games he scored 127 goals with 185 assists. In 80 playoff games he had 22 goals and 63 points.

"So who's next? Why, our best penalty killer and all-around player, Joe Klukay. He could mix and play with anybody, any position. He also went to Boston for zilch. His second year there he became a twenty-goal man, besides all the other things he did in helping them win.

"But that's not enough. Let's really put the knife into the team's heart and twist it. How about trading Gardner, Hannigan, Mortson, and goaltender Rollins to Chicago for Harry Lumley? They were mad, or determined to ruin the team."

Howie maintains that Mortson was traded because of an incident during training camp that year. Smythe was sitting in the front seat of a giant limousine one day after a team workout and, as the players were leaving the phys-ed field, Mortson spontaneously hopped into the back seat and briefly chatted with the occupants, who were acquaintances. Mortson's brashness and nerve so angered Smythe, Meeker maintains, that Mortson was history from that point on. "It was only a matter of time, and I said as much to Gus at the time."

The Leafs did miss the playoffs in 1952–53, but the blame could also be placed on the injury to Ted Kennedy, who missed 27 games, and the mental and physical decline of Max Bentley. Boston, with ex-Leafs MacKell and Klukay in the lineup, finished third, and Chicago, thanks largely to the addition of Gardner, Mortson, and Rollins, plus Vic Lynn by way of Boston, was fourth and made the playoffs for the first time since 1946.

Before the 1953–54 season, as Howie prepared to coach Stratford, Bentley was sold to New York, crippling what little offence was left. However, assistant general manager Day, coach Joe Primeau, and goalie Harry Lumley did a magnificent job. Lumley won the Vezina Trophy, the club finished first on defence and fifth on offence, good enough for third place overall, much better than predicted. In the playoffs Toronto faced Detroit and scored just five goals in the four games they lost. Obviously, offence had become the sticking point.

Smythe's string of questionable deals next began to focus on the Leaf defence. In July 1954 he sent Fern Flaman to Boston for Dave Creighton, a fellow who would score six goals over three years for Toronto. Flaman went on to win three All-Star positions in Boston and put the Bruins in the playoffs five of the next six years.

Next he dumped Leo Boivin to get back a tired and worn out Joe Klukay. Joe ended up playing down in Pittsburgh the following year. "When Boivin and Flaman originally came to the Leafs from Boston, they were very tough, very aggressive young kids, but they had absolutely no idea how to play individual or team defence. Day, Primeau, Kennedy, and others, with great pains and lots of patience, taught them how to adapt their special skills to a game plan. No sooner were they becoming an asset than Smythe handed them back to Boston. I couldn't believe it — especially Flaman."

There were other trades as well. Danny Lewicki, who looked like he might become a consistent goal scorer, was sent to New York for cash. He made the second all-star team that year. "Then it was so long to Harry Watson — keep him happy and he was a winger who'd get you twenty goals a season with a broken leg, just as easy as falling off a log." Harry went to Chicago for cash.

"Conn had to figure if the Leafs still made the playoffs with what was left, they were magicians."

At the start of the 1954–55 season, Smythe replaced himself as general manager with Hap Day, though the appointment was largely cosmetic since Smythe still controlled trades and player movement. Once again, though, coach King Clancy, GM Day, goalie Lumley, Ted Kennedy, and Sid Smith did outstanding work and the team finished in third place. Lumley was the first all-star goalie and missed the Vezina by one goal. In 1955–56, Kennedy retired, Sid Smith was in the rats, and Tod Sloan was the miracle man. The Leafs were nine games below .500. They scored just

153 goals, worst in the league, and allowed 181 goals — 46 more than the previous season — yet squeaked into fourth place by two points. Sloan had 37 goals and made the first all-star team.

"He gave a hell of a performance. I just shook my head time after time when I heard the Leaf scores. You didn't have to ask who got the tying goal, or who got the winner; it was Sloany. Anyhow, no one else in hockey but Clancy could have put the Leafs in the playoffs. The King loved people, loved life, loved the game and the players. He was a funny, bubbly character. He loved horses, the track, and the payoff window. What a man, what a pleasure. The players would walk on nails for Clancy, and that's mainly why they got there that year.

"So Hap, the general manager in name only, survived two years of hell thanks to the King getting super goaltending and great effort from everyone."

After the 1955–56 season, Clancy had had enough. "I'm sure at that time, because he and Hap were very close, that Clancy knew what was going on. I think he just said, 'That's it, I've had it, the pressure here is too much,' and just quit as coach." Clancy was reassigned as assistant general manager.

"To make sure Hap didn't survive another year, Smythe advised and insisted on selling Harry Lumley and Eric Nesterenko to Chicago for $40,000. Come on, there had to be other things moved from Toronto to Chicago besides money on that deal. Nesterenko wasn't going to be a superstar, but he was going to be a very good player, a top second- or third-line forward." Nesterenko played fifteen years in Chicago, appearing in 1,003 games, scoring 207 goals and 495 points, and playing in 115 playoff games — giving the Blackhawks an excellent return on their $20,000 investment.

"If Nesterenko had stayed in Toronto that year and scored 20 goals in 1956–57 we'd have made the playoffs. If Lumley stayed in Toronto and played 25 games we'd have won or tied ten of those and made the playoffs. Nine times the previous year he shut out or held the opposition to one goal per game; thirty times he held the opposition to two goals a game or less against. There is no way you can improve that kind of goaltending. No way."

Finally, at the end of the 1956–57 season, his web now fully woven, Conn held a news conference and Hap took the fall for the club missing the playoffs. Day quietly left hockey that day, and the company, C. Smythe for Sand, soon after.

If not for the business ties that bound Hap Day to Smythe, Howie suggests, he could have been coach with any team in the league that he wanted, and probably had the coach and general manager's job with at least three other teams.

V

Somehow Connie knew that Howie knew about the gravel-pit deal and some years later it came out. Smythe's horses weren't running so well that year, but horse owner Frank Stronach was having a fine season. Howie was a guest of Stronach's at Woodbine racetrack in Toronto one day when Stronach's horse won a big race. Howie huddled into the victory picture later with the horse, jockey, Stronach, and Howie's friend Gerry Petrie. While Stronach collected his winnings, Howie bumped into Conn and shook hands.

"Your horse ran out of gas in the stretch," Howie said.

Smythe muttered something about his trainer and then out of the blue said, "That Hap Day got a great deal when we parted company. I treated him all right."

Before Howie could answer, Stronach came into view, seven or eight tables down the way. Other owners and racing fans were congratulating him. Smythe stared briefly at Stronach, and said to Howie, "Look at that Johnny-come-lately S.O.B. His word doesn't mean a goddamn thing."

Howie looked Smythe right in the eye, and said, "You should talk, sir. Good day."

Twelve

On The Rock

"I couldn't believe my eyes. Not only was the place packed, but they hollered and yelled like they were at a game. We worked for one and a half hours and hardly a single person left the building; in fact, they kept on coming in. Right then and there I thought, 'Holy smokes Meeker, you better produce some good hockey in the next while.'"

A day or two before Howie popped Stafford, *Toronto Star* writer Milt Dunnell, a friend since Howie's junior days in Stratford, called about a column he was writing. The headline in the *Star*'s weekend edition read "Howie Meeker in the Hot Seat" and talked about the difficult task facing Howie as general manager, trying to put together a competitive club. Before it went to press Dunnell called the man himself for his opinion.

"Print it as is," Howie instructed.

Dunnell suggested Howie's job was akin to playing Russian

roulette and that he had little chance of surviving the job for a number of reasons: he was the only holdover from the Hap Day regime; Howie was appointed by Conn Smythe and not Stafford's hockey committee "Silver Seven," which was now running the Leafs. Stafford wanted his friend and business partner, Harold Ballard, as the club's general manager

A day after Dunnell's call, Conn Smythe summoned Howie to Toronto. The second he hung up the phone at home, Howie knew he was gone. When he arrived in Toronto, Smythe had a letter of resignation ready. It said they "had agreed to disagree," that Howie had resigned as manager, that he would be paid for the rest of the year. Verbally, Conn offered Howie a job in public relations "or whatever." Howie said he would think about it. No press conference was held, and since it was Grey Cup weekend, no reporters were on hand. The whole country was football mad. The story, "Meeker fired as general manager of the Toronto Maple Leafs," was on the fourth or fifth page of the sports section. "My neighbours and some close friends didn't know about it until the next week," Howie says. "The timing was a smart move."

So Howie Meeker, the father of four children by age thirty-three, who had been a machinist apprentice, soldier, hockey player, coach, general manager, and federal politician, was out of a job. What was he going to do next?

As often seemed the case for Howie, when one door closed other one opened — or else the phone rang. One of the calls was from Lorne Wakelin of St. John's, Newfoundland. When Howie coached in Stratford, Wakelin managed the arena in Goderich, Ontario, about sixty miles away, and the two men got to know each other well. Around 1955, Wakelin was hired to run a new arena in St. John's, but he couldn't solve a "hockey problem" they had, and had been told to find someone who could. He called Howie and asked if he was interested.

"When I explained the offer to Grace we both laughed. Newfoundland? Not likely!"

Howie phoned and declined the offer. Then Tommy Ivan called from Chicago, offering a possible coaching job in Sault Ste. Marie.

Next day, Newfoundland premier Joey Smallwood called personally and convinced Howie at least to visit the province and see what the offer was about. Howie accepted and in October of 1957 boarded a noisy TransCanada Airlines North Star for a grueling flight to Canada's most eastern geographical bookend. Grace wisely decided to wait for a possible second trip, "in the spring, perhaps." The long hours of travel suggested Howie was bound for another world. When he landed, in many ways it seemed that indeed he may have found exactly that.

There is good reason that the 42,734-square-mile island is nicknamed "The Rock," for in fact that is what it is. A massive, solid, rugged, beautiful, determined, harsh rock. Aeons ago The Rock was a piece of the continent. Geological upheaval over millions of years changed that. The Rock's unforgiving coastlines were hewn away by giant shards of ice as the Wisconsin Glacier ambled to the sea. A rugged land, yet hospitable . . . much like its people.

Steeped in an Irish ancestry, but separate as a land unto itself, Newfoundland is passion and hospitality at its finest. Straightforward, fun-loving, warm, and direct; Newfoundland people are fabulous friends and formidable foes.

Newfoundlanders work hard, and play harder. They live for life itself, for fun and music, family, and hockey. "They are a people like no other. There is only one Newfoundland.

"They say that it takes three years to tell a story about one year in Newfoundland so there is no way that I can explain our incredible and eventful nineteen years there in so few pages. It wouldn't do Newfoundland, or Howie Meeker, justice. My life in Newfoundland is a book in itself, which if I'm lucky I may live long enough to tell. But not today, and not here.

"Newfoundland was an experience like no other, and I'm glad we didn't pass it up, tempted as I was on those first couple of flights to Newfoundland to just head home."

The move to The Rock was a huge undertaking , and it proved to have an equally large impact on the Meekers' lives. For Howie it eventually led him in to the sports broadcasting world and the agency business, as well as inspiring the opening of his hockey schools around the country. As had happened to so many before him, from the moment Howie first landed in Newfoundland his life was profoundly changed.

His first taste of that unique Newfie spirit, passion, and hospitality was instantaneous upon his stepping out of the airplane at St. John's that first visit in October 1957. "It was 4:30 a.m. and I was shocked to see, aside from Wakelin, a number of newspaper and radio reporters, and interested residents gathered there. I guess maybe they thought I was really a somebody. Looking back now, they probably thought I was about to walk the plank, right into the ocean. They probably figured the St. John's 'problem' would chop me up pretty quick, if indeed I stayed long enough to discover what it was."

Howie met and talked with numerous folks that first visit, including mayor Harry Mews; town "boss" and council member Ned Foran; Leo Stead from the Memorial Stadium committee; and Gordon Sterling, chairman of the city council-appointed "hockey investigating committee" struck the previous summer.

"We talked and they explained their system and problems as best they could. Up until that moment, during school, work, hockey, and even in political campaigns, I never saw religion as a problem in my life. However, it took me no time to realize how religion dominated every aspect of life in St. John's; that even sports were run along the lines of the religious school system."

The city's large Roman Catholic population had three school systems: St. Bons for the rich and famous, St. Pats and Holy Cross for the rest. The Anglican Athletic Association was called the Feildians, while the United Church Athletic Association was known as the Guards. Each organization fielded teams in darts, five-pin bowling, basketball, soccer, rowing, hockey, and baseball. Soccer, and the annual St. John's Regatta, were the big summer events, while hockey, by far, was the most important championship of all. The Boyle Trophy, indicating local hockey supremacy, was the prized possession.

Each religious association had junior and senior high school hockey teams, and teams in the St. John's Junior and Senior hockey leagues. During the season, all-star Junior and Senior teams were chosen to represent St. John's in provincial championships. So severe was the religious rift and wrath, though, it was difficult to convince many players to compete for the Herder Memorial Trophy, emblematic of Newfoundland Senior hockey supremacy. Forming such a unit would mean a coalition team of Catholics and Protestants. Hell would have to freeze over before most of them would consider joining such a team.

Howie says that the St. John's sport set-up was good despite its shortcomings. But it certainly was a religious war, especially in hockey. Many of the toughest, hardest fought, most emotional games were between Catholic teams: St. Pats and Holy Cross against wealthy St. Bons. However, the Catholic groups united as one when playing the Guards or the Feildians.

The "hockey problem" was that St. Bons had won a total of twenty-four Boyle Trophy titles over the years, including sixteen consecutive championships. The key to their success was that they had their own small artificial ice arena on campus. It was the only school rink in town. Naturally, only St. Bons's students and parents could get ice time. Other teams tried hard to be competitive, but were at such a disadvantage that year after year the elite Catholics won the Boyle Trophy, "and they would never let anyone forget it. When St. Bons had the only ice in town, their advantage was so great that all the rest were farting against thunder."

Two years prior to Howie's arrival, city council agreed to build a public arena, the Memorial Stadium. F. M. O'Leary, who ran the new arena committee, convinced around eighty percent of working Newfoundlanders in the St. John's area to donate one percent of their salary for a year. Meanwhile, United Church Guards shaker and mover, Dr. Harry Roberts, wanted to beat St. Bons at hockey so badly he could practically taste it. Together with Don Jamieson, Ralph Atwell, Arthur Johnston, the Guards Athletic Association, and others, he spearheaded a fundraising campaign for another rink. Letters were sent to 110 prominent church supporters asking them to sign a note for $1,000 towards the new Prince of Wales Arena. Apparently more than 110 people signed the notes, on the strength of which the bank leant the Guards the $100,000 to get started. When the arena was completed Ralph Colyer was hired as arena manager.

After almost two years, however, the new arenas had failed to level the playing field, or resolve St. Bons's hockey dominance, so everyone decided it was time to change the "system." But no one was up to such a daunting, unprecedented task. The "system" was steeped in years of St. John's tradition and replete with shrapnel from an ongoing, nearly raging, religious conflict. As Howie's son Mike would suggest years later, "Playing hockey in Newfoundland then was like Northern Ireland on ice. It was a religious war with skates, sticks, and pucks." So they looked outside, all the way to the mainland, to find a hockey saviour — or scapegoat. Enter Howie Meeker.

"The smartest politicians in the British Empire had, for fifty years, been trying to settle matters in Ireland, and failed. What was I, a transplanted, hockey-playing mainlander, supposed to do about it?" Howie asks in amazed recollection.

Still, Howie and Grace decided Howie would agree to a job offer to coach a Junior all-star team for the remainder of the winter; after that, they would consider a more permanent move.

Once back in St. John's, Howie boarded with Ma Marsh and her sister. The elderly women owned a huge duplex on Circular Road, at one time one of St. John's finest areas, and a two-minute walk to the arena. There he met good friend George Anderson.

Howie watched most of the Junior practices and games for a couple of weeks and then submitted a list of players to try out for the all-star team representing St. John's at the provincial playoffs. "Despite the lack of early training, I found their skill levels pretty high. Every team, at every level, had four or five youngsters with great potential. Everyone, at every age, worked harder than anybody I'd ever seen at the amateur level." Of the twenty five skaters and two goalies who were asked to try out for the junior team, unbeknownst to Howie, thirteen were Protestants, thirteen were Catholics, and one was a Salvation Army kid.

Having spent more than ten years in the NHL, Howie thought he'd seen the most devoted of hockey fans. Surely no one was crazier about the game than the hard-working prairie folks, or those fanatics who swarmed regularly into Maple Leaf Gardens or the Montreal Forum. However, compared to Newfoundland hockey fans, the rest of the continent seemed to be in a stupor. Everything about the game appealed to Newfoundlanders, including the intensity, rivalry, and rough play. Newfies took their hockey almost as seriously as their religion. They lived and died for the game, and expected their players to do the same.

So Howie was not prepared for the scene that awaited him at that first Junior all-star practice held in St. John's Memorial Stadium. The candidates' names were announced in the papers and on the radio, as was the 7 p.m. practice time. Howie walked to the stadium at 6:15 and was surprised to see hundreds of people outside the rink, obviously waiting to get tickets for some special event. When the Junior team stepped on the ice that night the stands were packed with between 1,500 to 2,000 people. The special event was Howie Meeker running a practice.

"I couldn't believe my eyes. Not only was the place packed, but they hollered and yelled like they were at a game. We worked for one and a half hours and hardly a single person left the building; in fact, they kept on coming in. Right then and there I thought, 'Holy smokes Meeker, you better produce some good hockey in the next while.'"

Howie recognized that with only a few practices remaining in the season, and kids from four or five different teams being melded together, he'd have little time for teaching anything but basic defence: how to check and play behind their own blueline.

His instruction worked well, and in the opening round of the provincial playoffs St. John's defeated powerful Bell Island while in the finals, St. John's met and defeated the defending junior champions from Grand Falls. Led by Tolson Chapman in goal, and the superior play of defencemen Rolly Clarke, Dave Barrett, Clyde Green, and Joe Kenny, St. John's had cause to celebrate.

Howie was asked to handle the local Senior club, seeking the Herder Memorial Trophy. St. John's had been denied the trophy since 1949, and that didn't sit well. Again St. John's eliminated Bell Island in the opening round, and faced a Grand Falls squad in the finals, but failed to capture the coveted Herder hardware.

"Part of my job was to get to know not only the problem, but the people, which was the finest job a person could have, and then find a solution. Further investigation simply led to the original conclusion: the problem was that St. Bons controlled City Hall, the hockey executive, the referees' association, and about half the hockey talent in town. The others simply wanted a level playing field."

Howie could see a couple of long-term solutions, but for the short term there seemed to be none. "I talked to anybody, and everybody, who might fill in the many blanks, or could lead to a solution to the problem for the short term. I talked to St. Pats' Jack Conners and his executive, to Dr. Harry Roberts, Ralph Colyer, the Prince of Wales arena manager, to Ralph Atwell, Sid and Charlie Quick of the Guards, Gordon Breen and Jeff Carnell of the Feildians, referee association president Ted Withers, Hugh Fardy, Joe Smith, John Doyle, and Jack Reardigan from St. Bons.

"It wasn't long before I realized that St. Bons had such an advantage in the development of talent and control that, unless changes were made in philosophy and conditions, they would continue to dominate for years."

Howie met with Gordon Sterling and his committee and told him the only way to ever challenge St. Bons's hockey superiority was to take away some of their practice time at the Stadium, and give it to St. Pats, Holy Cross, and the Feildians, the teams that didn't have outside ice time.

"Give me the keys to the Stadium, let me be the boss, and within three to five years, under this new philosophy, somebody will legitimately challenge St. Bons for the Boyle Trophy," Howie said.

Naturally, word leaked out and, as Howie puts it, "the shit hit the fan. My name was mud with all the Catholic and United Church people. They argued that they'd paid for that stadium, signed notes, donated one percent of the money invested, and wanted their fair share of it."

Ɣ

When the playoffs ended, Howie was offered a five-year deal as head coach for the entire Guards hockey system: the Junior and Senior teams as well as the high-school teams. It offered enough security that Grace and Howie decided to make the big move.

After his two trips to Newfoundland Howie realized just how far out of mainstream Canada his family was moving, of how far St. John's was from Toronto. It seemed crazy to even consider such a shift. Not many people were moving to Newfoundland in 1958. The migration had tended to be just the reverse ever since Newfoundland had officially joined Canada nine years before, but in August that year the Meeker clan moved to the eastern seaboard.

They settled in a huge house, plunked in the midst of some colourful row housing on Maxse Street. The day after they arrived, there was a knock on the door and there stood a short, roly-poly guy with horn-rimmed glasses, a round apple-cheeked face, and eyes that sparkled. With his hand stuck out, he announced, "Welcome to St. John's. I'm Bob Grouchy [pronounced Grew-she]. Foot and I, and the kids, live in the house right beside your back door. How about coming over for a drink tonight?"

Howie knew right off the bat that Grouchy was something special, somebody a cut above the average, someone to enjoy life with, and how right he was. The Grouchys had a number of people over that night to help welcome the transplanted mainlanders, and two in particular became good friends: Myer Freelich and Bill McDonald. Myer was a piano playing character with a Newfoundland twang, and a witty sense of humour. "He was the master of great one-liners and jokes." McDonald was a strong Liberal and a firm Joey Smallwood supporter. He ran a small trucking company and was a constant fishing and hunting buddy of Bob Grouchy.

Much later, Howie discovered that he and Grace were the only Protestants in a house full of Catholics. Bob and Foot (her real name was Olga, but her large feet inspired the nickname) were strong St. Bons supporters and Bob was a member of the school/church executive.

"Despite that, they threw a party for us less than thirty-six hours after we arrived in the city, even though part of my job with the rival United Church Athletic Association was to end St. Bons's hockey dominance. At the time I still wasn't tuned in to the full circle of religious activity and its domination within the community and province. Bob was doing the neighbourly Newfoundland thing, but it took a lot of guts. In the following years, as we became good friends, Bob took a lot of flack both in his business and his church life due to his association with me."

Ɣ

A month after moving, in September 1958, Howie opened his sporting goods store. Friend and famed wrestler "Whipper" Billy Watson took part in the grand opening. Howie did fairly well with the business but with so many other jobs and commitments he did not have enough time to run the store properly and he eventually sold the business.

The Guards hockey program was huge, taking up any spare moments he might have. He worked with the Prince of Wales high school's Juniors and Seniors, as well as the Junior and Senior Guards teams. That meant practices every day from 7:30 to 8:30 in the morning and again from 6:30 to 8:30 every night, school games from 4:30 to 6 p.m. at least two days a week, and Junior and/or Senior Guards games from 7:30 to 9:30 p.m. twice a week.

Howie's life was further complicated with the unique Newfoundland religious spin-off factor. Most mornings he would leave home at 6:45 with four or five kids, drive by at least four elementary schools closer to home, and then drop his children off at three different schools, three miles apart. "It was a stupid educational system and the majority of Newfoundlanders finally realized it forty years later."

As a result of what Howie and his helpers began to do in the development of local players and Junior hockey talent, St. John's eventually became so strong they won consecutive Herder titles from 1973 to 1976. The all-star team from St. John's was so strong it was barred from competing in the league; the city had to be represented by a club team. Even that didn't stop them, as they claimed championships in 1978 and 1979.

Faced with the task of capturing the Boyle Trophy for the Senior Guards, Howie wasted little time in starting to assess the situation. "In comparison, the Guards were the weakest of all the clubs: St. Bons, St. Pats, and the Feildians. The Junior Guards were also the lowest in their level, but perhaps a little more teachable."

A key junior player who stood out from that first Junior practice was a wanna-be puck-stopper named Eggy. "We were rotating goalies during the practice and I saw this little guy, no bigger than a minute; his head didn't even come up to the crossbar." Howie noticed that the youngster found a perfect natural position on all shots, waited for the puck to come to him, was quick as a cat, and, best of all, stayed on his feet.

Howie couldn't believe what he was seeing, and as he skated over to him he said a little prayer: "Please Lord, let him have a goaltender's mind and attitude."

"Hey kid, what's your name?" Howie asked.

"Billiard, sir, Eggy Billiard."

"Eggy, don't you ever fall down?"

"I tries to stay on me feet, sir." Howie says he rode that kid to almost every championship they ever won in Newfoundland in those years. "He never did grow much physically, yet skillfully, he got a heck of a lot better. He developed into a goaltender with a great mind."

In 1961–62, Howie's teams won the Junior title and the Boyle Trophy. The Guards had help from various unexpected sources. When St. Pats put an end to St. Bons's twenty-four years of Boyle domination the previous year, the big boys couldn't stand the heat in the kitchen, picked up their puck, and dropped out of competition.

"I always admired their organization — they did what they had to do to win — but they didn't have the balls to stick around when they got a little competition."

Then, somehow, some open-minded Newfoundlanders got former St. Bons star, Ray Murphy, not only to play but also to captain the Guards team. "Sure as hell, that galled the old-time Guard supporters: a Mick captain on a Protestant team? No way! But, I guess they thought, 'Well, if it means the Boyle, we'll hold our nose and take it.'"

Y

During his final years of playing hockey with the Maple Leafs, Howie naturally thought about what to do after hockey. He wanted to remain connected with the NHL and contemplated becoming a newspaper sportswriter. He talked to Red Burnett of the *Toronto Star*, and Jim Vipond of the *Globe and Mail*, who encouraged him to submit some articles. So Howie wrote reports on his last two games played in the NHL, and on a couple of other Junior and Senior games. "It didn't take me long to realize that I couldn't make what was in my head readable and entertaining on paper."

Don Jamieson was not only one of Howie's bosses while he worked for the Guards, he was also co-owner, with Jeff Sterling, of CJON Radio and TV. With a sixth child just months away and low on money, Howie thought about giving radio a try. Since CJON studios were across the street from the Prince of Wales arena, Howie let George McDonald, head of the news department, know that if an opening in sports came along he would like to try out.

A few months later Howie walked into the news room around noon, and George was whapping away at the typewriter rewriting a 7 a.m. news story for the 1 p.m. news. McDonald looked up briefly, returned to his pecking at the keys, and said, "Howie. You still interested in that sports job?"

"When?"

"Now."

"Now?"

"Right now, I need something for the 1:30 sports."

"Where do I go? What do I do?"

"In that little room over there, the wire sports copy is stapled together and the morning paper is there to glean something from. You're on the air for about seven minutes. Good luck."

Howie quickly wrote down a few things, in his unique style, and took them to Charlie Peddle, the sound and recording engineer. Charlie showed Howie how to operate the microphone and other equipment. Several palm-sweating, nerve-grinding minutes later, Howie had completed the job. As he left the news room, George said, "You're on again at 6:30 tonight, and 7:45 tomorrow morning. Oh, yeah, you did good."

Howie's sports show was an immediate hit and quickly thereafter led to doing the TV sports show that followed Don Jamieson's newscast, which drew the biggest audience in Newfoundland. Howie didn't lose any of Jamieson's audience, and it wasn't long before Howie was rivaled only by Joey Smallwood in controversy.

Y

While living on Maxse Street between 1958 and 1960, Grace and Howie often drove the bumpy, dusty gravel road to a little fishing outport called St. Phillips, on Conception Bay. It was a particularly marvelous spot during the summer and the family would picnic, swim, fish, and boat there often. They fell in love with a glorious meadow, high on a hill behind a picturesque church which over-looked the bay, village, and in the distance, Bell Island.

Eventually, they purchased their dream fifteen-acre parcel of land for $2,500, hired a young St. John's architect to draw plans, contracted out the construction, and that fall moved into a beauti-ful home, practically all windows, with as great a view as found in Newfoundland. The locals thought the Meekers were nuts to move to an outport fifteen minutes' drive from anywhere in St. John's, where the wind always blew hard. "We had no power, and were on a party line; three longs and eight shorts was our call, what a night-mare." The extra room was nice, though, because on December 28, 1960, Andy Meeker hit the world. Howie had his sixth child, third boy, and first Newfie.

Howie still collected pigeons and built a two-storey barn with Harold Sheppard to keep them in. The birds drew plenty of spectators, especially tumblers, tipplers, and rollers, who entertained car loads of onlookers stopped on the roadside.

During the early 1960s Howie was asked to join Prime Minister Diefenbaker's newly formed National Sports Advisory Council with some twenty-five other knowledgeable Canadian sports people. "I'm sure my good friend, Hugh Latimer, was the person responsible for advancing my name. Also, I was probably the only Conservative in Newfoundland at the time, so they probably had to give it to me," Howie scoffs.

Don Jamieson saw it as big news and CJON did a live interview with Howie during his sports show. "Here I was, a Johnny-come-lately mainlander, and a Protestant at that, hated by all the hockey fans across the Island, and eighty percent of them in St. John's, and I was going to speak on their behalf in Ottawa? What a country!"

The National Fitness Council included many of Howie's sports friends and writers including Harry "Red" Foster (Special Olympics), James Warrell (Olympic Committee), sports writers Scotty

Melville, Charlie Mayer, Ted Reeve, Andy O'Brien, and Vern DeGeer, "Rocket" Richard, and football's Herb Trawick and Joe Porrier. "The leaders of almost every national sports organization and a lot of academics were there," Howie recalls.

Before Howie left The Rock for that first meeting, he met with a group of Newfoundlanders to find out what they considered to be most important if money was available. He ended up with a lengthy list, but at the top was a provincial sports centre. The plan was to renovate one of the large hangars at St. John's airport. Estimated cost for full renovation would be $150,000, plus funds would be needed towards operating expenses for five years.

There was a financial pie to be sliced up each year for sports, but it was quickly consumed. Quebec got more than its fair share, then the Olympic and Pan American Games committees got a considerable piece. The Amateur Athletic Association of Canada took another slice, by which time there was barely anything left for the rest of the representatives and organizations — though that didn't keep them from arguing over the leftovers for a day and a half. In the end, Howie and Newfoundland had diddly-squat.

But Howie had learned to play the political game during his stint as an MP from masters like Lester Pearson. He arranged a dinner and poker game, brought in some London Dock, and went fishing for funds.

"A year and four or five meetings later, the big wheels threw me a bone: $150,000 to renovate the hangar into a provincial sports facility and $25,000 a year for five years for expenses. Yahoo!" Graham Snow was named provincial athletic director and made good use of the facility.

Howie stayed in pretty good shape and one day was asked to play for the Senior Guards. At thirty-seven years of age he was still in better condition than many Senior players, and still good enough to have some fun. However, that announcement caused a huge stink in the local league. "They held special meetings everywhere, and with St. Bons and St. Pats holding the hammer I realized there was no way they'd let me play. Their reasoning was that it was an amateur league and once a professional, always a professional." Even though Howie would qualify as an amateur anywhere else in Canada, such was not the case in St. John's, Newfoundland, that year. Of course the league unanimously agreed that should Howie wish to play on the St. John's team competing for the provincial Herder hardware, that would be acceptable. "Somewhere along the line I was stupid enough to actually do that. I almost got killed, but that's another story."

Y

After four years of work, the Guards Athletic Association had a hockey system that, properly guided, would be very competitive at every level for years to come.

But Howie wasn't happy.

"I wanted to teach how to play the game, how to think. I wanted to teach creativity, offensive hockey, not just physical skills. It had been year after year of teaching skating, puck-handling, how to give and take a pass, back up and turn, how to come out of your own end . . . I was sick and tired of starting from scratch every year with my high school teams, being with a kid just three or maybe four years, and that was it. I was tired of teaching senior high school kids what they should have been taught between ages eight to fourteen."

After the 1962 season, Howie went to the chairman of the United Church school board, Bill Keeping, and told him to find someone else to run their high school teams.

But Keeping encouraged him to solve the problem rather than leave. "What's the answer?" Keeping responded.

"Give me a day or two and I'll draft up a plan on paper," Howie said.

Howie recommended the Guards start their own minor hockey house league and provided a three-page outline on how to do so. Two days later Keeping phoned Howie and said, "I've talked to everyone in the schools and have their complete cooperation. Go ahead with your program." Howie was shocked, but the Avalon Consolidated Minor Hockey program was born.

Howie arranged to have one teacher and one parent on every team. There were eight elementary schools, four junior high schools, and two high schools. Twenty-four hours of ice time per week was allotted for the program, over and above the five hours a week already given to high-school teams in the mornings. Each Saturday, games were held from 7 a.m. to 6 p.m. A budget was provided to purchase goal equipment and equipment for those who could not afford it.

Canadian Amateur Hockey Association rules were discarded for "Howie" rules.

Howie started the Avalon system with a dictatorial approach, then handed it over to others once it was on its feet and functioning. "Sometimes you need to have a dictator for a day, then take your views to others to modify, and gain a consensus." With a lot of thought and hard work he sold his minor hockey league philosophy to the board of education, the principal, teachers, and key helpers, "all people with no axes to grind."

With "participation for all" the main thrust of the program, it had to be an easy sell. "We had people in the executive who knew what they were talking about, and oh my, did it work. At the end of every season, Bill Keeping, the liaison teachers from the schools, Eric Crocker, my divisional leaders, and the travelling coaches all sat down and changed rules. We all agreed with the philosophy and found better and quicker ways to get there."

Howie needed people to help make the programs run, people with some common sense who enjoyed watching kids play hockey. He also needed a group of parents who would agree to the rules to run a division at every level.

He found those key people in Eric Crocker, Eric Rowe, and Dave Riche.

Avalon functioned as a two-tier system: a recreational league and a competitive league. Howie maintained that a competitive league was needed in order to raise the standards of play. But a competitive league meant a greater need for coaches and referees, obviously more help. "A young giant on my junior team, Rick Babstock, was the first to step up, and several others followed."

With the option of competitive or recreational play available, and interesting, challenging approaches to the game, the response was staggering. Howie had expected thirty-six kids from each of the eight elementary schools to form an eight-team competitive league, as well as having an eight-team recreational league with eighteen kids per team.

At the first school practice there were more than fifty kids on the ice, and that trend continued. At the end of the day Howie had eight teams of what were supposed to be the best in the age group, and eighteen teams of recreational players. The numbers continued to swell. Soon Howie had thirty-five recreational teams in Atoms and Pee Wees and he'd promised them one-hour games once a week. There was only one solution — divide the ice in half and have two games going at one time.

The next hurdle was the eight-team competitive league, which required four games and eight practice times per week, one for each team. Howie got creative and decided to have three teams practice simultaneously as one group, everyone working on one skill at a time: skating, puck-handling, and passing. Properly done, players would be kept busy, and all the ice would be used.

Such creative problem-solving techniques were behind much of the basics and teachings used later in the Howie Meeker Hockey Schools. His helpers at Avalon soon learned how to work effectively with forty-five kids on the ice, three teams, and six goalies. "Rick Babstock, Bob Babcock, Dave Butler, and my sons, Howie Jr. and Mike, along with the kids in the Junior and Senior system, made it work, and made it fun. Our hockey formula was taking real shape."

Howie's recreational playing rules dictated that players played the puck and not the man. Hitting from behind was prohibited.

Each team was divided into three units of five players, according to skill level. Each unit had a different coloured arm band: yellow, blue, or green. Units would be matched on the ice with each shift lasting two minutes and fifteen seconds. A bell rang at that time and unless a scoring chance was in progress, the referee would blow his whistle ending play.

Lines would change quickly while the referee retrieved the puck, held it above his head, counted to ten, and pitched it in the corner. "You never saw ten kids get off the ice, or ten get on so quickly." All minor penalties were solved by a penalty shot.

"No one could believe how much the average student in the recreational league had improved by early December. No scoring or personal records were kept in the recreational league. The kids and parents knew who the big scorers were, but we made out like we didn't know, or care. Eventually, Feildian Gardens joined the league."

The Consolidated Avalon Minor Hockey program met with great success and after three or four years had forty-eight recreational teams in four different age brackets on the ice. As well, there were forty-six competitive teams with well over 1,200 boys, and some girls, playing. "A great amount of that program's success was due to Bill Keeping. I owe him, not only for my ten most enjoyable, though hardest-working, years in hockey, but also for the opportunity to learn how to teach skills. I've had hundreds of happy and profitable hours, and met many wonderful people, through clinics and hockey schools all over the world. Without Bill Keeping, I'm not sure it would have happened."

One level of hockey participation continued to falter, though, and that was the involvement of teenagers in the game. There wasn't much room in Junior and Senior high school leagues, so what could be done with the rest of them? There were thirty to forty Midget age players with no place to go.

A few of the St. John's senior players were also RCMP members, and Howie convinced them to try to have the RCMP run a midget-juvenile hockey league. Once again Howie had cast the fly upon the water.

Sure enough, the police agreed — provided Howie could find available ice.

What happened next not even Howie imagined possible. "I had to do something, so I came up with a dream — it could have been a nightmare, but it turned into a pleasant dream."

Once again Howie went to Bill Keeping, and explained the development progress, the ice problem, the RCMP . . . Finally, he suggested that they bar all Protestant kids from participating in the city-run hockey program at the Memorial Stadium, and give almost the entire ice allotment to the Catholic school hockey system.

"Ever see a big, strong, healthy guy stop breathing and turn white? I mean white white? When he finally regained some colour he said, 'Almost all the ice time?'"

Howie laid out two exceptions. "We get a minimum of four and a maximum of six hours per week for an RCMP juvenile league, and we invite the Catholic school system to play in our system, those fourteen years of age and under."

Keeping took a deep breath and said, "I'll run it by my people, but don't get your hopes up."

The next most important fellow in town was city clerk, Ed Foran. When Foran heard Howie's plan, he laughed. "You're mad, Meeker. But just in case it's yes, I'll get everybody, the Stadium and the church, on my side. I'll get them in line, and if you can do it, we'll do it."

In a week Bill called back and said, "No problem. Go ahead." Howie took his proposal to a St. John's minor hockey meeting, and when he was finished he could have heard a pin drop. The astounded looks exchanged between the two Jesuits and George Fardy, the Catholic layman, were hilarious.

The president, Gordon Duff, a Protestant and good buddy of Howie's said, "Jeez, boys, you don't expect me to make that public. I will resign before that's announced. The only way out of this thing is to have Howie Meeker do it. Make him president, and let him make the announcement." And that's what happened.

The Juvenile RCMP league was a huge success, with 165 kids showing up from everywhere. They started the league with six teams, then eight; and eventually had a two division, ten team league. Many times over the years an RCMP officer would mention the program in glowing terms.

Ⱶ

While with the Sports Advisory board, Howie was reunited with Roly McLenahan, then Minister of Recreation and Sport in Louis Robishaud's New Brunswick government. Roly had once belonged to the Montreal Canadien chain and played in Hershey in the American league for years. He was there when Howie coached Pittsburgh. Roly was running hockey clinics all over the province and invited Howie, along with three other Maritime members of the sports council, as observers to the clinic. The main lecturers were Dr. John Meagher, Vance Toner, and Pete Kelly, all from the University of New Brunswick.

It didn't take Howie Meeker long to pontificate his theories and views on the game and in no time he was invited to become part of their travelling clinic. "My, oh my, what an education. There were others I learned from in the clinic such as Ed Meagher, director of athletics at Loyola High School in Montreal, and Father Kehoe, dean of men at St. Francis Xavier University — a marvelous guy. I'd go to his church any day."

All of them had the same objectives in mind: to increase the participation of teenagers in the game of hockey, and to increase skills for more personal enjoyment.

Howie parted company with the city hockey management as coach after some of the influential members of the executive decided they wanted to chase the provincial Herder Cup and brought in Fleming MacKell to do so. Howie felt that at the time the team was not big, tough, or mean enough to handle the other clubs.

MacKell played exceptionally well, but he couldn't overcome the club's main problem: too many boys in a man's league. He couldn't perform both roles, and the club's lack of toughness did him in. Ewart Hillyard and Kelly Grant then took control of the team and brought in Les Calder as player/coach. Calder had played minor pro. "He had a strong shot, was very competitive, and a great guy, but at the time he wasn't a coach."

Halfway through the 1970–71 season Les said he couldn't do it all, so Les, Ewart, and Kelly asked Howie to take over the bench, and he agreed.

"In the finals against Gander, the series was tied 2–2 and the fifth game was back in St. John's, one that we just had to win, and they smoked us good. So we went back to Gander for the sixth game and everyone thought, 'school's out.' Our reputation wasn't too good on the road, so nobody gave us a chance. But thanks to some of the veterans from Bell Island and Conception Bay, and some great young guys from the local league, and goalie Eggy Billiard, we came through."

Halfway into the third period, with the game tied, Calder let go a howitzer from the blue line, and the St. John's Capitals led 3–2. George Spracklin put in the clincher and St. John's tied the series. That road victory swung the momentum, and the final game in St. John's was over before it really started. The Capitals dominated right away and grabbed a two-goal lead. They won the final game by three goals and St. John's had its first Herder Memorial Trophy in twenty-two years. The city went crazy.

ꙮ

After leaving the Guards and Senior hockey, Howie spent his time with the Avalon programs and at CJON. The financial rewards for coaching local minor hockey teams, even when combined with the radio and television shows, weren't enough to house, feed, and clothe six kids, and care for numerous dogs, pigeons, and horses.

The number-one participant sport in St. John's at the time was five-pin bowling, with about ten lanes in town, six at St. Pats. Supplies were hard to get, though, because the local agent had died.

Howie eventually contacted the Brunswick Bowling company and got the job as agent for equipment and supplies. Soon after, he went to Don and Colin Jamieson at CJON and suggested that he host a one-hour TV bowling show. Don said, "Why not?" It wasn't long before the bowling business improved considerably.

"We got lucky. Jack Cranshaw, a thrasher and a basher, won twelve straight weeks while the women's champion Bernice Cook was just the opposite. She was all style, skill, poise. Immediately we had the number-one TV show on the air."

All of a sudden everybody wanted to bowl. In two years St. John's went from ten lanes to more than 100 lanes, and from one building to four. Selling and servicing became a very big and profitable business and Howie decided to pursue other agency openings.

Woolco had just built a new store and when Grace and Howie went on tour they were amazed at the size and the stock and the variety of the same. Grace said, "Look at the toy department." Shelf after shelf was filled with Tonka trucks, Mattel toys, Barbie dolls, talking dolls. Howie went over to the luggage department. There was Samsonite everywhere, and in the guns and sporting department it was Winchester equipment everywhere.

Once again Howie discovered no one was servicing the stores, or not regularly and not from the island. So he went to work. He phoned Tonka in Toronto and got a hold of their sales manager, Rod Harding.

"Howie Meeker, the hockey player? You want to work for us?"

"Yes, I do."

"You got it. I'll be down next week."

Then he called Samsonite. "Howie Meeker? Jeez, that was a great Junior B team you had here in Stratford. What can I do for you?"

Almost everywhere Howie called the result was the same. Hockey had opened so many doors for the man, some he had obviously not even thought to knock on. Soon he was an agent for Samsonite Luggage, Leggo, Mattel, Winchester Guns and Ammunitions, and other companies.

Howie did well in the agency business, especially with Tonka and Mattel. He tripled Tonka's sales on The Rock; their commission check came in December every year and often made the Meekers' Christmas.

Suddenly Howie was back in a furious work groove, with his booming agency business; an increasing number of appearances on CBC TV's *Hockey Night in Canada*; three five- to seven-minute sports programs on the radio every day; the Saturday one-hour televised bowling show for twenty-five weeks of the year, and in the summer, a regular one-hour outdoor show on everything and anything: fishing, camping, cooking, golf, tennis, boating.

During the fall and winter months, Howie hosted a morning physical fitness program for women and kids. Just before Christmas, Grace and Howie were twacking (window shopping) on Water Street when along came Foot Grouchy. From fifty feet away, she screamed, "Howie Meeker, I'm pregnant and it's all your fault."

Howie turned white as passers-by turned and looked at Foot and then at him. Just how was the guy going to talk his way out of this situation, with his wife on his arm? Grace gripped Howie's hand like a vise as Foot continued to bellow, "I just came from my doctor. He confirmed that I'm pregnant and it's because of you." When the four finally met a few feet apart, Foot was chuckling away at a red-faced Howie and grim-faced Grace.

"I'm on the rhythm method for birth control and the doctor said I upset my metabolism by doing your exercise show. I'm eight weeks' pregnant," Foot laughed.

Y

Newfoundland provided Howie with his first opportunity to catch big fish, like tuna. One day he joined Al Vardy, director of tourism, on his Cape Ann fishing boat, complete with a skipper and big-time fishing equipment. Howie watched Big Al hook and boat a 500-pounder before he got his turn.

"It wasn't five minutes and bang — the reel was just screaming. So I got into the chair and the tuna was peeling line as if I were hooked to a jet. The skipper wisely turned the boat and followed this wild thing and finally it stopped running. Yeah, now what? Well, I'd watched Mr. Vardy play his fish, so I slid forward, reeled the loose line in, bent my knees, and then kept my back straight and straightened my legs. That got the tuna three or four feet closer to the boat. I began to take in line as I slid forward; ten minutes later the fish was thirty feet off the port side. After seeing the boat it ran another 250 yards. This time Al tightened the drag, and ten minutes later this 400-pound tuna was beside the boat. We tagged him, cut the leader, and away he went. Well, you never forget your first tuna."

For the majority of his time in Newfoundland, Howie says the people lived under a dictatorship. Premier Joey Smallwood ran everybody: the butcher, baker, candlestick maker, the fisherman, businessman, the opposition, and finally, the news media.

When John Diefenbaker took over the federal government as prime minister he made Donald Fleming his Minister of Finance. One day the Rotary Club of St. John's invited Fleming to be a guest speaker. On the day of the event, with the lunch set for noon, Smallwood walked in at 11 a.m., sought the chairman for the day and said, "Mr. Fleming will not speak today."

"What do you mean? He's here, flew in yesterday, so is the press. We've advertised it; our members expect it, and you're telling me he can't speak."

"Yes, I am."

The Rotary Club's executive hastily assembled and reluctantly threw in the towel. When they informed Fleming, he said, "Just let me speak. I've got a million funny stories I'll tell and I'll avoid politics entirely." But Joey would not budge.

Howie snorts at the memory. "So our Canadian Minister of Finance left town with his tail between his legs, and big John Diefenbaker and his marvelous cabinet sitting on their asses up in Ottaw did nothing about it. I knew right then that the guy didn't have the balls to successfully run our country. He was all talk, which I suspected when his office was just down the hall from mine while I was in the House of Commons. I saw just enough of J.D. in caucus, in the town hall, in the house, and in private to suspect that he was fine on his feet in front of a crowd but was terrible when sitting on his butt making business and political decisions."

In early March 1996, Howie and Grace returned to St. John's for a reunion of the 1970 Herder Cup team. Former Capital team co-owner Kelly Grant, a Catholic, was talking to Howie remembering the fun they had. "Howie, you really left your mark on the game here," he said.

Howie responded, "I don't know about the actual playing of the game, or individual players, but in November 1957, if you would have told me that a St. Bons player would one day captain the first Guards Boyle Trophy team, I'd have ordered a straight-jacket for you real quick. Or that Howie Meeker, a Protestant, would be president of a Catholic minor hockey system, I'd have said absolutely no way."

Howie didn't stick around St. John's long enough to know if his nineteen years there did anything positive for the game of hockey, but he is confident that he did help change the thinking of sport, particularly hockey. He left Newfoundland feeling he had done a good job.

"I didn't set out to do that, but certainly it came about, and I was proud of the fact that the people who played the game, and the executives, had some respect, not only for each other but for the game, and maybe I had something to do with that."

Y

Howie believes that over the years, with a lot of talking, hard work, and family sacrifice, he reduced the hockey friction in St. John's by seventy-five percent.

"Twenty two years after leaving, I don't miss The Rock, but I miss the people, the great friends I made, and the many enemies while in competition; we didn't let it spoil our social existence together. I fished, hunted on land and sea, and travelled the rugged land from one side to the other. At the same time, the Newfoundlanders gave me the opportunity to learn how to teach hockey skills and to develop a philosophy and style in the television business. Both assets have brought personal happiness and financial rewards, far above the norm. My, oh my, what a province, what a country."

Howie says he only left left the place because of its weather and climate. "The people were something special, which you just can't replace or explain."

Y

Perhaps Howie's impact on The Rock is best described by another Newfoundlander In March 11, 1996, newspaper columnist Don Johnson, who was also a strong Catholic and former Canadian Hockey Association president, wrote:

"When there is an election, you hear a lot of talk about the undecided vote. I can assure you when it came to Howie Meeker and the sports fans of this city (St. John's, Newf.) there was no such thing as the undecided. You either hated Howie Meeker or you loved him.

"In fairness to Howie, a lot of people made up their minds on the basis of religion rather than on Meeker as a person. It was lots of fun back in those days and if you wanted to be part of a lively discussion, all you had to do was bring up Howie's name.

"When it came to players who played for him, it was a whole different story. I know of no one who played under Meeker, regardless of the person's religion, who did not think the world of him and have the greatest respect for him.

"Reflecting back on those years, I feel respect may not be the appropriate word. Howie was able to create a tremendous bond between himself and his players. There was always a fierce loyalty there, one for the other. I know for certain to this very day many of the people who played for him unquestionably believe he was the finest coach they ever played for during their career."

Thirteen

When the Train Whistle Blows

"What am I doing out at sea in a twelve-foot rowboat, in the pitch dark, with two armed and impaired Newfoundlanders?"

When people around the world talk about the vast country of Canada, the descriptions and impressions are as varied as the land and people itself, and for good reason; it seems as if each province and region of the country is different, not only geographically, but also economically and socially. However, even allowing for Canada's vastness and diversity, nothing quite compares to Newfoundland, an island apart.

Indeed, "The Rock" itself is distinctive in its landscape, with foreboding forests and wild, rugged coastlines, but even more unique and inspiring are the people of the province. Few other pockets of land in the world can claim to cradle such warm, fun-loving folk. Few cultures display the same wild, good-natured, heart-on-the-sleeve lust for life in work, and, of course, play.

Since neither the average Newfoundlander nor Howie Meeker was keen on letting a good time slip by, the combination was bound to create a few memorable tales. Howie's favourite hobbies, fishing and hunting, provided the perfect arena for such frivolity, and there was no shortage of game Newfoundlanders happy to help him out with either; Bob Grouchy especially.

One day Bob invited Howie on a trip to Trepassey, where his friend Joe McNeil had a boat and would gladly take them up the narrows to the mouth of the Northwest Brook to fish for salmon. Howie jumped at the opportunity. A few days later they were headed along the southern shore to Trepassey on a gravel road, but not before loading Bob's car with all the necessary supplies: a case of scotch, six cases of beer, enough food for four people for a week, one fly rod and just three flies. "I should have had some idea of what was in store if I continued to cultivate our friendship. My, oh my, what a wonderful person he was, and what a character."

Bob suggested they leave at 9 a.m., arrive at Trepassey about 11 a.m., head up the narrows, and be at the head of the river by 1 p.m.

"Isn't early afternoon a bad time to fish?" Howie queried.

"Naw, we'll hook them morning, noon, and night," Grouchy replied. In the years that followed, Howie would learn that Bob had the knack of getting whatever he sought — fish, moose — whenever he pleased.

An hour into the trip, Bob asked Howie if he fancied a cup of tea. Howie nodded and a few minutes later, as the two travelled through the small fishing village of Ferryland, Bob pulled off the road and parked beside a house next to a huge church. He opened the trunk, grabbed a case of beer and a bottle of scotch as gifts, and said, "Let's go."

Newfoundlanders tend to be big on hospitality and are not fussy about formalities. Hence, friends are not expected to knock before entering, and front doors of homes are rarely used, except by strangers. So, much to Howie's amazement, Bob simply opened the back door and walked in, yelling, "Jimmy, it's Bob. Where are you?" A few minutes later, on the path between the house and the church, Howie met Father Jimmy, an old St. Bons school chum and the first of at least twelve priests Howie would meet through Bob.

After some tea and cookies, with scotch and beer for chasers, the two soon were back on the road. Forty-five minutes later, going through Papdahaden, it was the same procedure: big church, small house, bottle of scotch, and a case of beer. "Howie, this is Father Arnold. He and I went to St. Bons together."

An hour later, when they arrived at Trepassey, Bob stopped at a gas station and general store. The familiar routine was repeated yet again; Bob grabbed a bottle of scotch and a case of beer from the trunk, and barged through the back door of the home. "Howie, meet Joe and Nancy McNeil." By 4:30, and with the case of beer consumed, Howie suggested they finally try some fishing. The McNeils' youngest son, Francis, asked if Howie had ever fished East Coast salmon before. When Howie replied that he hadn't, the youngster immediately said, in his thick Newfoundland drawl, "Well, Mr. Mayker, let's be seein' yer rod 'n' reel. Heh, the reel, she be too small; we'll only be gettin' 150 feet of backin' on 'er."

Soon after, the foursome floated up the waterway, where the bay narrowed fairly quickly. When they arrived at a small, shallow stream and beached the boat, Howie was surprised by the choice of location. The stream was no more than fifteen feet wide and about a foot deep, with occasional deeper sections and holes. Just as Howie convinced himself there was no hope of there being any reasonably sized salmon submerged in the shallow liquid, an eight- or nine-pound salmon broke the surface and catapulted at least two feet in the air as young Francis hollered, "Yahoo! Got one!"

Before Howie had managed to get his fishing rod into the water, Francis had beached and released his fine catch.

"What did you let him go for?" Howie asked.

"It's foul 'ooked, Mr. Mayker."

"Foul hooked? What's that?"

"Well, round 'ere the rules are, Mr. Mayker, you 'ave to keep yer fly on top of the warter. She can't be a-sinkin'. If the fish idn't 'ooked in the mouth you 'ave to release 'im."

Just then Joe sauntered up, rod in hand, and led Howie down to where the fresh water flowed into the brackish water. Just as they arrived at the shoreline Howie heard another loud splash followed by another, "Yahoo! Got one!" The two men ventured out fifteen or twenty feet into the stream where the water was finally knee high and Joe explained that Howie need use only twenty to thirty feet of floating line in his fly casting, to cast at about three o'clock and let the fly drift in the current. Joe explained that fish tended to rest near certain boulders and that the fly should be floated over a rock three times: once about two feet in front, once on the near side of the rock, and the third cast over the far side. "After three times leave 'er alone 'n' go try anudder rock. In five minutes go back and try 'er agin." As a parting comment he added, "See that big boulder over dere about twenty feet out? Try her first."

Howie was certainly no stranger to a fly rod, but the rust had set in. It took him a dozen casts or so to gain back some timing and finesse. The first time through the advised routine of over the rock, beside the rock, behind the rock — nothing happened. So Howie moved to another rock, and another rock, and another rock — still nothing happened. When he returned to the first rock his first cast accidentally went over the far side and just as it started to swing behind the rock a huge fish head appeared and Howie's line began to sing. "Very soon my 100-foot casting line was gone and I was into the backing, recalling Francis's early analysis of my reel. I'd landed quite a few large fish in my life to that point, but nothing like this. I remember thinking, How the hell do I stop it?"

Howie had tremendous hand pressure on the spinning reel, but the rod was bent like a horseshoe. "It was like a locomotive that just kept going and going, like the rabbit in that battery advertisement."

Just as Howie finally looked down at the reel, he heard Joe holler, "Hang tough, b'y." With only a few turns of line left and the fish still motoring, Howie did the only reasonable thing he could do to stop his prized fishing rod from breaking like a twig — he lowered his rod, pointed the tip at where the line went in the water, and hung tight. When the line snapped it was the greatest and loudest *zing* Howie had ever heard.

When Howie snapped back to reality, Joe was standing beside him. "I've got a thirty-five-pounder in me deepfreeze that I caught yesterday over that very same rock," he said, "but yers was as big or bigger. Come on, let's join the others up the river."

As Joe and Howie ambled the fifty or sixty yards back to Bob and Francis, they heard the now-familiar "Yahoo! Gotcha!" It was Francis's sixth catch within the half-hour the party had been there. Howie wisely decided to watch the young hot-shot fisherman, and after Francis beached and released another solid sized salmon (this one "foul 'ooked" in the dorsal fin), Howie could contain his questions no longer. "Francis, your Dad and I have hooked three fish between us; you've hooked six. How come?"

"Well, Mr. Mayker, I'll gladly show ya. Try on these tinted glasses. Look in the middle of the stream, down two or three feet, 'n' tell me what you sees."

Howie saw salmon, dozens of them, all between eight and fifteen pounds. Francis said, "Give me me glasses 'n' yer rod, and I'll 'ook you one." Francis cast upstream, let the fly sink, and tightened the line just a little. As the fly floated past him, and when the hook was nose to nose with a salmon, he pulled downstream. Francis then quickly handed Howie the rod just as the water exploded and the fish cleared the surface. It took off upstream along the bank, with Howie in hot pursuit. Ten minutes later, when Howie finally beached the ten-pound beauty, it was hooked in the chin. As Howie released the fish, Francis apologized. "Sorry, Mr. Mayker. When I try real 'ard, I can usually 'ook 'em in the mouth. Give me yer rod and I'll get ya anudder."

"Thanks, but no thanks," Howie replied. "Give me your glasses and I'll try on my own."

At the end of the afternoon the group had five nice East Coast salmon, and had hooked and released another twenty.

A few weeks later, in early September, Bob invited Howie on yet another long weekend expedition with a crew of characters. "Some buddies and I always go over to Swift Current for three or four days to play cards, eat lobster, and drink dark rum. Do you want to come along? I got a friend over there who has a lodge with some cabins. We'll have a great time. We'll catch a few sea trout, and I'll take my .30-30 in case we see a moose."

Howie considered the idea for about three seconds and agreed.

With Bob's station wagon loaded up with a case of scotch, twelve cases of beer, and guns, Howie knew it would be another *long* weekend. "When he was loading, I thought, 'Wow, are we going to have a party!' Six guys and all that booze, plus apparently plenty of rum, which his friend Smitty would supply. At that time I only drank beer and very little at that."

When Bob and Howie arrived at Smitty's place he had everything ready for them, including two cabins and a case of dark rum, but he didn't have any lobsters. "Nobody around here has any lobsters that I know of," Smitty lamented.

"No problem. Come on, Howie, let's go." Howie hardly had to guess where Bob was headed. A few minutes later Grouchy stopped his car outside a church, grabbed a bottle of scotch and a case of beer, and headed in the back door of the adjacent house. "Hi, Father Jiggins, how are you? This is Howie Meeker, a mainlander friend of mine. Say, Freddy, remember the day in class you set fire to the waste-paper basket?" Twenty minutes later, with school experiences and other memories hilariously rehashed, Bob asked, "Freddy, where can we get some lobsters?" Three phone calls later,

Freddy had found a parish member who lived five miles up the road in Goose Cove with a large pen full of lobster at the exorbitant price of $1.25 each. Normally they sold for 75 cents to a dollar. By the time Bob and Howie returned to the cabins with thirty 2-pound lobsters, Bob's friends had a huge fire burning under a very large iron pot that was almost filled with salt water.

A half-hour later, with red lobster everywhere, Bob introduced Howie to what he considered to be the best rum ever distilled, London Dock. Smitty smuggled it into Newfoundland from the French islands of St. Pierre et Miquelon — for a quarter of the normal price. Bob explained, "Howie, you just can't eat lobster without drinking dark rum, and London Dock is preferred." London Dock is available in proof and overproof versons and, if taken straight, after three drinks one tends to find oneself staring up at the underside of the table. Bob taught Howie the secret of using the cap on the bottle as a jigger, then adding Coke until one can't smell the rum. "Follow the formula, you can drink London Dock all night with no harmful effects the next morning," Howie advises. "Don't follow the formula, and you're a piece of cake."

With a menu of beer, scotch, London Dock, lobster, and a deck of cards, an all-night session of poker was in the works. Around 1 a.m., Howie packed it in for the evening but at 3 a.m. he awoke briefly, watched the poker game still in progress, cracked open and ate a whole lobster, then went back to sleep. At 7 a.m., Howie awoke again, spied Bob at the table still playing cards, and said, "Let's go fishing." Much to Howie's amazement, Bob looked up and said, "Sure, b'y," while the others headed for bed.

The two men drove through Swift Current and continued on for what seemed like hours, with a gorgeous view of the ocean on their immediate left. As the long bay began to narrow they came to a bridge over a river named Piper's Hole, which flowed into the sea. Smitty had told Bob there was a small pool upstream that they should try first.

Howie had never fished for sea trout before, and when he saw

Bob dig out a spinning rod and not a fly rod, he asked what the plan was. "Bob, how are you going to fish flies with a spinning rod?"

"Watch this," Grouchy said as he dug out a huge, weighted cork with a quill sticking out of the top about six to eight inches long. It was the funniest-looking rig Howie had ever seen. It also worked like a charm. Bob hooked the cork quill to the line and tied a six-foot leader, with three flies attached, to the top of the quill. Bob walked to the edge of the pool and cast out into the current, just below the rapids. When the line straightened out, Bob gave no more than two turns of the handle before the cork went half under, the quill dipped into the water, and the reel started to sing. "Fish on," he hollered, his bloodshot eyes popping wide open. Howie could see the infectious smile on Bob's face through his two-day beard, and heard his unmistakable, mischievous giggle. Once again, his partner had a fish on the hook long before Howie had even finished preparing his rod and tackle. Two minutes into Bob's fight, the fish slowed down and he started to reel it in slowly. Then all of a sudden the cork took off downstream at full speed, with the line singing loudly, and one of the two fish now on the line broke the surface.

"Jeez, Grush, you've got breakfast for the two of us," Howie grinned, as Bob landed the two beautiful trout, each about a pound and a half. While Bob was trying to net his catch near shore Howie could see other trout trying to get fly number three. Howie then laid a single fly in the rapids, it drifted ten feet into the pool, and Howie had his first sea trout.

On Saturday afternoon, Howie had to return to Goose Cove for more lobsters, and soon after he returned, Father Fred arrived with some huge crab. "What a brunch we had: sea trout fried with butter, lobster freshly cooked, roasted chicken that Bob had brought, a salad full of crab and lobster, potato salad, red and white wine, beer, and London Dock."

Saturday night was more of the same: more poker, more lobster, and Father Fred dropped off six more huge crab. Sunday morning at 7 a.m., all was quiet in the kitchen where the men had played poker just hours before, but the snoring emanating from the two large bedrooms was almost deafening. Howie awoke, looked at the bacon and eggs, looked at the lobster, and opted for the latter before waking Bob. "I just about died of shock when he sat up at the side of his bed, unshaven, hair all over the place — what little he had — and said, "Okay, b'y, let's go get some trout."

Before leaving, Bob put his .30-30 rifle in the car, mentioning that Smitty had said there were quite a few moose just past the bridge on the road to Terrenceville, on the Bonavista Peninsula. Just over the bridge, Howie looked for a spot to park so they could start fishing, but Bob said, "Let's run up the road a mile or two and maybe we'll get lucky."

"I don't want to get lucky, I want to fish, but okay."

Sure enough, five minutes up the road, Bob hollered, "Stop the car; there was a moose back there in the woods." Howie hadn't seen a thing, but before the pickup was at a full stop, Bob had grabbed the .30-30 and was out the door and across the road.

Hunting can be a tricky procedure at the best of times but hunting in a Newfoundland bog is a whole different story. "It's like walking in glue," Howie says. "You sink a foot for every step you take and you practically need a block and tackle to get your foot out. If your boots are the slightest bit too big, your foot comes out of the bog but not the boot."

Deep in the bog, Bob crouched down and tiptoed from one small clump of trees to another, all the time advising Howie to "stay low; keep quiet; get behind those small trees." Howie chuckled, looking at the sparse saplings and thinking, "Those aren't trees, they're twigs." Nothing was healthy in the bog but the bog itself. "Since then, every time I see a cartoon of some person or animal sneaking up on something I remember Bob Grouchy and me on the Bonavista Peninsula."

After fifteen minutes Howie still hadn't seen the moose. A .30-30 rifle packs a kick, but it isn't a powerful gun. One has to be pretty accurate to kill anything more than 150 yards away, especially a moose. In light of Bob's last two days of frivolity, Howie didn't think Bob was capable of hitting an elephant at fifty feet. Just as Howie had decided that a moose near Bob would be as safe as a church mouse, they noticed something browsing about fifty yards away. Bob laid his gun in the crotch of a tree and took aim just as the animal lifted its head.

Howie managed to yell, "Bob, don't shoot! It's a cow!" a split second before the gun's explosion rocked the bog.

"Cow be damned; that's a moose," Bob argued, but on closer inspection Howie was right. "Bob hit the poor thing right between the eyes. Sober, he probably would have missed it."

Sunday night the great hunters returned home to St. John's with sea trout, crab, lobster, and a six-brace of rabbits. Bob, through Father Freddy, relayed a message to the owner of the cow to come to Simpson-Sears the next time he was in St. John's, and Bob would settle up for the moose he shot.

Ɣ

Not long after, Howie was invited to go on his first real moose-hunting trip with friend and business partner, Charlie Riddle. Howie would find out later that, compared to Charlie, Bob Grouchy was a regular Daniel Boone.

"The closest spot to hunt moose is the Terra Nova area near Port Blandford. I know the area well and have shot several moose there," Riddle said, adding that there were plenty of cabins in that area, left in pretty good shape by the loggers when they moved out. In those years Terra Nova had not yet been made into a provincial park.

Howie did not own a high-powered rifle, but his sporting goods store had a half-dozen old Lee-Enfield rifles on sale for $29.95. A few days later, the two men set off in Howie's Vauxhall packed to the roof. "As we loaded the car with three days of supplies — food, drinks, clothing, sleeping bags, tarps, guns, axes, propane stove and lights, cooking utensils, brin bags, a cheesecloth — in case we got a moose — I thought to myself, 'The only way we could get a moose home is ride it or hire a truck.'"

The paved road ran out fifteen miles out of St. John's, giving way to a horrid, bumpy gravel road. Five bone-rattling hours later the two drove through Terra Nova, and headed to Lake St. John.

Since leaving home, Charlie and Howie had been telling each other lies. "There was no radio so we had to talk about something. Charlie was telling me what a great marksman he was, that half the little gold things on his uniform were for excellence in shooting, and that he had a wide and varied experience in hunting, shooting, and paunching a moose. The constant theme was that he had the best moose rifle, a 30-0-6 Remington with the best scope made, and that he could hit an apple at 200 yards."

Howie was no slouch with a Lee-Enfield rifle in the army, but he hadn't fired the one he was carrying from the store. The wholesaler told Howie the guns had been sighted in before shipping but Howie still wanted to put up a target and find out. Charlie argued, however, that firing off a gun to sight it in would scare away any moose and anger other hunters. Howie conceded his case.

When they arrived at the lake they passed three or four rundown cabins filled with hunting parties and Howie knew he would be sleeping under canvas or in the car that night. Sure enough, there were three cars parked in front of what they had supposed to be their cabin. Howie and Charlie built a lean-to, cooked supper, and spent a miserable night under a cold, cloudy sky.

By 7:00 the next morning, Charlie and Howie had started driving the roads and walking the wood cuts, which they continued to do all day without ever seeing a sign of a moose. The next day their luck improved, and while walking yards apart, parallel to a small trail, they came upon six moose scattered in a small area.

"All of a sudden, I heard a bang and up came all the moose heads, then another bang and they began to move. To gain cover they had to move right in front of us in an arc and they were caught out in the open. They were no more than seventy yards away, running full out. I heard another bang and the moose kept running. I had a bullet in the chamber, silly of me but I did, and four in the clip. I fired them all and didn't touch a hair."

"Well," Howie thought, "no problem. Charlie will have one, maybe two, down. He's a hell of a shot."

Thirty seconds later Howie spied Charlie furiously reloading his gun, so he walked over and asked, "How did you do?"

"I think I hit one," Riddle replied.

"Excuse me, six shots and you *think* you hit one?" Howie fumed. "That's it, let's go back to the car. We're going home." Just in case Charlie had hit one they walked the area where the animals went into the woods, looking for signs of a wounded animal, but discovered nothing. Under normal conditions Howie knew he would have hit at least one of the moose that boogied by him, so, ignoring Charlie's earlier pleas, he put up a target two feet square, stepped off a hundred yards, and fired. He missed.

"I thought, I can't miss that thing. So I aimed for the bottom of the target and hit the top, dead centre. I was two feet high at 100 yards." Some sight adjustments and three shots later, Howie was dead centre.

As the two men sat in uncomfortable silence while driving the bumpy, potholed road, they passed numerous bogs and small lakes. Negotiating a corner, just past a small treed area, Howie slammed on the brakes. There, some 150 yards away, was the biggest bull moose he'd ever seen. The two men hopped out of the car, grabbed their rifles, and hedged a little closer. On the count of three, they fired simultaneously and down it went.

Having never hunted moose, Howie admittedly had no idea what a job he was now in for, paunching and cleaning a 1,500-pound animal that had been brought down in a bog 250 yards from the road.

The men were huffing and puffing by the time they got to the moose and Howie immediately saw the folly of their actions. "Okay, Charlie. What do we do now?"

"Paunch him."

"How?"

"I'm not sure."

"Jeez, Charlie, you've done this before," Meeker said, holding his knife.

"Well, not really. I was there when my friends did it."

Howie looked at his knife for a few seconds, contemplated paunching Charlie instead of the moose, and then shook his head in disbelief. Charlie was saved, however, by the timely arrival of two Newfoundland men who were also out hunting.

The two real hunters had been searching for three days and hadn't had a sniff of moose. John and his buddy Bill were from Cape Broyle, about an hour and a half outside of St. John's, and John ran a taxi service in and out of St. John's. It was obvious to them that Charlie and Howie needed help.

"They took one look at our knife and brought out their own tools. While they were working away, I headed for the car and got the bottle of dark rum Charlie and I had been working on, and four mugs. They not only helped us paunch the moose, but also helped quarter him and carry him through the bog. There is absolutely no way that Charlie and I could have carried that moose through the bog; he was huge. I was in pretty good shape in those days but there is no way in the world I could have carried even the rear quarter, which is the easiest to carry."

Getting the moose to the road was one problem, but finding a place to put it on Howie's little Vauxhall was quite another. They managed to get one quarter into the back of the car, on top of everything else, which they covered with plastic. They lashed another quarter to the back bumper, put two on top of the car, and tied the head to the front bumper.

"We looked like a moose travelling down the road. There has never since been a Vauxhall loaded to the hilt like that one was. John and Bill headed for home, half-snockered, since we finished the half-bottle of rum and I gave them a full one to take home for all their help. About two hours later we finally got back out to the road, but by now the motor was boiling over, so we stopped at the garage and got some water. I was smart enough to pick up a good sized can for water, and phoned home to tell Grace we had a moose and should be home in four hours, by 10 p.m."

Murphy's Law kicked in, though, and every few miles the car boiled over. As well, everywhere they went, people were waiting for them because John and Bill were ahead of them, telling everyone that Howie Meeker was coming down the road with the biggest moose they'd ever seen. They finally got home at two o'clock in the morning, but Murphy was not quite done with them.

Howie tried the back door of his house but it was locked, as was the front. Howie went around the back again and tried to jiggle the door. A couple of minutes later there was a screeching of brakes and the sound of people jumping out of their cars. Howie looked up to see several policemen running down the alley who, upon spying Howie, shouted, "Stop where you are, put your hands in the air." Finally one officer, shining his flashlight in Howie's eyes, said, "Howie Meeker, it's you!"

Inside the house later, Grace explained she had finally given up on Howie making it home that night and went to bed. She awoke and heard someone trying to break in and called the police.

Ɣ

Howie's best outdoor experience in Newfoundland took place in September 1959. Grouchy and Bill Macdonald, once again, were the catalysts of the campaign.

The three men headed for a friend's cabin on nearby Gander Lake, right on the mouth of the Southwest Gander River. The area was well known for its bounty of moose and excellent salmon fishing. The plan was to overnight with other friends in Gambo, and leave for Gander Lake the following morning. When they arrived at Cyrl's and Junior's house in Gambo around 8 p.m., a party was already in full swing. With Jack, Joe, and their wives, and Bob,

Bill, and Howie, there were nine or ten people at the party.

Around 9:30 p.m. the festivities were going strong when Howie saw Junior and Jack head for the closet, put on jackets, pick up a shotgun, and head for the back door. His curiosity piqued, Howie asked where they were going.

"We're going fer a boat ride, wanna come along?" Howie hesitated; both men were half-snockered and getting into a boat, with shotguns. Then a little voice, the one we usually avoid, said, "Go ahead and live dangerously."

Junior and Jack fished out an extra pair of gumboots for Howie and in a swoop, the trio were out the back door and into the dark crisp night. Jack, with his flashlight, led the way to a rowboat tied up at the small wharf. In the boat were two big square flashlights. Howie quickly climbed aboard and sat in the bow.

Junior weighed about 225 pounds and Jack was easily pushing 200, so any sensible man would have climbed ashore after they both fell into the boat. Had it not been securely tied to the wharf all three men would have been in the water.

Junior grabbed the oars and to a rousing hurrah started rowing. Howie wondered where they were headed as he peered uselessly into the darkness, seeing only the scattered lights on the shore. Then it hit him, "Jeez, how are we going to get back? What am I doing out at sea in a twelve-foot rowboat, in the pitch dark, with two armed and impaired Newfoundlanders?"

Junior stopped rowing after a bit, and the boat drifted slowly and silently over the water. Howie was just about to ask "What's next?" when he heard honking sounds. The boat had floated into a large gaggle of Canada geese.

"Jeez," Howie thought, "we are in the middle of the village and we're going to shoot geese, out of season, with no licence. We are also probably going to be charged with discharging firearms in the dark. They are going to lock me up and throw away the key."

Since the tide was going out they drifted slowly with it and soon arrived at the railway bridge that spanned the narrow gap between the ocean and the large bay that runs down into Gambo. The gaggle of geese had increased in size. "If she be on time she should be 'ere any minute," Jack whispered, slinging his rifle.

Junior grabbed onto one of the bridge pylons and there they sat, surrounded by big geese and a shroud of inky darkness. The world became silent, except for the soft lapping of water against the boat, the occasional ruffle of a goose feather, and the muffled sounds of a town fast asleep. Soon, Howie could hear a train coming, rumbling down the distant rails. As the sound grew louder, a faint light began to illuminate the top of the bridge and the water's edge. Junior broke the silence, "When the train whistle blows, blast away; till then don't be shootin'."

The instant the locomotive reached the far end of the bridge, the engineer hauled down on his whistle and held it there. Junior shoved away from the bridge, which caused them to float closer to the geese. The roar of the train over the shaking bridge, combined with its whistle screeching full out, was deafening. Suddenly, thanks to the engine's headlight, the geese were as visible as in broad daylight. *Boom, boom, boom* . . . Five minutes later, in deathly quiet surroundings, they gathered in eight geese.

"Okay, fine. Now, how do we get home?" Howie thought, gazing again towards the few lights back on the beach, and then, as if by magic, there was a bright red light. Back at the cabin there was already a huge bucket of boiling water ready, and a giant pan to put the goose in. In jig time, one bird was in the oven.

Sometime around 2 a.m., accompanied by a London Dock, Howie was into the biggest drumstick he'd ever seen.

The comforting smell and sound of frying bacon woke Howie in the morning, and when he eventually sauntered out the back door he looked at the bridge. "All of a sudden it dawned on me — we had been hunting in the middle of town, less than a quarter of a mile from the police station."

The next morning Jack asked Howie to drive him to the train station. "I've gotta deliver me a parcel, b'y," he said to Howie. Jack grabbed two brin bags, ran into the shed, stuffed three geese into one bag and one goose into the other, tied both bags tight, and jumped into the front seat next to Howie.

Howie followed the train tracks, which parallelled the beach, and when they arrived Jack jumped out, grabbed a bag, and hung it on the signal-tower that tells the train engineer to stop. When Jack returned, Howie asked, "What did you do that for?"

"They're fer the crew what's operated the train las' night. They turn aroun' at Gander 'n' come back through 'ere at eleven in the mornin'." Then Jack looked Howie in the eye and said, "Jesus, b'y, if they didn' blow that there whistle fer us there'd a been nuthin' but Mounties everywhere when we come ashore." Howie realized the Canada goose caper was actually a conspiracy. "Little did I realize they were almost as proficient at hunting moose."

Friday night the boys got into the whisky, beer, and cards in that order. About 11 p.m., Howie realized they were going to continue that same frenzy all evening. Trying to conserve some drinks for the morning, Howie opened Bob's trunk, took three of the six bottles of whisky left, and two cases of beer, and hid them in the woods.

Once again, Howie woke to the sound and smell of sizzling bacon, with Bob and Bill obviously getting ready to go hunting. As usual, they'd been up all night into the booze and were in no condition to be doing anything, but they were determined to go no matter what Howie said.

"Boys, you won't even get up the hill to the main road before you're in the ditch. At least let me drive you." Howie quickly slurped down two coffees and they were off with Howie driving and Bob and Bill slouched down behind the cab in the back of the truck. Howie had driven no further than 200 yards when he spotted a huge cow moose, standing 100 yards away, in the middle of the road, at the bottom of the hill. The cow was staring right at them.

Howie slid to a slow stop, expecting to hear a shot. Silence. Someone knocked on the window with orders to get going. Howie knocked back and motioned for them to get up and look. "They thought I was kidding, and both of them just sat in each corner on the floor, huddled up because it was cold." When Howie knocked again, Bob finally got up and looked. *Bang, bang* — the moose turned sideways. *Bang, bang* — the moose turned back on and looked at the truck. Then slowly she turned and started to cross the road and head into the woods. *Bang* — down she went.

Howie figured it was finally safe to get out of the vehicle.

He didn't think there were any live shells left in their guns, so he shut off the motor and went to get the guys off the back of the truck. They were standing there arguing furiously.

"I shot the moose," Bob barked.

"No goddamn way you shot the moose; I shot the moose. Hit it first shot," Bill countered.

"Like hell, I clearly hit him first."

Howie reached over and borrowed a rifle and a shell and walked down to kill the wounded animal. When he returned, Bob and Bill were still arguing. Howie shook his head, hopped into the truck, and drove to the bottom of the hill where the moose was. It had ended up ten feet off the road, crashed in amongst some small birch trees; Howie had to chop down two of the trees to get at the moose.

"When I looked at the weaving Bob and Bill, I said to myself, 'Howie boy, it's your turn to paunch a moose.'"

After splitting the rib cage, Bob held one side open and Bill held the other, while Howie tried to do the rest. He was making such an awful mess that Bill finally said, "Here, give me the godammed knife and I'll do it."

"Good, please do," Howie said, and grabbed Bill's side of the rib cage and pulled it open.

"Bill got his knife, bent over, lost his footing, and fell head first into the open rib cage, in all that mess. Grouchy laughed so hard he let go of his side; at which point I broke up in laughter, lost all strength, and let go of mine as well. The ribs snapped together just like a vise. We both stood there, howling in delight, while Bill unsuccessfully tried to get out, legs flailing away. Suddenly, we both realized Bill might be drowning, so we opened the ribs, and out he crawled. What a mess! I've never seen anything so bad in my life."

Bob and Bill argued about whose moose it was the entire time it took to quarter and load it onto the truck, and drive back to the cabin.

"I shot it."

"No, damn it, I shot it."

At the cabin the three men hoisted a quarter section onto a tripod and Howie began to skin the moose, sending the other two off to make breakfast. "The boys wanted to help, but I didn't want either of them close to me with a knife in their hand."

The fire had gone out and, since they were having trouble getting it started, Howie suggested using a little kerosene. A few minutes later a loud *kaboom* startled Howie, and when he spun around and looked, fire was licking about everywhere inside the cabin.

"It looked like the take-off of a rocket. There was even fire coming out of the chimney." Howie ran into the building, while Bob and Bill ran out. On the floor, on its side, was a red gas can spewing out fuel, which immediately turned to flames as it gurgled out. Howie grabbed a sleeping bag, picked up the gas can, and ran outside. He told Bob and Bill to get back inside, grab blankets, and smother the flames on the floor. Five minutes later, thanks to the three or four layers of linoleum on the floor, the fire was out. Obviously, Bill or Bob had grabbed the gas can, instead of the kerosene.

Fortunately, the only casualties were some singed sleeping bags and blankets, along with several sets of singed hands, hair, and eyebrows.

While inside the cabin before breakfast, Howie noticed the five guns leaning against the wall, beside the front door. Considering the state of his partners, he decided a safety check might be in order.

"Obviously I was feeling the effects of London Dock as well, because there certainly are better ways to check a gun than I did." Howie picked up the first rifle, cocked it, pointed to the roof, and pulled the trigger — click, sigh of relief. Second gun, same —

click. Third gun, Howie cocked it, pointed skyward, pulled the trigger — *blam!*

Bob, his plate loaded with breakfast, was headed for the table when the gun exploded two feet away. Everything on Bob's plate went straight to the roof. Bill, the only one sitting on his side of the table, jumped up, and the weight of the three on the other side tipped the table. Everything on it, hot coffee and all, landed on top of them.

"Boy, was I in trouble. They thought I did it on purpose. The mess from the fire was easy to clean up, compared to that."

Ⴤ

Cyrl eventually sold the cabin at Hunts Pond to Howie, Bill, and Bob for $600. Howie says it was the best deal he ever was part of.

"Grace and I maintained it for the next fifteen years. Eventually, as the roads improved, we could get to the cabin in six or seven hours. My, oh my, what a wonderful place it was. The family would always spend at least a week there during the summer.

"I can't remember any of the girls, Jane, Peggy, or Kim, complaining about spending time in the woods, fifty miles from the nearest people; and the boys, especially Mike and Andy, just loved it. They had their own private salmon river with all kinds of salmon in it, Hunts Pond filled with one-pound trout, and great swimming."

Howie has great memories of the turbulent times when he solved the hockey problem, his introduction to broadcasting and writing at CJON radio TV, and his experiences in sales, as well as the formative years of the hockey school business. But, he says today, the best times by far were spent with Grace, the kids, and the dogs, as well as Bob Grouchy and all his wonderful friends, at the cabin on the Southwest Gander River.

Fourteen

Potsdam to Parksville

*"In a lot of cases with the pros, during their minor and
amateur hockey days they weren't taught to think.
Now at $1,500,000 a year, some of them
still can't think."*

During the mid-1960s, Roly McLenahan ran the biggest hockey schools in the Maritimes, if not the entire country, in picturesque St. Andrews, New Brunswick. Roly imported top NHL stars to his schools, and by adding Howie Meeker's name to the roster, he made a good move.

In early 1967, Roly invited Howie, who'd previously worked with him at a number of coaching clinics, to come to his school as an instructor for two weeks. Howie and Grace quickly accepted the invitation, especially after Roly said he would provide the Meeker family with private accommodation as part of the offer.

St. Andrews is at the other end of the earth, even from Newfoundland, but the Meekers now had a roomy Volkswagen bus with a sky vent in the cab (the best moose-hunting vehicle in the world) and decided to drive it there. Grace and Howie packed up the six kids, the dog, hockey equipment for three, and they started out on the first leg of their journey, 500 miles to Port aux Basques, where they caught an evening ferry off the island. The vessel docked at Sydney, Nova Scotia, at 4 a.m., after which Howie drove another 500 fabulous miles to get to St. Andrews.

Roly escorted the tired clan to the house. He told them to use a specific grocery store, to order anything they wanted, and "just sign the bill." Roly handed Howie a stack of meal tickets for breakfast, lunch, and dinner for the entire family. He then showed them around the other facilities at their disposal: the dining hall, swimming pool, recreation centre, arena, and bowling alley. Roly also handed over a wad of bowling tickets..

"Registration starts tomorrow at noon, Howie, so see you then. Oh, see that huge white house over there on the corner? Eight or nine of us stay there. We're having a lobster dinner tonight, so please come if you like; we have ample."

When Howie and Grace returned to the house, they discovered the refrigerator contained a half-dozen beers, a bottle of wine, bread, butter, cheese, eggs, bacon, and fruit. "My, oh my, what a guy. I made sure in the following years, when I ran a hockey school, that everyone coming in from a trip had something in the refrigerator. What a marvellous two weeks. Grace thought she'd died and gone to heaven, and the girls lived on the sandy beach; they had movies, bowling, and plenty of attention from boys, I'm sure. I had three scheduled ice sessions a day."

Howie watched and learned. It was the best school he'd ever attended, and his insatiable appetite for learning new, or better, ways to teach the game was well fed. There was certainly plenty of talent there to learn from, including such people as Jacques Plante, Scotty Bowman, Don Marshall, Doug Harvey, Buster Harvey, Mickey Redmond, and the Plager brothers: Barclay, Bob, and Bill.

At the end of the first week Roly handed Meeker an envelope with a cheque in it for $400 pay, plus $300 for expenses and $150 for travel. Howie protested, saying, "Roly, no way. Some expenses are okay, but we've got a fully furnished house, free food from a grocery store, two bottles of wine and beer delivered twice a week, three meals a day for the kids, and you're going to pay me? No way."

But Roly was calling the shots. "Everybody here gets that," Roly grinned. "It's either that or go home; so c'mon, let's go have a beer." Howie was very impressed with a figure-skating professional from Toronto who specialized in teaching proper balance on skates.

When Howie returned home that first summer from St. Andrews he asked Colin Jamieson for a month off the next year. He wanted to attend Roly's school for two 2-week sessions, and would do extra work for CJON to earn the time off. Jamieson made sure Howie did get the time off — and that he did the extra work.

Howie continued with Roly from 1967 to 1969, but stopped once his own hockey school at Feildian Gardens took off. He operated his own school in St. John's from 1968 until 1972. The three years there taught Howie what not to do in the teaching of students and helped him learn that the key to skating is really in balance. Using all the facilities of CJON, Howie sold out the Howie Meeker Hockey School locally each year. It served as a great training ground, not only for the students but also for Howie and his hockey school staff. Slowly the school's unique Meeker imprint evolved.

For the most part, Howie emphasized the basic skills as well as the thinking ability needed in the game of hockey. "In the 1940s and '50s, and well into the 1960s even, no one in all of pro hockey believed it was possible to teach the physical and mental skills of the game. I was thirty years of age, had played high school, Junior B, Junior A, Senior, and seven years of pro hockey, and no one ever attempted to improve my skating, passing, shooting, puck carrying, or my *thinking* skills. It was an accepted fact, back then, that you either had the skills or you didn't.

"How many times did I hear from the scouts, 'Jeez, that kid is a great prospect, looks super, but he can't skate well enough,' or 'Man, can he skate, but he can't handle a puck around the net.' Even today, when most kids come out of Junior hockey at least semiskilled, they still know as much about *playing* the game as I know about flying a spaceship."

However, Howie does see some positive changes. "All professional teams now have high-speed skating, passing, and thinking drills that they run through hour after hour, day after day, month after month, and year after year. Gradually, the highly drafted kid improves to the point where he can help his team play .500 hockey. They also have assistant coaches who can regularly go to the kid after games and give instruction, lend advice, and support. In a lot of cases with the pros, during their minor and amateur hockey days they weren't taught to think. Now at $1,500,000 a year, some of them still can't think."

Howie was one of those players who could skate as well as anybody and who, after three weeks with Hap Day in his first training camp, could check as well as anybody. However, he certainly could have improved his puck-handling, passing, and thinking. "Most of the players from my day could really have used the skill drills that the Oilers started in the 1980s. Everyone uses those drills today."

Howie has always been a strong proponent of teaching the basics and fundamentals of the game early on. One of the easiest and first skills he taught when coaching was how to check and play defence behind the team's own blue line. "Finish the check, and stay with that guy until your team takes control. In amateur hockey, the basic rules to winning are: When you have the puck, never pass it towards or into the middle; when you get into a little bit of trouble in your own end, ring it gently around the boards, away from the traffic, or bang the puck up against the fence as high as possible."

V

During the 1960s and early '70s, Howie kept himself very busy with coaching, hockey schools, his sales work, radio and TV shows at CJON, and as an analyst on *Hockey Night in Canada*. His successful bowling show ran for five years and during that time he sold more than a couple of million dollars in new bowling equipment.

In the spring of 1973, Howie received a telephone call from Gerry Petrie in Montreal. Petrie was a successful agent who represented Guy Lafleur, Jean Beliveau, and other athletes. "We've got this little college in Stanstead in the Eastern Townships of Quebec, on the U.S. border," he said. "They want to start a hockey school and run it."

"My way, my system? I'm the boss?" Howie asked.

"Yes sir," Petrie replied.

"Sure, boy."

"Why don't you fly to Montreal; we'll get all the parties together, work out a deal, and take you down to Stanstead."

When Howie got there, Gerry, a senior partner in the project, had already made a deal to have Jocelyn Guevremont and Rick Martin of the Buffalo Sabres as guests that year.

Howie agreed to work that year for a flat fee rather than a share of the profits, because he doubted there would be any. He estimated there would be about 150 students, making up about ten teams of fifteen players each. He said he'd bring his own staff and suggested they advertise in *The Hockey News* all summer for three 2-week sessions.

Grace and Howie arrived a week ahead of time to get things organized, and the weather was baking hot.

Registration that first year was not good, and Howie figured "somebody was about to lose their shirt." So they called everyone booked in the third session and transferred them to the second session, eliminating the last two weeks.

"Our two pros were great with kids, but they knew nothing about teaching skills. They did however, kick our butts in golf. Rick

Martin could hit the golf ball a mile, straight as an arrow."

Petrie informed Howie before they headed to Stanstead that headmaster Tom Russell had suggested, as part of every hockey day activity, that students attend scholastic classes in one of three different subjects: French, math, or general learning skills. Each student would pick a class. Gerry had agreed to the idea.

When Howie met with Russell, he explained that a lot of parents would appreciate a little help in their son's and daughter's educational program. "We thought we would offer one-and-a-half-hour classes every day." Howie agreed, and said to put it in the brochure as an option. "Much to my surprise, 80 percent of the students, or at least their parents, indicated their choice of subject, and 100 percent attended classes. On the survey we took, the education component received very high marks. Any class I visited was well-organized, very quiet, and everyone seemed interested. We later dropped the educational aspect, and I can't remember why we did. If it was Gerry and I who advocated it be dropped, against the wishes of the people at Stanstead, then we were wrong."

Howie agreed to run the school again the next year as long as he and Petrie looked after the registration and advertising and no pros were hired.

"I still haven't met a pro who could teach a skill, except maybe Bobby Smith," Howie says.

That winter, late in October, Howie was talking to *Hockey Night in Canada* producer Ralph Mellanby, and Ralph inquired how the school in Stanstead had faired.

"Fine, but I didn't get nearly enough customers," Howie admitted.

"I can help solve that, Howie. Schedule a coaching clinic in Stanstead two weeks from today, a Friday, Saturday, and Sunday, and we'll do a show on it for a clip between periods. I've got a friend here in Montreal who can gather twenty-five coaches to go down, and you can get another ten to fifteen locals. That will get you thirty-five to forty people."

Howie phoned Stanstead, who agreed to the plan. Stanstead also supplied food, beverages, and beds. Sure enough, the *HNiC* people showed up with two cameras, shot tons of film, and produced a six-minute package on Howie's school to show between periods of a Montreal-Toronto game.

"What a great guy Mellanby was. We had an audience of at least a million people that night, at least half of them from the Toronto or Montreal area. Well, we sold out Stanstead by March that year, and had eight sellouts in a row after that."

Between the board of directors at Stanstead College and Howie Meeker Hockey School Ltd. was middleman Stewart Cowan. "We got along fine. He understood both me and them, and I think we met all financial obligations that we were supposed to." When he resigned, Captain John Dawson took his place, and everything went smoothly with the Captain. "They were both fine, talented people. We often had differences, but they were usually piddly little things, and no problem to settle."

Then the board wanted John and Howie to work with a lawyer son of one of the directors. The two men agreed and figured it would not be a problem. But it was. When "this lippy punk came down and tried to tell me how to run a hockey school, both financially and physically, I knew it was time to look for greener pastures.

"In my budget, which I had already presented to the board, I'd requested another three or four hundred dollars for air fare. He wrote back and said, 'No, you're not going to get it. I fully expect you to live within your budget.' In past years, from my salary budget for all staff, I often returned $5,000 to $10,000 unused to Stanstead. I expected to do it again that year, but there was no way I was going to after that rude correspondence from him. So, I went to both Stewart and the Captain and told them I was going to give everyone bonuses until I had spent my full amount of salary budget. Neither of the two disagreed; they just stood there and shook their heads."

Every time a door had closed in Howie's life to date, another door had opened. Uncannily, it was about to happen again. The summer before, while gliding around the ice surface at Stanstead, a young student named Jim Young Jr. cruised up to Howie and said, "Mr. Meeker, would you move your hockey school from here?"

Howie grinned at the young teen and said, "Maybe. Where?"

"My father is president of Clarkson University in Potsdam, New York, and I think your hockey school would be a smash hit there." Howie tousled Jim Jr.'s hair and said, "Thanks son, I'll remember that." Soon after his budget confrontation, Howie was on the ice conducting a class when he suddenly recalled the conversation.

Howie tracked the young man down, and yes, he thought his dad might be interested. Howie told Jr. to call his dad and find out. While walking back to his accommodations Meeker thought, "Jeez, it makes sense. Seven years ago when we started here we had 70 percent Canadian and 30 percent U.S. students, and now it is reversed. We'll be closer to our main targets, New York and Boston, and only one and a half hours from Ottawa and Montreal and three from Toronto."

Soon after, Jim Young Sr. and his wife came knocking at Howie's door. A few days later, with Gerry Petrie and Don Wells in tow, they toured Potsdam. Howie was impressed with the facility. Five huge acres under one roof, a huge quarter-mile track, nets set up all around for volleyball and tennis; the hockey rink seated three thousand; there was an Olympic sized pool, gym room, wrestling room, eight squash courts, a theatre, three basketball courts, and meeting rooms. Outdoors there were thirty-six tennis courts, basketball and volleyball courts, and soccer pitches. The dormitories and teaching facilities matched the gym. They were first-class. In 1981, the Howie Meeker Hockey School moved to Potsdam.

Y

Early in his Stanstead days, CBC St. John's offered Howie a $5,000 raise to switch jobs from CJON-TV and Colin simply couldn't match the offer. "We shook hands, I thanked him, he wished me luck, and I was on my way. Don and Colin Jamieson were very good to me and I owe them a lot. Cameraman Wally Daniels is the guy who got me into cigars and scotch; how many cables did I pull with that guy during my outdoor shows, and lug cameras as well? It felt like another portage with Andy Dole.

"Those people took me in, green as grass, with the worst possible voice for television and radio," Howie recalls. "They were very patient, taught me all the tricks, let me try whatever I wanted, and fifteen years later I thought I was good enough to take on the world."

Howie had his own priorities. He wanted to produce a half-hour hockey school television program, and on one of his previous trips to Toronto he again cast the fly upon the water. He visited Gordon Craig, head of CBC Sports, and after talking about the recent 1972 Canada-Russia hockey series, Howie mentioned his idea for a hockey school show. He left Craig with scripts for twenty-five half-hour programs.

A week later Craig called, said it looked interesting, and that he'd cost it out for production in Toronto.

Howie nixed that. "No way, Gordon, it just won't work in Toronto. It's got to be done here." A week later Howie received a phone call from Craig, who said, "Okay, fine, we're going to send Pat Ford down to do a survey. He'll be in tomorrow and you two can get together and see what it's going to cost us."

"We went to the Prince of Wales Arena and the second he turned the lights on he said, 'Oh, hell. We can't do it here. It will be too costly to light this place.' But we did. At the end of the day we had laid out a budget for all the costs, including travel, and it was just over $100,000. We were at least $15,000 over budget.

"Pat, if I can save you $15,000, what are our chances?"

"I think they'd be pretty good," he replied.

"Where did you get the figures for the cost of ice?"

"In Toronto we pay close to $100 an hour and that's $12,000."

"What about the cost of the cast? What's that all about?"

"Kids up in Toronto want $25 a day, so with thirty-six kids at $25 a day, for five weeks, that's $9,000."

Howie grinned. "The ice here will cost you one-third of your figure, and the kids here won't want a nickel for doing the show. If you put away two or three thousand dollars in the budget and buy them something when it is all over, that would be great."

So Pat Ford went back to Gordon Craig with the costs $15,000 to $20,000 less than their Toronto budget, and the Howie Meeker TV show had the green light.

"We all did a little dance, had a cigar, a feed of flippers, and killed a bottle of London Dock. Those who came down from CBC Toronto — John Spalding, Ron Harrison, Audry Phillips, and cameraman Jack Vandermay — were great people. Bob Ota was the producer. Without him we were dead."

Pat Ford turned out to be another interesting character in Howie's life. He and Grace enjoyed Pat's visits to such an extent they would create crises so he would come home. "When he stayed at our place he would go down to the harbour in the evening where the kids were catching conners and flat fish off the wharf. He'd give a kid a dollar for his pole and come home with six to eight fish, fillet them into the pan, and open a bottle of wine. I can still see the smile on his face as he sat down to a midnight snack of fresh fish."

Pat couldn't get over the fact that Newfoundland children would catch the fish and throw them back in. He started paying five cents for a flounder and soon every kid in the village was fishing for him and he would always take home twenty pounds of flat-fish fillets. Pat later went on to host his own successful children's TV show.

Y

After the Howie Meeker Hockey School had been on CBC, coast to coast, for three years, Howie was getting three to five invitations a week to run coaching clinics. He finally went to station manager Darce Fardy and said, "Darce, we've got a monster by the tail. Here's seven or eight invitations to run clinics that I've said 'I'm sorry' to. Here is another ten to twelve that I haven't answered. We've got to have a policy. If you want me to stay and work, I'll write them and say, 'Sorry, I can't get time off from CBC.' If you want me to go out and do some public relations work on behalf of CBC, just let me know. I have to have something on paper."

The two men agreed that Howie should do two or three clinics a month, over the weekends.

Howie had already scheduled a coaching clinic for the Arbutus Club in Vancouver in October. One foggy Newfoundland day, the telephone rang in Howie's office.

"Hi, Mr. Meeker? I'm Brian Storrier, arena manager at Parksville, Vancouver Island, British Columbia. We're opening a new arena soon and have a minor hockey meeting scheduled. Would you like to be our guest speaker?"

"When?"

"Whenever you can come."

"I'll call back in a day or two," Howie said. He went to Darce. "I'm scheduled to go to Vancouver, on Friday, Saturday, and Sunday, and I just had this call from Parksville, Vancouver Island, to be a guest speaker." Howie pointed to his son Andy, there as a demonstrator. "Why don't Andy and I leave here Wednesday, do the banquet Thursday, over to Vancouver Friday, work Saturday and Sunday, and leave for home Monday?"

Darce, having made the flight before, said, "Fine, but you'll not survive that. Leave Tuesday. You'll need a day to recuperate when you get there."

The banquet went well, and over a dark rum Brian Storrier suggested salmon fishing the next day. At six in the morning, with pal Bob Brown, they were in the boat, just off French Creek, chucking about in the Strait of Georgia. They were bucktailing, trailing a fly along the top of the water, and Andy was holding his rod tip up in the air. Bob hollered, "Andy, drop your tip, quick." The fish missed the fly on the first try, but when the rod tip dropped, the fly sat still for a moment. The fish turned and then smashed the line. A huge, silver, northern Coho was on the hook.

"It reminded me of the Calgary Stampede, with the cowboy on

the back of a bucking horse, 'cause this thing was in and out of the water like nobody's business." Ten minutes later Andy had a twelve-pound beauty in the net, and a half-hour later Howie had the same thrill.

While the happy fishermen were devouring a scrumptious breakfast at Bob's seaside restaurant, Brian asked, "Why don't you come out here in September and run a hockey school?"

"Sorry, I've got six weeks at Stanstead and I don't think I have the time." Later that day though, the light bulb came on again. During the second week in the third session at Stanstead, he could get away, run two weeks in Parksville, and go back.

Howie took brother Tom, nephew Dan, and all his Newfoundland instructors out to British Columbia. "We went first-class. The school took in $21,000 and it cost me $23,000, but we had a ball. Grace and I arrived a couple of days early and had booked three cottages at Parksands Beach Resort, a stone's throw from the arena, and right on B.C.'s best beach. Gordon Bannerman and his wife owned Parksands, and Gordie was a veteran, a hockey fan, and we got along fine; still do." Howie also gets along fine with the huge oyster bed on Gordie's beach. "One of the real pleasures of life, and I don't do it often enough, is to get a small bottle of Screech and go down to Gordie's place and shuck oysters to my heart's content."

After the third day at Parksville, with gorgeous weather and stunning country, someone suggested they take the two-and-a-half-hour drive to Long Beach. "The majestic scenery is out of this world, and I got to thinking, 'How long has this been going on?' Grace, let's move."

"No way we're going to move across the country again," she countered.

At hockey school registration that first year, a black-haired guy with sparkling eyes and a grin like he just got caught in the cookie jar stuck out his hand and said, "Hi. Remember me?" Howie didn't, but he did remember the nose. "I was at the Arbutus Club,

295

last October. I was the guy that gave you all the trouble. I'm Don Skoyen and these are my kids. I want to see if you are as good as you say you are. I brought my skates, track suit, and gloves; can I come on the ice and help?"

"Sure boy," Meeker said.

Howie laughs at the memory. "What a gem he turned out to be. Skoyen is an amazing person and it's almost scary the way he can handle people and solve problems; how he can calm the water. We've worked together in the hockey school business all over Canada and the United States for the past twenty-five years."

In 1976, Howie and Grace bought property in Parksville, and one year later they had moved all the way across the nation. Howie Meeker had literally become the *Hockey Night in Canada* guy "from coast to coast."

Fifteen

Golly Gee, Look at That Guy!

"I remember, during the opening ceremonies, that the 2,500 to 3,000 Canadian fans sang the national anthem with such pride and such gusto that I cried, something I did three other times before the series ended."

To put it simply, Howie Meeker still missed life in the NHL. He had moved on and was happy, but the wish to somehow be involved in the game at the National Hockey League level again nagged away at him. Ever since his last full season in 1952–53, he had felt severed from the big-league camaraderie. Sure, he'd coached the Leafs in 1956–57, and for the following summer was — superficially — the general manager, but that really didn't count. As a coach and manager he'd felt like an outsider.

During the winter of 1968 Howie was in Montreal attending a toy fair as a Newfoundland sales representative for Mattel and Tonka. Howie stayed at the Mount Royal Hotel, and on a Thursday afternoon he bumped into *Hockey Night in Canada*'s Montreal host, Ted Darling. During conversation, Darling said he needed someone to do colour work during Saturday night's game between Montreal and Chicago. Would Howie do it?

"Sure, I'd be delighted."

Dick Irvin and Danny Gallivan made it easy for him. Howie says now, "Knowing that it was a one-shot deal, I had fun with it. I was very critical on some plays and tremendously excited about others. Game over, show over, that was it — or so I thought. Whatever I did that night must have been all right because I was invited back."

Howie headed for home Sunday morning, and by Tuesday he received a phone call from Ralph Mellanby, the main producer of *Hockey Night in Canada*, asking, "Could you work in Montreal next week when the Toronto Maple Leafs are there? We want you to do game analysis. You'll have to leave Friday, and won't be home until Sunday." Howie said he would call back. A few minutes later Howie bounded down the stairs to Colin Jamieson's office like an excited kid at Christmas. "Hi, Colin. Just had a call from *Hockey Night in Canada*; can I work in Montreal on Saturday night? I have to leave Friday. Can I?"

"Sure, Howie, but don't let it become a habit," Jamieson said. But Howie did, and Colin and Don were good enough to roll with the punches.

Eventually Mellanby asked Howie if he would work games on a fairly regular basis in the 1969–70 season. In 1969–70 and 1970–71, Howie worked about a dozen games each year, weaving them around various jobs on the Rock. During that period he worked mainly in Montreal with Danny Gallivan and Dick Irvin on the Canadiens' broadcasts. When he managed to work games at his beloved Maple Leaf Gardens, it was usually with the talented Brian McFarlane, Dave Hodge, and Foster and Bill Hewitt. In 1971–72,

Meeker did at least fifteen matches for *Hockey Night in Canada* while keeping his job at CJON.

"When my *Hockey Night in Canada* schedule took me to Toronto or Montreal every second week, and often for a week at a time during the playoffs, Colin would complain a little bit, but eventually tell me to go ahead."

Most of the time Hurricane Howie managed to juggle his horrendous schedule of commitments; however, he recalls one time when he overtaxed himself, and paid the price publicly.

While shooting the *Howie Meeker Hockey School* TV series in St. John's, he worked every day from four in the afternoon until eight o'clock at night, and a double shift on the Saturdays he didn't do games. On Sundays he rested — though he often helped prepare an entire script of another episode. The actual hard work was after the filming, and they were stuck with a "half a million" feet of film that had to be developed and packaged. The series was shot with three cameras, so Howie and the crew had three different angles on every scene and had to sit down and edit every shot. Howie and film editor Bob Ota spent endless hours together, working like madmen, editing the film.

"Often, I'd go to Toronto on a Friday, do a hockey game Saturday, then work all day Sunday from seven in the morning to seven at night, keeping up the pace until the next Friday. It was long, tedious work, but I got to know how to operate a Steenbeck machine and how to splice and put film together pretty good."

During that insane haul, Howie faltered. He'd been in Toronto for four days editing film, worked all day Saturday, then rushed to the Gardens to work a *Hockey Night in Canada* match against the New York Rangers.

During his between-periods analysis, Howie used a wrong name for a player and Dave Hodge corrected him. Less than a minute later, another player appeared on the screen and Howie again used the wrong name, so Hodge corrected him again. Says Howie now, "I knew what the problem was; I should have been home in bed.

But I don't think the *Hockey Night in Canada* people realized it."

In the second period Howie misidentified another player and was corrected once again. "This was all coming down in front of a national TV audience, and when it was all over I felt like two cents. The technical crew were on the money, doing a great job. Normally the on-air guy is supposed to just add to what the technical crew produces, enhance the show, or fill in when they have technical or transmission trouble. But here they were doing everything right, and I was screwing up."

Ralph Mellanby was the fellow who made *Hockey Night in Canada* happen, hiring, firing, and working with the on-air announcers. Howie and Ralph played a lot of tennis together when Howie stayed in the big city and Mellanby, who was handy with a tennis racquet, regularly thumped Meeker. The day after Howie's bad night the two played tennis and, following a solid pasting by Ralph, went for lunch. Between mouthfuls, Howie apologized for his errors the evening before.

"Had it been your first or second time on television, there might have been a problem, but we decided that over two or three years a guy could have a bad night, but not two," Mellanby warned, with a smile on his face.

During his first few years on *HNiC*, Meeker was primarily hired as a game analyst and between periods would point out key factors in scoring plays, or highlight other significant action. "I'd watch my own video screen and, with an engineer, select the thirty or forty seconds I wanted, package it with a replay, and then describe what was happening, or wasn't happening, while the film rolled for TV audiences.

"After about four or five years of game analysis, *Hockey Night in Canada*, for some reason or another, thought I should do colour. That's a pretty tough job, doing colour. I have an excellent idea of what's going on, and what should be going on, but I have a terrible memory for names. I just can't look at a guy and have the name pop onto my tongue."

Howie's first time doing colour "officially" was in St. Louis, after Mellanby had left *HNiC*, and Don Wallace was the head honcho. Wallace had been in charge of the Montreal production the first few years Howie was in the business. "Don, or who ever had the idea of me doing colour, probably kicked himself in the butt soon after."

That night in St. Louis, Howie was not yet aware of all that his new role required. He didn't know the trick was to take control and announce who he wanted to talk about at the next play stoppage. Instead, when play stopped, the director would put up anyone at random on the screen, and Howie was expected to babble away.

Producers and directors are scared to death of dead air. The play-by-play broadcaster that night was Jim Robson, who had a habit of dropping his head and making notes the second the whistle blew, letting the colour guy take over. Sure enough, the sorry scenario unfolded quickly: the whistle blew, Robson's head went down, Howie's head went up, his mouth opened, dead air. Some player's sweaty mug was on the screen, and Howie was scrambling about looking for notes. Wallace could no longer contain himself, and through Howie's headset came an urgent and slightly agitated voice saying, "Talk! For Christ's sake, someone talk; somebody say something!"

When the game was over, Wallace was steaming. It was a couple of days before he would talk to Howie.

Howie's lapses were few and far between, and soon he was wanted for both his colour work and analysis on a regular basis, and by more than one TV station.

In time, Howie had developed a pretty good book, an information package on every player with notes for fifteen- to forty-second clips. "I know it came across exceptionally well, but I had to call the shots to be effective. While the play was going on, I would tell the director who I wanted to talk about next. Nine times out of ten, I got him, whether he was on the ice, or sitting on the bench. Then I was really ready and had solid information." There was a lot of work involved in preparing material on the twenty players on each team. Howie had to continually update his notes and, when he did use somebody, go back and update them again.

"I think I could have stayed a colour man, but I really didn't enjoy it when they snuck in someone other than the guy that I was looking for. I was basically lost. If it was one of the top 25 or 30 percent of the players, I probably knew them, but you can only talk about them once or twice during the game, and that's it. There's all kinds of other people that I didn't know. I could have lost my job there."

The best tool of all, though, Howie stole from football.

"Thank God for the telestrator. The second I saw it used in a Canadian Football League game, I said, 'That thing's for hockey.' Ron Harrison, Mellanby, and other people made sure I got the telestrator and that saved my duff for sure."

V

By 1972, Howie had honed his analytical skills in hockey broadcasting, and gained a reputation for being an opinionated, yet knowledgeable, critic. His skill was such that he was chosen to help answer the biggest NHL broadcasting bell of all time — the Canada–USSR Summit Series.

Howie never did find out who chose him to be an analyst in the legendary series. When Mellanby asked him if he was interested in working the series, he replied, "Heck Ralph, I'll swim to the mainland and walk from there to Montreal to get to work that series."

As it turned out, not only was Team Canada's lineup filled with stars of the game, so was the broadcast crew. The men behind the microphones and controls were a who's who of the hockey broadcast industry at the time.

"I knew I had really made the big leagues when I looked around and saw folks like Foster Hewitt, Rene Lecavalier, Johnny Esaw, Bill Good Jr., and Gordon Craig, all working together on the broadcasts."

Few Canadian events, if any, created the same frenzy of national pride as the epic eight-game battle. Work and study stopped for three periods on game days as men, women, and children across the country crowded around the television set. Businesses and schools had TV sets brought in, in recognition that no TV would have meant no staff or students.

"I think the feeling, clean across the country, was that our boys were far too good for them, that the Soviet boys wouldn't have a chance," Howie recalls. "We had some people, scouts and former pros, who went to the Soviet Union and said their goaltending was 'iffy' and that we would have no trouble with them."

The players in August of 1972 figured they would have a leisurely three- or four-week training camp in Toronto, get into 75 or 80 percent condition, and beat them maybe six games to two. I know the hockey players themselves, the people in the hockey business, newspaper writers, radio, television, and the average fan, were in no way, shape, or form ready or expecting what we eventually got from the Soviet Union."

The first four games of the series were held in Canada, with opening night at the Montreal Forum. Due to his busy schedule, Howie did not have a chance to see the Soviet team practise before the first game. In the pregame warm-up, though, he knew the Soviets had sent a competitive hockey team. "The Soviets were zipping the puck around with deadly accuracy. I thought right then that something was up."

Canada jumped out to an early 2–0 lead in the first period, but before the first twenty minutes of play were over the USSR had tied the score. Between periods Howie told hockey fans, "The Canadian players have more than their hands full. We are in deep, deep trouble, folks."

"I was ecstatic about the USSR play," Howie recalls. "I said, 'These people skate as well as we do, handle the puck better than we do, don't give the puck away as often as we do, and that young goaltender, Tretiak, looks sensational.' I talked about nothing but Soviets."

In the second period it got worse for Team Canada as the Soviets' speed and pattern plays left Canadian players reaching at the air. Canada attempted to skate with, and hit, the swift Soviets, but the plan failed. In fact the USSR appeared to be speeding up while the Canadians started to sputter. The Soviets scored twice in the middle frame, and twice more in the third. At the end of the night, the USSR skated off the ice with an impressive 7–3 win.

"It became obvious during Game One, and for at least the first four games in Canada, that our team faced a tremendous disadvantage. They were now not only physically and psychologically in trouble, but challenged skillwise as well. The most obvious disadvantage was that the Soviet puck handling, and puck movement, was just so much better than ours, all of which Team Canada had to overcome."

In Game Two, Team Canada coaches Harry Sinden and John Ferguson inserted some much-needed toughness into the Canadian lineup, including Bill White, Serge Savard, Pat Stapleton, and Wayne Cashman, and the move paid off. Before a standing-room only Maple Leaf Gardens crowd, Canada won 4–1.

At the end of the second game Art Harnett, a member of series organizer Alan Eagleson's entourage, burst into the broadcast studio and berated Howie for his "pro-Soviet praise" and comments after the first game, accusing him of "not liking" Canadian hockey.

"I just stood there and took it, but actually there is nobody who admires Canadian hockey or NHL hockey more than I do. I found out later that a lot of people, including some of the players, were put off quite a bit by the way I supported and admired the Soviets' play."

Game Three, held in Winnipeg, while robust and eventful, was the least spirited game of the series, a match Howie admits he hardly recalls. That may have been because on that early September evening, the hockey series seemed far less significant than it had just two days before. Prior to the opening face-off, one minute of silence was observed in memory of the eleven Israeli athletes who'd been brutally executed the previous morning by Arab terrorists at the Olympics in Munich, Germany. The aftershock of such butchery was felt around the world, and in Winnipeg, Manitoba, that night, it seemed to diminish the physical, aggressive side of the contest.

The game, perhaps appropriately, ended tied 4–4.

Injuries to defencemen Serge Savard and Guy Lapointe hurt Canada in the fourth game at the Pacific Coliseum in Vancouver, which they lost 5–3. Disenchanted Vancouver fans displayed their frustration with Team Canada's performance, loudly booing the players as they left the ice. That incident wounded some Team Canada members, particularly team captain Phil Esposito, who later told TV reporters his teammates deserved better treatment and respect from Canadian hockey fans. Esposito suggested the players' dedication and willingness to take part in the exhibition tournament was being forgotten and suggested many Canadians, including his teammates, had been duped into believing the tournament would be an easier affair for Canada.

"For some reason I did not get to hear Esposito's reaction to the booing 'live,' but I saw it on tape later. In true Esposito fashion it was straight from the heart. He was dead-on; you just don't go from August conditioning to a January or February level of play, either physically or mentally. Esposito's performance right there had as much to do with winning the series as his on-ice performance."

Despite the fan reaction in Vancouver, Canadians were still caught up in the series. Every game was vital, now that Team Canada trailed the eight-game event.

Team Canada lost the first game in Moscow by a nail-biting 5–4 score. Howie maintains that the most significant factor from Game Five was not the game at all, but the Canadian fans, stuffed in a block at the north end of the dull, cold, Palace of Sports at the Lenin Central Stadium.

"During the opening ceremonies the 2,500 to 3,000 Canadian fans sang the national anthem with such pride and such gusto that I cried, something I did three other times before the series ended. I didn't feel awkward, though, because when I looked at Foster Hewitt he had tears in his eyes, too."

That same unabashed Canadian pride, and fan support, never

diminished throughout the remainder of the game — nor the rest of the series. Even after Team Canada blew a three-goal lead late in the third period, the dedicated Canuck fans stood to a person and cheered, hollered, and waved Canadian flags at the players. The fans treated their players as if they had won the game.

"They gave them a standing ovation, and I just couldn't believe it. There were a lot of things about that series that I will never forget, but those fans are at the top. They were telling the players, 'We're Canadians, we're proud of you, you're going to win,' and that message got through to the players. Next day at practice you could see that confidence."

The return of Serge Savard to the lineup, and the fine play of the blueline brigade, helped Canada to win Game Six. Canada won despite picking up seven penalties at key times. "The guy who made it all happen, who put it together, was Savard. The defence played consistently better with each game: Gary Bergman got better every game; Pat Stapleton was consistent; Brad Park not only played good defence but also joined in on offence; big Bill White mugged everybody within reach, and he could reach a country mile; Savard kept his coolness under fire, and Guy Lapointe played well. All played outstanding games."

Goalie Ken Dryden also played well, particularly in the third period. "When he stood up, there was nobody better in the game, but like most goaltenders, he'd start to go down early." But that night the lanky lawyer was hot between the pipes, and Canada won 3–2. Paul Henderson scored the game-winning goal.

Back in Canada, even the least likely of hockey fans were drawn to their television sets in what had already become a piece of Canadian history and folklore. Team Canada was deluged with more than 50,000 telegrams of congratulations and encouragement. The telegrams were pinned up around the dressing room as the players prepared for one of the biggest games of their lives. With the Game Six victory, the expected, turned improbable, now seemed conceivable.

In Game Seven, the Esposito brothers, Phil and goaltender Tony, hit the ice and went to work. When the evening was over Phil had scored two goals and brother Tony had kicked out 28 of 31 shots on goal. Canada won the game 4–3, with Paul Henderson scoring another game-winner.

"One thing I noticed at that time was that, all of a sudden, Tretiak looked to be human. Most people thought he could walk on water after his four-game performance in Canada, but some goals beat him in Moscow that he would have stopped in Canada."

The two teams had each won three games, and they'd tied in Winnipeg. Canada needed to win the final game in order to win the series. Two nations remained suspended in anticipation. Two nations sat fixated in exhilaration . . . and fear.

Dryden started in goal for Canada and, while he had his occasional moments of brilliance, he was very shaky throughout the first forty minutes.

"After the first two periods Canada was down 5–3, and I thought Dryden had just played terribly, absolutely terribly. But he redeemed himself in the third period. The Soviets entered the third period with a two-goal lead. It was essential that Canada get a goal early, so who else but Esposito scored to make it 5–4 early in the period, and suddenly Team Canada is back in the game."

Next, Yvan Cournoyer tied the game, set up by Esposito. "The key to the win, though, was that between the score being 5–4 and 5–5, Dryden made three big stops. The Soviets did have some excellent chances, but with the outcome of the whole series on the line, Dryden more than made up for his occasional mediocre performances. Without his key stops from about the two-minute mark to the ten-minute mark of the third period, we'd have been in trouble."

Eventually Phil Esposito stole the puck again in the corner and gave it to Henderson. Henderson shot the puck, Tretiak made the save, Henderson snagged the rebound and put it in the net with thirty-four seconds left in the game, and Canada won an unbelievable series.

With two or three minutes left in the game, Howie had to leave his broadcast perch high up near the arena roof and head down to the ice-level broadcast studio for a postgame show. At the bottom, Howie paused at the north end of the rink behind Dryden, the opposite end from where the final goal was scored. Above the boards there was a heavy wire fence, instead of glass, surrounding the ice surface.

"I remember that when Henderson scored his famous goal, I climbed up the wire fence behind the net about ten feet. The 2,500 Canadian fans sitting at the north end all around me went absolutely bonkers. It was perhaps the happiest night of their lives. It certainly made me feel great to see the team come from behind and win the series.

"There will never be another series like it. A single game, yes, but not another series. I'm not sure how much we learned from them at that time. I think we are learning more from the European players now, than we did back in the '70s and the '80s, but we learned some lessons."

For Howie, the real hero of the series was Phil Esposito. "No one has ever played in any sport, at least in my lifetime, who was as responsible for a team winning, not only a game, but also a series, as Phil Esposito. I have never seen anybody excel both in leadership and in play, both on and off the ice, as Esposito did in that series. He forced his team to win and he played so galdarn good. He was the guy who won the series. It was the most outstanding performance I've seen."

Gordon Craig was on a headset connected with Canada at all times during the final game, making sure the television signal got from Moscow to Canada.

"None of us over there were aware of how caught up Canada was with the series," Howie says. "No one told us this Soviet-Canada series was building in excitement and in audience size."

No one told them that an entire nation was holding its breath.

Gordon told Howie that when Henderson scored the winning goal there was an unbelievable noise on his headset. Everyone at every broadcast relay centre across Canada, listening to the same feed as Gordon, screamed and hollered. "My God, listen to that," Craig said, pulling the headphones away from his ears.

It was only then that he realized, and told Howie and the others, that the eighth game was such a huge thing back in Canada.

Ɣ

Adapting and adjusting to the Soviet hockey skill on the ice was only part of the quick shuffle the Canadians had to do. Despite the recent impact of Western culture on their lifestyle, the Soviet Union of 1972 was still another world.

Howie and the broadcast crew arrived a few days early to try and establish, in the television world, how they were going to get their work done: what they could do, and what they couldn't do. They soon found out there was a whole lot of things they couldn't do.

After Game Five, Howie and the crew had to prepare a highlight package for opening the next game's broadcast. To do so, they would take their tapes to the Soviet broadcasting centre. "We had to get permission from the Soviet intelligence people, and we had to have a special pass to get into the place. It was trouble enough getting in, but one time we couldn't get out. The person who was supposed to sign the release wasn't there. After half an hour waiting around, we just said, 'To hell with this,' and walked out. We fully expected to get arrested, but it never happened."

At the broadcasting building, it would take them three to four hours to get a forty-five-second clip and get it transferred to another tape.

"In the Soviet Union they used to brag about having full employment. Well sure, because it took at least two people to do one person's job. If we needed a videotape operator, not one person in their system knew the full job from A to Z. One guy would know A to M, and then another guy would come in for N to Z. It was total inefficiency."

The Canadian broadcast people were not allowed to touch a

machine, but finally Ron Harrison decided enough was enough and started to use the oldest bargaining process in the world.

"Many of the technicians were women and Ron would con them with sweets, lingerie, perfume, or that sort of stuff, and they would let him run the tape machines. He taught them as they watched, so that eventually the Soviet people just sat back and enjoyed watching what we were doing. By the fourth or fifth visit Ron was running the place."

Soon after returning from Russia, Howie wound up in the hospital battling huge kidney stones. While he was recuperating, a vaguely familiar giant walked into his hospital room and introduced himself as Darce Fardy, head of CBC Newfoundland. Would Howie consider coming to work for CBC as a TV sports director?

"My first job at CJON, I didn't ask how much money I was getting paid. My first job at *Hockey Night in Canada*, I didn't ask how much, and the fact is I never did again after that day, but I looked Fardy in the eye and said, 'How much?'"

"Ten thousand dollars."

Howie gulped, turned a little white, and asked if he could still keep his agency business, hockey schools, and work *Hockey Night in Canada* as often as requested. The answers were, "Yes, yes, and yes."

Howie couldn't believe his luck. He had just doubled his TV salary aside from *HNiC*, from $5,000 to $10,000. He hired a staff person to cover for him when he was away. Scott Oake took on the task, before heading off to Winnipeg to further his career in CFL and NHL broadcasting.

Howie worked with CBC St. John's from 1973 until 1976 as a sports broadcaster and from 1970 to 1990 with *Hockey Night in Canada*, logging thousands of travel miles a year and seemingly running through as much film footage. He was constantly in demand for shows and public relations events or charities, and always tried to fit every one into his schedule.

During that period, Howie worked with Brian McFarlane for three or four years on a popular series called *Showdown*, which again featured Howie's colourful views and opinions. He also produced a show with Mellanby and Petrie called *Pro Tips*, which ran between periods and featured such stars as Guy Lafleur, Larry Robinson, Bobby Smith, and Mark Messier.

Howie covered thirty-five games a year, as well as playoffs, for *Hockey Night in Canada*. He also occasionally worked for NBC television in the U.S.

One of the unique attributes about Howie Meeker which inspired fans to either love him or hate him was the collection of expressions which became known as Howie-isms. In reality, many such as holy smoke, jumpin' Jehoshaphat, golly gee, and Jiminy Crickets, were ways of curbing an otherwise occasionally coarse tongue.

"I'm not much for cussing and swearing, but I'm no angel. My father had a sharp tongue and I spent a lot of time in the army and in hockey dressing rooms, so rough language is not foreign to me. I learned early in radio and TV that foul language has a way of popping out, especially during exciting moments such as a goal or fight. That split second between putting my mind in action and my mouth in gear saved me a lot of embarrassment."

Howie says his years of broadcasting in the NHL, starting in 1968, have been some of the best times in the game.

"What a wonderful time to be around the game and watch it grow and improve. I watched Bobby Orr and Esposito haul off the Stanley Cup in Boston; the incredible Montreal Canadiens, with stars like Kenny Dryden, Gump Worsley, Jean Beliveau, and Yvan Cournoyer; Chicago, with the likes of Bobby Hull, Glenn Hall and Stan Mikita; Philadelphia, who had Bobby Clarke and crew; the Islanders with Mike Bossy, Bryan Trottier, and Billy Smith, who was always a joy to watch.

"There is no other league like the NHL. It will continue to change and grow, and I fully expect European cities to be in it some day, but I'm glad I had a chance to be a part of it then, and even a little bit now."

Between *Hockey Night in Canada* and *Howie Meeker Hockey*

School on TV every week, his mug became familiar to Canadians everywhere. The exposure also began to open doors in the lucrative advertising field.

Eventually, agent Gerry Petrie suggested Howie write a how-to book about hockey. "Use all the things you've talked about and demonstrated in your hockey series, all those techniques," Petrie encouraged. Petrie made some arrangements, and Howie and Grace hit Florida for a couple of weeks while Howie worked on his book. The first, *Howie Meeker's Hockey Basics*, written in 1973, did well, selling 100,000 copies. The second book, *More Hockey Basics from Howie Meeker*, written in 1975, was also popular. Howie's brother Ken, a veteran news-paperman who'd also moved to St. John's and become editor of the *Herald*, made the books readable and funny.

Peter Gzowski read the book and interviewed Howie on radio. He asked about skates, and Howie said a lot of good things about Bauer and was less complimentary about CCM. A week or so later he received a call from Bauer in Kitchener: Could they talk to him about representing their product?

"CBC, at first, violently objected to my lending my name to Bauer and in fact threatened to fire me. I'd been through that kind of struggle with Conn Smythe, however, and was not about to do it again, so that was resolved quickly. I won, and they didn't fire me."

When the Meekers moved to Vancouver Island in 1976, it opened up another potential TV market. Sure enough, that year Gordon Craig moved to Vancouver to run CBC Television's western operation. A year later, in the summer of 1977, Howie mentioned that he would love to work some Vancouver Canucks games on BCTV, but wouldn't give up *Hockey Night in Canada* to do so. "In no time, Gordon was on the phone and said a deal had been worked out and Howie could do Vancouver games when available. So Howie had the pleasure of working with the accomplished Jim Robson, as well as the talented, hardworking, and funny John McKeechie.

In 1985, once again, the telephone rang.

"Hi, Howie. It's Gordon. I've left CBC, moved to Toronto, and I'm working for Labatt's. We're opening a sports network, and we'll be doing hockey. We'd like you to come and work for us."

"I'm already committed to *Hockey Night in Canada* and to BCTV, but if you can get permission from them, I'll come."

The next day the phone rang and it was Gordon again. "We'll send you our schedule."

"My, oh my, but The Sports Network has come a long way in the last eleven years, thanks to Gordon Craig, president Jim Thompson, producer Gord Cutler, director Rick Chisholm, and technical producer Maurie Jackson. Very talented and fun people.

"It's just amazing what you can accomplish with hard work, a little talent, a little knowledge, and the right portion of pizzazz. In my business, if you haven't got pizzazz, you haven't got nothing. I learned to stir the pot in St. John's at CJON, then the entire island. When the chance came to do it nationally, it was a piece of cake."

Y

For the record, Howie says he's retired, but no one takes him seriously. He retired once before, in 1989, and Parksville hosted a big retirement party and roast, complete with a golf tournament. But Howie was back behind the microphone the next year. He's already discussing a couple of guest appearances on TSN in 1996–97.

In the world of broadcast, Howie says the real heroes of television hockey are the talented cameramen, directors, switchers, and technicians. "The people who get the picture onto the sets in living rooms around the country are a real marvel and a big part of the reason I lasted so long. No one has ever told the story of what a great job they do, or showed the viewer the mental and physical skills it takes to get that picture on the screen."

On November 23, 1996, Howie Meeker turns seventy-three, but he shows little sign of slowing down. He still makes about twenty public-speaking appearances a year — "when time permits" — and runs a hockey school in Parksville every summer as well as other camps around the country. He continues to try to change the approach to minor hockey by making it fun for those participating. Fun, he maintains, can't exist when 50 percent of the players drop out from between ages twelve and sixteen.

"Minor hockey has to be fun for everyone and it has to be a skill-learning experience," he says. "It's the duty of the adult to create an on-ice atmosphere where the boy can improve his skills without the fear of being constantly under attack. There is no skill teaching at all going on in this country. If the boys had the skills, they wouldn't be dropping out because they would be having fun."

In 1996, Howie made two trips to Newfoundland and three to Toronto, not including the dozen games he did for TSN across North America. He recently attended a "Make A Wish" camp for children, and managed to fit in two major fishing trips on B.C.'s coastline.

For Howie Meeker, the world virtually never stops moving. He still approaches life with the same tenacity and work ethic that have made him so successful and allowed him to overcome incredible odds on several occasions over the years. So what's left for Howie?

He says his main goal is to "walk healthy into the year 2000," and to do so with Grace, his partner of more than fifty years "and best teammate ever.

"I've had a wonderful life. Not only because of Grace and my kids, hockey, the wonderful people I have met, and places I have been, but also because of the world in which I have lived. I've lived in probably the best fifty or sixty years in the world's history. I grew up in the best times to ever grow up, during the 1920s, '30s, and '40s.

"My life in one sentence? Oh jeez, that's easy, I can give it to you in one word: suuuper!"

Epilogue

I have a problem. I have to find an ending to this book, and I don't know where to begin.

How do you sum up a man like Howie Meeker — the many faces, moods, mind-sets, passions? Who is this Canadian icon who has overcome so much, and yet will tell you he's just lucky and has really done nothing at all? One minute he is puffed up in storytelling, and the next he's humbly dismissing some spellbinding success.

The pages of a book hardly seem enough room to properly reveal the life story of the average seventy-three-year-old, and there is nothing average about Howie Meeker.

I suppose I could write about Howie's dedication and work ethic. How he spent so many hours transcribing notes and tapes for this book when he would much rather have been out in his beloved garden, or walking his dogs on the beach, or better yet, fishing. Working with me on this book has mainly been a pain in the butt for Howie, but I convinced him to share his life, to draw on some of his vast memory banks of times, places, and faces, for others to enjoy.

I suppose I could write the story about Howie's first big bass, back behind the Baden hills at seven o'clock in the evening, the leaky rubber raft, fly-rod, cork popper, the lily pads. *Boom!* This thing, eight to ten pounds, exploded out of the water. While trying to get him out into open water, the excited, scared, clumsy Howie . . . lost the sucker. "That's living, that's life, that's fun," he said later.

Perhaps I could dispel that myth about him being "cantankerous" or a grouch. Watching him run his hockey school, barking at kids everywhere, can make you wonder, until you pay attention, as the kids do, and see the rest of the man there. He's a no-nonsense, military man, all right, and it saved his rear end more than once. But he's also a gentle, caring man who will never turn down an autograph, or a talk with a youngster, or a media interview.

I could tell the story his brother Tom relates about Howie's school in Newfoundland. Howie was upstairs in the press box of the arena with his skates off, talking to Tom. Down below a small flock of young tykes milled about on the ice with sticks and skates. One youngster was skating around pylons and had successfully finished a series of turns. Howie, in midconversation with Tom, stopped, looked down at the lad, and tore out of the box, down the bleachers, and onto the ice. Tom looked out to see what the problem was. Howie ran across the ice, picked up the tyke in his arms, and held him over his head in victory. "Attaboy, you did it. See I told you you could do it. Suuuper, what a guy," Howie said, dropping the beaming youngster back to the ice. He turned and scampered off the ice quickly, the ice cold on his bare feet.

I could share the numerous stories told by his brothers Tom and Ken, or sons Andy and Mike, but there's no more room.

I could tell you about all his work with the Special Olympics (eight straight years of charity golf games in Campbell River, B.C.), Big Brothers, and other such groups, or his nonstop playing and organizing old-timers' hockey tournaments with his Parksville Panters pals; and the Golden Oldies.

There's Grace, of course, and all of her stories, wit, and kindness. How Howie feels Grace "got the dirty end of the stick" when he worked seven months of each year in hockey, then returned to New

Hamburg in the first years and worked on the railroad and played in the intercounty baseball league, then in later years was so involved in building and operating their hunting and fishing camp 1,500 miles from home and fifty miles from the closest village for three or four months every summer.

I could talk about Howie the dad. He taught his children to face adversity square on, that it won't go away just because it is wished to. "He taught me to stand up for things and not be shy," son Mike recalls, "to stand up for what I believe, and when I absolutely had to, to stand my ground and fight for me. Being a Protestant child growing up in a Catholic neighbourhood in Newfoundland, and being the son of outspoken Howie Meeker, meant I was picked on a lot by other kids. So Dad took us boys down for boxing lessons, saying, 'I can't always be there to look after you, so you better learn how to yourself. Stop running now, or you will never learn how to stop later.' He could be a hard dad, and a hard man, but a whole bunch of that is simply a facade, a well-orchestrated bluff. Inside, my Dad is a teddy bear with a heart for others, especially kids."

Y

But none of that seems right. Instead, I decide to give Howie the chance. I track him down at the arena, of course. It's hockey school time.

I lean against the arena boards, waiting for a moment to talk to him. He knows I'm there. He seems to see everything in an arena. Slowly he skates across the blue line, all the time watching, like a mother bird over her brood.

"No, no, Eddy, you're getting ahead of yourself on that pass . . . ya, ya, ya — that's it, boy. Lord t'underin', b'y, I knew ya could do it," he hollers at a youngster swooshing past me.

Ten feet away from me, and again the man's attention is diverted to a skill drill in kinetic state. As he studies the play unfolding, I study the teacher. He stands erect, much bigger in some ways than his battered and bashed five-foot eight-inch frame. His healthy salt-

and-pepper hair crowns a rugged, attractive, friendly face. Even his face can tell stories.

To look at the man it is hard to believe he is nearly three-quarters of a century old. Trim, lean, strong, he makes wine envious. However, it has come at a price, and he wears that, too. It's in his eyes. Those eagle-like glinting orbs, piercing grey-blue. They do not have that cold blackness of the Rocket, or Conn Smythe. Instead, they glint out in concentration, intense study, microscopic. The Professor is in. Then, in a wink, they flash a sparkle of blue, pleasure, success. A student has learned.

He turns to me, with a deep grin for a friend, "Hi, Charlie, good to see ya."

"Hi, Howie. Listen, I won't keep you but I need some help. I thought maybe you might have something to say to end the book. Maybe something you haven't said. Something profound."

He looks at me. The eyes say, "Surely b'y, you must be kidding. After a year, a zillion stories, and only 300-plus pages to do it in, you want another story?" But instead, his mouth said, "Not really; like about what?"

"Hell, I don't know what I want, Howie, something, um, er . . . Howie-ish. Maybe some advice on life or something."

"Charlie boy, I don't know what to say to you, except what I've always said to everyone, especially kids, when it comes to advice: 'Have fun.' See what you can do with that," he grins, and skates away.

Index